Revenge versus Legality

In the wake of Guantanamo Bay, extraordinary renditions, and secret torture centers in Eastern Europe and elsewhere, *Revenge versus Legality* explores the relationship between law and wild or vigilante justice, between the power to enforce retribution and the desire to seek revenge. Examining a variety of narratives from the eras of Romanticism, Realism, Modernism and the Contemporary Period, the authors address the conflicts and complex compromises that can occur between legalistic courtroom justice and the vigilante variety. *Revenge versus Legality* also analyzes some of the main obstacles to justice, ranging from judicial corruption, to racism and imperialism. It culminates in a consideration of that form of crime or lawlessness that poses the most serious threat to the rule of law: vigilante justice masquerading as legality. With its mixture of politics, literature, law, and film, this lively and accessible book offers a timely reflection on the enduring phenomenon of revenge.

Katherine Maynard is a Professor of English at Rider University. She is the author of two books: *Thomas Hardy's Tragic Poetry*, and *Men and Women at Work: Warriors and Villagers on the Job*, as well as numerous scholarly articles on literature, American culture, and ideas of justice.

Jarod Kearney is the Curator of the Woodrow Wilson Presidential Library and Museum. He publishes scholarly articles on American history and film, and writes short stories and plays.

James Guimond is a Professor of English and American Studies at Rider University. He is the author of *American Photography and the American Dream*, and his research interests include law and literature, imperialism, and American culture.

Revenge versus Legality

Wild Justice from Balzac to Clint Eastwood and Abu Ghraib

Katherine Maynard, Jarod Kearney
and James Guimond

Birkbeck
LAW PRESS

First published 2010
by Birkbeck Law Press
2 Park Square, Milton Park, Abingdon, Oxon, OX14 4RN

Simultaneously published in the USA and Canada
by Birkbeck Law Press
270 Madison Avenue, New York, NY 10016

Birkbeck Law Press is an imprint of the Taylor & Francis Group, an informa business

© 2010 Katherine Maynard, Jarod Kearney and James Guimond

Typeset in Garamond by
Taylor & Francis Books

Printed and bound in Great Britain by
CPI Antony Rowe, Chippenham, Wiltshire

British Library Cataloguing in Publication Data
A catalogue record for this book is available from the British Library

Library of Congress Cataloguing in Publication Data
Maynard, Katherine.
Revenge versus legality : wild justice from Balzac to Clint Eastwood and Abu
Ghraib / Katherine Maynard, Jarod Kearney, and James Guimond.
p. cm.
ISBN 978-0-415-56016-0
1. Criminal justice, Administration of. 2. Vigilantes. 3. Rule of law.
4. Terrorism–Prevention. 5. Revenge. I. Kearney, Jarod. II. Guimond, James.
III. Title.
K5001.M39 2010
809.3'93556–dc22
2009044981

ISBN13: 978-0-415-56016-0 (hbk)
ISBN13: 978-0-203-85437-2 (ebk)

with love for Sophia Isobel

Contents

Acknowledgments

We would like to thank Mike Britton for his drawings that capture the allure and danger of revenge. We are grateful for financial assistance from Rider University and for our supportive colleagues at Rider and at the Woodrow Wilson Presidential Library and Museum. Most of all, we would like to thank Michael, Heather, Arnold, Sophia, Katy, Laura, Pete, Gee (and Hoppy and Bob whose love of narratives remains an inspiration), and our extended families who supported our endeavor with thoughtful ideas and good humor.

Preface

"Revenge! Revenge for Wanda!" rages Michael Palin in the film *A Fish Called Wanda* (1988). Mounted on a steamroller at an airport construction site, Palin confronts the film's villain, Kevin Kline, who had earlier sadistically swallowed alive Palin's prized pet fish, Wanda, for lunch. Now is it Palin's turn for payback? The villain gloats; surely he will be able to outrun an avenger on a steamroller, but he's wrong. His feet are caught in the hardening cement of the construction site's tarmac. It's a perfect example of poetic justice and revenge, and a relatively rare instance of a comic version of a serious theme.

Revenge is a powerful and attractive emotion. From revenge in Sherlock Holmes' *Study in Scarlet* (Doyle 1930: 31) where "*RACHE*" ("revenge" in German) is scrawled in blood on the wall above a corpse, to revenge against races, Imperialist revenge, and revenge for the toppling of the Twin Towers, revenge takes many forms and shapes. Lynch mobs embrace it, ghosts do it, rogue cops enjoy it, and governments can authorize it. The rule of law is supposed to control it. The law is supposed to channel anger, hatred, and rage into legally sanctioned punishments.

Faded but still legible, a bumper sticker on a pick-up truck orders, "Never Forget 9/11." This message, with its implied demand for some type of revenge, is obviously not a new sentiment, nor one that is uniquely American. Before 9/11 there was "Remember Pearl Harbor" and "Remember the Alamo." The Serbs and the inhabitants of Ulster, for example, presumably also had similar sayings about their past and recent battles and "times of troubles." But these are nations or communities with long histories of ethnic or sectarian conflicts, and so we were not surprised when they seemed trapped in cyclical waves of revenge, repression, and retribution. It is more worrisome when one learns, first, that two prisons in Iraq built by Americans—Camp Bucca in the south and Camp Ganci (part of Abu Ghraib)—were named after firefighters who died because of the 9/11 terrorist attack, and, second, that there are disturbing revelations about prisoners having been tortured and abused at these prisons as well as at Guantanamo. Not only are the firefighters' memories being dishonored, so is the United States' credibility as a modern, civilized nation whose citizens are, in the words of former President George W. Bush, "a lawful people." "Modern" countries are supposedly removed from the cyclical trap of vengeance, yet when circumstances elicit powerful emotions in their citizens, these countries can easily fall back into the blood-feud mentality of old, at least for a time. So, when more disturbing news arrived about "extraordinary renditions," and secret torture centers in Eastern Europe and elsewhere, it seems appropriate and timely to reconsider the subject of revenge and its relationship to topics such as justice, rationality, and modernity.

In 1983, Susan Jacoby wrote an excellent book whose title—*Wild Justice*—was taken from Francis Bacon's essay, "On Revenge." (We have used the same Bacon passage for our epigraph for Chapter 1.) As her choice of subtitle, *The Evolution of Revenge*, suggests, she presumed that the justice process was evolving to become "tamer" and less vindictive as many nations were abolishing the death penalty and public opinion disapproved of victims who insisted on dwelling on their injuries. "Justice is a legitimate concept in the modern code of civilized behavior," Jacoby wrote; "Vengeance is not" (Jacoby 1983: 1). And she ascribed major exceptions to this rule—such as the American enthusiasm for capital punishment and vigilante films such as *Death Wish*—as motivated by frustration caused by the ineptitude or indifference of conventional justice systems. Nevertheless, she believed that such systems serve to remove private animus from the justice process and replace it with public retribution and punishments.

Our presumption is quite different. We emphasize that justice and revenge are coded discourses whose keys and patterns may be discerned particularly well by narratives—since revenge is inseparable from narrative. Analyzing such narratives, mainly stories, novels and films, we find much evidence of wildness, and we believe that the boundaries between public retribution and private animus are often porous. Like some of the characters portrayed by actors such as Clint Eastwood and Gene Hackman, the wilder elements in modern societies may wear suits and ties and occupy positions of power and authority, but they barely conceal their contempt for civilization and legality, their preference for violent reprisals, and the difficulty they have in controlling that violence. Add the element of emotion aroused by particularly large-scale or heinous acts, and the line between civilized retribution and barbaric vengeance becomes as blurred as the distinctions of civilization and modernity.

This dispute between legality and wild or vigilante justice, between the state's power to enforce retributions and individuals' desires to revenge themselves for injuries they have suffered, is the main theme of this book. The conflicts that result can be complex and involve serious ethical and legal concerns. Moreover, the desire for revenge can be a powerful communal passion as well as an individual one. Tribes, communities, nations, and even empires want to "strike back" when injured or insulted, and sometimes they do this by violating their own laws or international ones. A secondary and often related theme deals with the causes and consequences of injustice. Legal justice is a delicate and vulnerable process. It can be disrupted or subverted by hatred and fear, and by factors such as racism, ethnic and class prejudice, and also by incompetence or corruption by participants. When such factors discredit legal justice, groups or individuals may be motivated to "take matters into their own hands" and consider vigilante or extralegal justice an attractive alternative.

To deal with these issues in a broad but in-depth way we have selected a range of nineteenth- through twenty-first-century narratives. We have included representative texts from four cultural eras: Romanticism (Balzac and Le Fanu), Realism (Twain and detective stories), Modernism (Forster and Wright), and contemporary literature and films as well as political issues (Brink, *Mystic River* (2003), *Unforgiven* (1992), Iraq War, etc.). We give each text social and historical antecedents, particularly any factors that involve revenge and make it seem difficult to attain a just outcome according to the rule of law and its normative standards. As our table of contents suggests, the texts we have selected have an ascending degree of difficulty in this regard. Our Romantic and Realist works deal with relatively simple revenge and justice problems such as homicides (all three detective texts), judicial corruption (Le Fanu), criminal masterminds (Balzac), and slavery, racism and the science of fingerprinting (Twain). Our Modernist texts are more complex and involve issues such as racism and the power of the media (Wright), and imperialism and the power of colonial discourse (Forster) that make justice problematical. This pattern culminates in our final chapters on state (i.e., government-instigated) terrorism in Brink's *A Dry White Season* (1984) and governmental lawlessness in post-9/11 America since we consider that form of crime or lawlessness the most serious and insidious threat to the rule of law: vigilante justice masquerading as legality.

In the final chapters on Brink's novel about apartheid South Africa and America's twenty-first-century policies we analyze how revenge and the violence it encourages can be a seductive but ultimately self-destructive political force. As part of this analysis we discuss opposition to the redemptive lawlessness itself, and why it has taken different forms in the two countries. In South Africa this lawlessness was chiefly associated with the National Party's vision of Afrikaner history, and Brink and other dissident Afrikaner intellectuals opposed it by creating an alternative history and national identity that denied the legitimacy of apartheid. In the United States, we employ theologian Walter Wink's concept of the myth of redemptive violence to analyze how this myth, that originated mainly in the popular mass media, has furnished America with a vision of itself as a nation of vigilante superheroes, many of whom believe they can transform chaos into order by becoming as violent as the evildoers they are attacking. Rather ironically, since he was a major example of this myth in his spaghetti westerns and Dirty Harry roles,

Clint Eastwood has emerged as one of its chief critics by making films such as *Unforgiven* and *Mystic River* that deny the efficacy of violence. Vigilante violence in particular is portrayed in both films as being deeply flawed, and torture is depicted in *Unforgiven* as being unequivocally evil.

In contrast, although understandable to many, the US government resorted to redemptive violence after 9/11. In both Afghanistan and Iraq it was a kind of payback that occurred either as public, military violence or as the more secretive, clandestine violence of torturing prisoners, "extraordinary renditions," "extrajudicial executions," and other practices that violate US and international laws and treaties and the Geneva Conventions. Among the negative outcomes of these practices occurring at Abu Ghraib, Guantanamo and elsewhere that we analyze in this chapter, the one that is perhaps most notable is the way in which they have inverted the justice process. Instead of putting captured terrorists on public trial and revealing their guilt to the world, the American government has itself become a kind of defendant or prime suspect being investigated by a global coalition of lawyers, journalists, and human rights activists. For many Americans this was a new and disturbing development. In the legal courts of the nineteenth and twentieth centuries there were hard fought battles to dismantle institutional vengeance. For many decades Americans took it for granted that their nation was a liberating, civilizing, humanitarian force in the world. Now Americans have to find solutions to regain that vision of America.

Chapter 1

Introduction

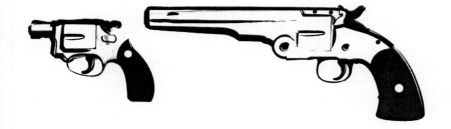

Revenge is a kind of wild justice, which the more man's nature runs to the more ought law to weed it out.

(Sir Francis Bacon, "On Revenge," 1625: 15)

It certainly may be argued, with some force, that it has never ceased to be one object of punishment to satisfy the desire for vengeance. The argument will be made plain by considering those instances in which, for one reason or another, compensation for a wrong is out of the question. ... In all these cases punishment remains as an alternative. A pain can be inflicted upon the wrong-doer, of a sort which does not restore the injured party to his former situation, or to another equally good, but which is inflicted for the very purpose of causing pain. ... The statement may be made stronger still, and it may be said, not only that the law does, but that it ought to, make the gratification of revenge an object. ... If people would gratify the passion of revenge outside of the law, if the law did not help them, the law has no choice but to satisfy the craving itself, and thus avoid the greater evil of private retribution.

(Oliver Wendell Holmes, Jr., *The Common Law*, Holmes 1992: 247)

"I'm going to kill him, Katie. Somehow, I'm going to find him before the police do, and I'm going to kill him. ... And don't you worry whether I'm up to it, baby. Daddy is up to it."

(Jimmy Marcus speaking to his daughter's corpse in *Mystic River*. Lehane *Mystic River* 2000: 289)

Revenge, retribution, payback

As even a brief excursion into Google will illustrate, revenge is a subject that is both extensive and debatable. In response to a recent inquiry, "revenge quotes," the search engine claimed to have millions of entries available. BrainyQuote, CoolQuote, and their competitors offer opinions and definitions by the dozens or the hundreds from a plethora of sources. Moralists, celebrities, religious leaders and sacred texts, philosophers, social scientists, and humorists, all have their contributions—many of which are wise and few surprising. Mahatma Gandhi and Martin Luther King, Jr. did not approve of it, which is to be expected, whereas Joseph Stalin enjoyed it immensely, also not a surprise.[1] The Bible famously gives us a choice: "Eye for an eye, tooth for a tooth" (Deuteronomy xix: 21) versus "Love your enemies, do good to those who hate you" (Luke 6: 27–28).

Luke 6 may seem ethically superior by modern standards, but Deuteronomy xix may be a better plan for evolutionary survival. According to Animal Behavior scientists, some species are so adept at attacking their enemies that they are called "punishers," a varied group that includes blue-footed boobies, moorhens, elephant seals, and side-striped jackals. Primates, such as chimpanzees, have larger brains and use them to plan their punishments (surprise attacks) and carry on what might be called feuds or vendettas (attacking an attacker's relatives) ("Revenge Motivates"). Anthropologists study how "blood revenge" is an impetus for feuds, violence, and wars in exotic past and present "tribal societies" in places such as medieval Iceland, the Balkans, New Guinea, and the Middle East. Instead of being an arcane and rather old-fashioned academic specialty, this subject began to seem surprisingly timely when troops from the United States, Great Britain, and other nations were sent to impose peace and/or democracy on nations where tribal loyalties and concepts of blood revenge still seemed powerful or capable of being revitalized despite the veneer of modernity that had been imposed by rulers such as Tito or Saddam Hussein. Hollywood and popular culture publishers have given us hundreds or perhaps thousands of pulp fictions and films whose heroes, more inspired by Deuteronomy than by Christ, return from the dead or escape from unjust imprisonments, like the Count of Monte Christo, to avenge the injuries they have suffered. Major characters in many canonical, high-culture operas, dramas, and novels are just as concerned with avenging wrongs suffered by themselves or by others: Verdi's Rigoletto, the Greeks' Orestes cycle, the Elizabethans' revenge tragedies, most notably Shakespeare's *Hamlet*, and of course Cervantes's Don Quixote who believes his "profession is none other than that of helping those who cannot help themselves, avenging those who have been wronged," especially ones wronged by "haughty foes" (Cervantes 1951: 179).

Near the end of *Mystic River* there is a scene in which Jimmy Marcus confronts his erstwhile friend, Trooper Sean Devine of the Massachusetts

State Police, at dawn on a deserted street. This scene dramatizes the theme implied by our choice of the Francis Bacon "wild justice" quote for our title and epigraph and the quotes from Holmes and *Mystic River* we have selected for this chapter. For what this scene reveals are the conflicts between the extralegal, vigilante, or "wild justice" based upon revenge and driven by passion and grief, represented by Jimmy Marcus versus the tamer, cooler, more rational and institutional legal justice practiced by Trooper Devine. As our table of contents suggests our book does not deal with wrongs or injuries inflicted by kings, queens, windmills, or amorous dukes. Instead, it is focused on nineteenth-, twentieth-, and twentieth-first-century narratives involving modern societies with competent police—such as Balzac's Detective Gondureau, and Lehane's Sean Devine. These narratives are located in nations and empires that have courts, judges, and legal systems that can supposedly avenge wrongs and thus make what Holmes called "private retribution" unnecessary. Yet in every narrative there is some flaw in the justice system that is either criticized or must be corrected by some form of extralegal justice. But extralegal justice also can have flaws, and "private" revenges or retributions can be as disastrous as those imposed by corrupt judges or biased courts. Judge Richard Posner has summarized these flaws in his comments on revenge as a motive for seeking justice:

> As soon as centralized institutions for the enforcement of law emerge, vengeance ... comes to be regarded as an archaic and destructive passion. This is partly because exact retaliation does not work well. It is not feasible for all wrongs. ... It is not adequate in situations where the aggressor can count on avoiding retaliation much of the time. ... And a commitment to limited retaliation is hard to stick by in the highly emotional circumstances in which revenge is administered. So vengeance falls out of favor, not only in ethics but in law, where taking the law into your own hands becomes a crime.
>
> (Posner, *Law and Literature: A Misunderstood Relation*, 1988: 31–32)

However, another plausible reason for this insistence that retribution and revenge is the state's prerogative (exercised through its governmental agencies) can be related to Weber's claim that "legal coercion by violence is the monopoly of the state" (Weber 1954: 14), and that nation states are unwilling to share this monopoly with mere citizens, no matter how much they may have been wronged or treated unjustly.

In the confrontation between Jimmy and Sean in *Mystic River*, on a street in Somerville, Massachusetts, both men have done what they sought desperately to achieve, and both have failed. Jimmy has kept his vow to kill the man he thought was his daughter's murderer, but it was the wrong man. Sean has arrested the actual murderers, but he was a few hours too late to prevent the death of Dave Boyle. There was no middle ground or compromise that could have saved Boyle from the lethal chain of coincidences, mistakes, and circumstantial evidence that destroyed him as Marcus and Devine each followed their own ideas of justice to their bitter and logical conclusions.

One such compromise was suggested a century earlier by another Bostonian, Judge Oliver Wendell Holmes, Jr. As our quote indicates, he was willing to sacrifice some of the law's rationality and logic so that it could accommodate individual and communal passions like Jimmy Marcus's—the kind of judgment that has caused Holmes to be praised as America's greatest "realist" jurist by his admirers and condemned as its worst "cynic" by his critics. For despite the hundred years in time and the differences in class that separate them, Holmes, the Cambridge Brahmin, and Marcus, the Boston Southie, might understand one another. Though Holmes the jurist would condemn Marcus's course of action in *Mystic River*, his murder of Dave Boyle to avenge the death of his daughter, Katie, he might have understood Marcus's "craving" for revenge. Hence, Holmes' insistence that the legal justice system, what he calls the "law," must act as the agent for the passions of persons needing revenge. In addition, both Holmes and Marcus would almost certainly have agreed that Bacon's prescription was not a realistic one, that the desire for revenge is often so powerful that it is naïve to believe it can be uprooted by the law as if it were a weed.

The scene from *Mystic River* can be considered an emblem of the relationship that exists between revenge and legality. By bringing Jimmy Marcus and Sean Devine together at the moment of their estrangement, when Devine realizes Marcus has murdered Boyle, it eloquently symbolizes not only the conflict between Marcus's extralegal or vigilante justice and the kind of lawful procedure that Sean Devine has used to discover who really killed Marcus's daughter, but signals also how the two men are inextricably linked by their shared past and their future hostility with one another. For the street where they are standing, the place where both have instinctively returned at this moment of crisis, called Gannon Street in the novel, is the street where Dave Boyle was abducted by two pedophiles when they were all eleven years old—an event that, as Marcus realizes, both changed and inextricably intertwined their lives. Moreover, behind the two men, linking them visually, is a bridge, the US1-Tobin Bridge over the Mystic River where Jimmy "buried" Dave. Analogously, as this book will show, there often are inescapable patterns, linkages, and connections—as well as conflicts—between the legal and extralegal paths to justice that the authors we have selected describe.

Special crimes and wild justice

One such pattern is the way in which certain kinds of crimes, mysteries, injuries, and transgressions seem to incite extralegal responses particularly strongly. Whether they occur in historical or fictional circumstances, these are the crimes or injuries that appear so mystifying or disturbing that ordinary, conventional legality—the usual, normative police procedures, judges' rulings, lawyers' motions, and jury verdicts—seems inadequate. A Sherlock Holmes or a Dirty Harry is needed to solve or avenge such a crime; cruel or unusual procedures or punishments are called for; the law must be bent, broken or at least supplemented to achieve a just revenge. In *The Secret Agent*, Conrad describes Scotland Yard as having a "Special Crimes Department" (Conrad 1924: 83), a fictional version of the actual C.I.D. (Criminal Investigation Department). Borrowing Conrad's terminology, and excluding cases in which it is the injured party that seeks the revenge, we have focused on four categories of Special Crimes.

Special crimes: locked rooms and magic bullets

First, there are crimes that confound our conventional sense of space, time, and/or agency. Though the examples we have selected and analyze in Chapter 2 are fictional—detective narratives by Doyle, Christie, and Glaspell, all involving revenge as a motive—there are enough unsolved, or semi-solved, actual crimes in this category to make it significant. The assassinations of Martin Luther King, Jr., President John F. Kennedy, and Prime Minister Olof Palme of Sweden, to name only three prominent examples, all contain enough mysterious details and inexplicable facts—such as the notorious "magic bullet" in the Kennedy case—to keep conspiracy theorists busy for decades. The arrests, convictions, and even the confessions in the three cases only served to undermine the credibility of the legal systems that produced them. In contrast, our fictional detectives solve their cases with exemplary certainty, and this certitude contributes to the moral authority they exercise by deciding that the homicides that occurred were justified and the victims deserved to die.

Special crimes: crimes against kin

Second, there are the crimes against kinship, especially children or parents, as in *Mystic River*, but sometimes against extended family members or close friends; for example, William Munny's ferocious revenge on the town of Big Whiskey in Clint Eastwood's *Unforgiven*, after its sadistic sheriff kills his friend, Ned Logan. Or it may even—in the case of Glaspell's "A Jury of Her Peers"—be an attack on a pet. Like Munny or Jimmy Markus, persons seeking blood revenge for these crimes are not much interested in legal rules or niceties such as evidence, fairness, or extenuating circumstances. Impelled by grief and anger, they want revenge, and they want it to be deadly. A student in a class, who had discussed *Mystic River* and Harper Lee's *To Kill a Mockingbird* (1960), was asked what she would do if someone harmed a "dear family member." Would she hire Jimmy Markus or Lee's idealistic lawyer, Atticus Finch, to remedy the situation? If the family member were a distant cousin, she'd hire Finch because he "knew the law," she said, but if someone harmed her seven-year-old son, then she would hire Jimmy. "He's the kind of man who'd get the job done," she said, implying that homicide was exactly the kind of "job" she had in mind. Nor are some persons seeking this kind of revenge influenced by concerns for their own rational self-interest or even their own survival. Thus Ben Du Toit, speaking of the South African police who killed his friend, Gordon Ngubene, in Brink's *A Dry White Season*, tells his daughter that someday, "we'll have all of Gordon's murderers lined up against a wall" (Brink 1984: 202, 208), a judgment that, in apartheid South Africa, leads to Ben's own death.

Special crimes: crimes against symbolic places and persons

Third, there are what we call symbolic crimes. These are attacks on persons, places, or objects that are considered so significant a part of a community's identity that an attack on them is considered an assault on the entire community itself. The community in question may be a nation, a religion, a political party, or even an empire. What matters is that the attack is seen as injury to something that is—to use religious terminology—"sacred," and, therefore, it must be avenged—either by legal or extralegal means—or else the community will be irreparably weakened. A major recent example of this kind of attack would be the explosion that wrecked the Shiite Golden Dome shrine in Samarra in February 2006, an event that led to dozens of Shiite attacks on Sunni mosques throughout Iraq and caused "a tragic escalation of sectarian rage and reprisal" (Worth 2006). The Al Qaeda attack on the World Trade Center and the Pentagon in September 2001 is an obvious equivalent for this type of attack but on a secular institution. So also is the fire that destroyed the Reichstag building in February 1933, a catastrophe that the Nazis (who may have started the fire) used as a pretext for attacking their enemies, destroying German democracy, and establishing Hitler's dictatorship. An important fictional equivalent is Conrad's *The Secret Agent*, and Mr. Vladimir's plot to cause a "dynamite outrage" attacking the Greenwich Observatory, because he considers it a "sacrosanct" symbol of the British faith in science (Conrad 1924: 33, 36).

If this category is expanded to comprise attacks on persons who have a charismatic, symbolic importance—as well as a conventional political significance—to their followers, then the King, Kennedy, and Palme assassinations mentioned earlier might be included. So also might the murders of charismatic political activists and dissidents, such as Steve Biko and the Chilean folk singer, Victor Jara, though obviously achieving any form of retribution for their deaths was possible only after the apartheid and

Pinochet regimes, that were responsible for their deaths, had reluctantly relinquished power. In addition, if one adds race and sex as "sacrosanct" topics of discourse, then certain crimes against women, such as rape, take on a strongly symbolic significance. When such crimes violate "racial purity," they are likely to be avenged by the harshest possible legal or extralegal means, and two of our chapters—those on E. M. Forster's *A Passage to India* (1952) and Richard Wright's *Native Son* (1940) deal with this issue in the context of the racial mores that prevailed in the British Empire and Jim Crow America.

Special crimes: the police as criminals

The murders of Jara and Biko introduce us to our fourth category of "special" crimes, injustices, and injuries: ones that are committed by persons operating within—not outside of—an established legal system. In the cruder, simpler society of Big Whiskey, Wyoming, in 1881—depicted in Eastwood's *Unforgiven*—injustices perpetrated by the town sheriff, a sadistic bully, are speedily revenged. William Munny, the film's aging but still lethal gunman, rides into town with a shotgun in one hand and a Smith & Wesson .45 Schofield revolver in the other. Minutes later, the sheriff and his henchmen are dead or dying. In less primitive, more complex societies Munny's kind of wild, extralegal justice is rarely possible. Corrupt, biased, unfair, and even criminal legal officials can be adept at hiding behind the skirts of the law, manipulating it, and using it to protect themselves as they subvert the justice process. News stories and the popular culture media are replete with examples of rogue cops, crooked judges, and shyster lawyers, and this book is equally well stocked with the mendacious, the prejudiced, and the malevolent. In our chapter on Sheridan Le Fanu's "Mr. Justice Harbottle," that novella's title character, an unscrupulous hanging judge, uses his position and legal skills to make sure that his mistress's husband is executed for forgery. Buckley, the ruthless State's Attorney in Wright's *Native Son*, is an ambitious politician who is running for re-election and uses inflammatory, racist rhetoric to guarantee that Bigger Thomas receives a death sentence. Forster's Police Superintendent McBryde in *A Passage to India*, the best of a bad lot, is also a racist, but he is a thoughtful, "scientific" one. He bases his prejudices on a "theory about climatic zones," according to which, "all unfortunate natives are criminals at heart, for the simple reason that they live south of latitude 30," and therefore he assumes all the Indians he arrests are guilty (Forster 1952: 184). As for Captain Stolz and the Special Branch police Andre Brink describes in *A Dry White Season*, they are not only racists but also criminals as they torture and kill prisoners in their custody. Determined to protect South Africa's apartheid regime at all costs, they maintain a façade of public legality while secretly resorting to blackmail, terrorism, and murder to silence anyone who dares to question them and their methods. But how, especially in cases like these, can revenge, retribution, or genuine justice be achieved? When position, privilege, and prejudice are allied with power and force, including lethal force, how can injustice be avoided or injuries be avenged? Our answer is a corollary of philosopher John Gray's comment that, "Justice does not speak always with one voice" (Gray 2000: 7). In the texts and examples we analyze there are two recognizably different but equally eloquent voices.

Legality and carnival

> Our courts have their faults, as does any human institution, but ... our courts are the great levelers, and in our courts all men are created equal. I'm no idealist to believe firmly in the integrity of our courts. ... that is no ideal to me. That is a living, working reality! ... I am confident that you gentlemen will review without passion the evidence that you have heard, [and] come to a decision.
>
> (Atticus Finch addressing the jury in *To Kill a Mockingbird*,
> Lee 1960: 233)

> When Gen. Augusto Pinochet breathed his last ... this much seemed clear to everybody in Chile: The man who had lived his whole life and never paid for even one of his crimes had done it again. ... everybody in Chile thought that Pinochet had escaped judgment. Everybody, that is, except for a young man named Francisco Cuadrado Prats, who decided some sort of punishment, no matter how symbolic, was merited. So he walked up to Pinochet's coffin and deliberately, calmly spat on the dictator's face as he lay there in full regalia. [Ariel Dorfman describing an event in Santiago, Chile, 12 December 2006.]
>
> (Dorfman, *Los Angeles Times*, 17 December 2006)

The first voice is that of Atticus Finch and, like the voice of Oliver Wendell Holmes, Jr., it is the voice of law and legality, of retribution tempered and controlled by reason. This voice demands judgments and verdicts based on objective rules, precedents, and evidence, rather than those influenced by subjective, arbitrary, or capricious personal opinions. In its ideal form, as epitomized by Atticus Finch, it may be zealous and passionate as well as rational as its participants narrate their stories. But this passion must be disciplined and regulated by judicial procedures that are meant to establish clear boundaries between legal narrations and "ordinary" storytelling. "Maintaining the boundary between the courtroom and ordinary life," explains Paul Gewirtz, "is a central part of what legal process is all about. ... The mob may have their faces pressed hard against the courthouse windows, but the achievement of the trial is to keep those forces at bay. ... there is always a struggle between this idealized vision of law ... and the relentless incursion of ordinary life." "In the context of the criminal trial," Gewirtz says, this "struggle is in large measure played out over narrative construction and reception—a struggle over what stories may be told at trial, over the way stories must be told and even listened to. ... [Legal storytelling] must conform to certain distinctive legal rules of storytelling contained in the law of evidence and procedure," so that the wrong kinds of storytelling do not "invade the criminal trial with their anger, fear, and ignorance as well as their concern and curiosity" (Gewirtz 1996: 135–36).

Like Atticus Finch, Francisco Prats is an agent of justice, and a courageous one. In *To Kill a Mockingbird*, Finch, unarmed, faces down a lynch mob armed with rifles and shotguns until he is rescued by his children when they remind the mob that Finch is a friend, as well as a lawyer, who has performed legal services for them for "entailments," payments in crops rather than cash that—in Alabama in 1935—they do not possess. Prats is the grandson of General Carlos Prats who, along with his wife, was murdered by a car bomb in Buenos Aires in 1974 at Pinochet's instigation. A patient man, the younger Prats waited many years, and then for 12 hours in the line filing past the dictator's coffin, for the opportunity to spit on the dead man's face. He did this in full view of hundreds of ardent Pinochet supporters who began beating and kicking him until he was rescued by a group of military policemen who briefly arrested him and then freed him without making charges. His act, says Dorfman, was a kind of revenge, a voice that "spoke for his murdered grandparents and for all the missing and mutilated bodies of his land. It expressed what millions of Chileans had long dreamed of doing and what one of us finally dared to do" (Dorfman 2006). But it is a very different kind of voice than Finch's voice of law and legality. Along with the Chileans who celebrated Pinochet's death in Santiago and Madrid, it is the voice of what we, influenced by Mikhail Bakhtin, refer to as carnival justice: a form of revenge and a kind of justice derived from what Bakhtin calls the "carnival sense of the world," which is embodied in motifs and symbols that occur with an almost obsessive frequency in many narrative texts dealing with justice and revenge. These motifs, as described by Bakhtin, include masks, dualisms, dismemberments, carnival feasts or Saturnalias, scandal scenes, "parodies, travesties, humiliations, profanations, comic crownings and uncrownings" (Bakhtin 1984: 11).

Legality and carnival: their antecedents

The differences between carnival justice and conventional legality are numerous and significant. Their cultural antecedents, for example, are virtually antithetical. Modern legal systems are based upon the stable, rational norms of what Jürgen Habermas and his followers describe as the bourgeois or "modern public sphere" created by Enlightenment intellectuals and the civil societies that flourished in Western Europe and North America in the late eighteenth and the early nineteenth centuries. Two related developments, which were almost as significant, were the humanitarian campaigns to reform criminal justice systems, led by intellectuals such as Voltaire and Cesare Beccaria, and the movements to codify existing laws (e.g., in France, Germany, and Austria) or to write new constitutions establishing republics, bills of rights, and constitutional monarchies (in the United States, Poland, and France). For participants in these civil societies, says Keith Baker, rational "public opinion" would replace absolutist edicts and decrees as

> the ultimate source of authority in [society because it] was construed as the universal reason of the generality of thinking individuals continuously engaged in open discussion. Under its aegis, power and domination in human life were to give way to free acceptance of the enlightened order of human rationality. ... Publicity, the essential condition for rational discussion, was now opposed to the secrecy shrouding the mysteries of absolute sovereignty. Reason—abstract, universal, constant reason—was invoked against the disordered commands of arbitrary will. ... These, finally, became the legal principles of the constitutional states through which bourgeois civil society eventually secured its interests in the early nineteenth century.
>
> (Baker 1999: 183, 185)

By being rational, modern legal systems promote order, stability, and consistency in relationships, particularly legal ones, so individuals can precisely "calculate the consequences of their own and others' behavior" (Habermas 1996: 143). By conducting their proceedings in public, rather than before secret royal tribunals or Star Chambers that might rely on torture and anonymous informers, modern criminal justice systems enable communities to judge whether trials are conducted in accordance with the rights and principles guaranteed by—to cite one influential example—the 1776 Virginia Bill of Rights which states that in criminal cases, a "man hath a right to demand the cause and nature of his accusation, to be confronted with the accusers and witnesses, to call for evidence in his favour, and to a speedy trial by an impartial jury of his vicinage, without whose unanimous consent he cannot be found guilty, nor can he be compelled to give evidence against himself; that no man be deprived of his liberty except by the law of the land, or the judgment of his peers."

In contrast, what Bakhtin calls "the carnival sense of the world" (Bakhtin 1984: 11) is derived from medieval folk pageants and festivals, Menippean satires, Renaissance literary texts by Rabelais, Cervantes, and Shakespeare, novels by authors such as Dostoyevsky, and contemporary carnivals that still flourish, albeit in attenuated form, in cities like New Orleans, Rio de Janeiro, and Venice. Rowdy, bawdy, disorderly, and sometimes subversive, carnival feasts and events, as Bakhtin points out, are linked to "moments of crisis [and instability], of breaking points in the cycle of nature or in the life of society" (Bakhtin 1984: 9). Mardi Gras/Carnival, Saturnalia/Twelfth Night, and Halloween/Todos los Santos/El dia de Los Muertos, plus insurrections, protests, and street theater—all of these "breaking points" are potential sites for carnivalistic behavior, motifs, and symbols. In contrast to the legality of the public sphere, which is monitored by rational public opinion and tries to keep law "separate from politics, passion, and public resistance" (Gewirtz 1996b: 135), carnival expresses public or communal feelings that can take many forms and sometimes be highly irrational and/or political. Thus, at one extreme, carnival justice and punishments can be as apolitical as the innocent revelry of Shakespeare's comedies, such as *Twelfth Night*, in which prudes and bores are ridiculed, or they can take the form of the brilliant comic buffoonery satirizing knight errantry in *Don Quixote*. At another extreme they can be as violent and as explicitly political as the scene in Isabelle Allende's novel, *Of Love and Shadows* (1988), in which protesters disrupt a ceremony dedicating a monument to her fictional version of Pinochet's regime. "Popular fury was translated into street demonstrations so riotous that not even the police shock troops ... could control the people pouring into the streets," Allende writes.

> At the construction site of the monument ... an enormous pig was released, costumed in cockades, a Presidential sash, a dress uniform cape, and a general's cap. The beast ran squealing through the throng, who spit on it, kicked it, and hurled insults at it before the eyes of irate soldiers who used every trick ... to rescue the trampled sacred emblems; finally, amid screams, sticks, and howling sirens, they shot the beast. Nothing remained but the enormous humiliated carcass lying in a pool of black blood on which floated the insignia, the kepi, and the tyrant's cape.
>
> (Allende 1988: 274–75)

Legality and carnival: order and disorder

Both carnival and legality can be, as Atticus Finch says of America's courts, "great levelers" that may enable communities and societies to achieve justice and avenge injuries by transforming private concerns, interests, and feelings into public ones. Both make "private life public," as Bakhtin said of criminal trials (Bakhtin 1982: 124) and help individuals or groups fight "all modes of settlements that are somehow unjust" as Habermas claimed in 1992 (Baker 1999: 462–79). Either by insisting on the rule of law, according to which all persons must be treated alike irregardless of their race, gender, class, or other considerations, or by claiming that even dictators can be spat upon and depicted as pigs by people whom they have harmed, both demand that no one is "above the law" or immune from scathing criticisms if they deserve them. However, the manners in which the voices of legality and the carnival square speak to achieve this leveling are radically different.

Above all, modern legality seeks to be orderly. As that form of justice became established and refined in eighteenth-century England, Douglas Hay writes:

> strict procedural rules ... were enforced in the high courts and at assizes, especially in capital cases. Moreover, most penal statutes were inter-preted by the judges in an extremely narrow and formalistic fashion. ... If a name or date was incorrect, or if the accused was described as a "farmer" rather than the approved term "yeoman," the prosecution could fail. ... [This] punctilious attention to forms, the dispassionate and legalistic exchanges between counsel and the judge, argued that those administering and using the laws submitted to its rules. The law thereby became something more than the creature of a ruling class—it became a power with its own claims, higher than those of prosecutors, lawyers, and even the great scarlet-robed assize judge himself.
>
> (Hays 1975: 32–33)

This concern for order extends beyond procedures to all kinds of protocols, rules, and customs. The ways that judges and attorneys dress, for example, the English with their wigs and gowns, the behavior of witnesses, attorneys, and magistrates in courtrooms, the swearing of oaths, and the prescribed order in which judges, lawyers, and witnesses are allowed to speak—all emphasize the formality of legal speech and its goal of achieving the highest degree of certainty. Thus, whenever possible, legality aligns itself with for-ensics and the hard sciences. Careful distinctions are enforced between admissible and inadmissible kinds of testimony; witnesses may be cross-examined to test their credibility; confessions made by defendants who have not been properly informed about their rights may be ruled inadmissible; expert witnesses must have credentials proving their expertise. Even the placement of furniture, railings, and other barriers enforces order. The judge sits behind her bench with a flag beside her; jurors and witnesses sit in their respective enclosures. Barriers and boundaries, both physical and procedural, are ubiquitous. Designed to protect what Gewirtz calls "legal storytelling" from contamination by "ordinary" life and language, these rules and bound-aries create a Newtonian sense of time, space, identity, guilt and innocence.

Ideally, in this kind of justice story a crime occurs at a certain time and place, and through reliable evidence a jury can reasonably decide whether the prosecution's or the defense's story is true and thus whether the defendant is guilty or not. To use *To Kill a Mockingbird* as an example, the narrative definitely has a victim, a young white woman, Mayella Ewell, who suffered a black eye and bruises on her face and had choke marks on her neck. The question is whether these injuries were inflicted by a black man, Tom Robinson, who raped her (Mayella's story) or by her abusive father, Bob Ewell (Tom's and Atticus's story). Through a masterly cross-examination,

Finch proves a left-handed man attacked Mayella. Since Tom's left arm is crippled, he is innocent, and Bob Ewell (who is left-handed) is really the guilty person. Even though a racist jury finds Tom guilty, the narrative's audience knows that Atticus is certainly right and his story is the true one. And a small sense of satisfaction occurs when the jury deliberates much longer than expected.

In contrast to legality and its quest for order and certitude, carnival justice seems messy or even chaotic, a mélange of revenges, vendettas, and mis-alliances, a world of masks, hidden identities, and ambivalent or concealed realities. And of course, whether it takes the form of a Halloween parade in Greenwich Village, orgiastic Mardi Gras revelry in Rio and New Orleans, or a political demonstration in Madrid's Plaza del Sol, carnival flourishes in the streets; it loves to mingle with "ordinary" life, and it is no respecter of boundaries, rules, and decorum. Instead of being based on conventional rationalism as legality is, this mentality takes the form of carnivalistic images, symbols, and motifs that have, says Bakhtin, their own "characteristic logic." But this is, he acknowledges, a "peculiar logic": the logic of "change and renewal ... of the 'turnabout,' of a continual shifting from top to bottom, from front to rear, of numerous parodies and travesties, humiliations, profa-nations" (Bakhtin 1984: 11, 275). Or it can be seen as the "logic" of dual-isms that "unite within themselves both poles of change and crisis: birth and death ... blessing and curse ... praise and abuse, youth and old age, top and bottom, face and backside, stupidity and wisdom. Very characteristic for carnival thinking [are also] paired images, chosen for their contrast (high/low, fat/thin, etc.) or for their similarity (doubles/twins)" (Bakhtin 1988: 126).

Legality, as Hay points out, strives for precise, punctilious identifications and language in which a man must be a "yeoman" and not a "farmer" if a case is to succeed. But a common carnivalistic dualistic pattern is that of masked or hidden identities. And a second related motif is that of a secret language with special or double meanings that may be used, for example, by lawyers to mystify clients or by criminals to communicate with one another. In some cases these languages are presented as being so secret that the authors claim they need to translate them for the benefit of other characters (and, by implication, for the benefit of readers) as Balzac's detective, Gon-dureau, does in *Père Goriot* (Balzac 1998: 145). Similarly, in *Oliver Twist* Dickens declares that the thieves' cant spoken by Sikes and Fagin is "unin-telligible," but he then communicates what the two criminals say through signs. When Sikes warns Fagin about the gallows, says Dickens, he "con-tented himself with tying an imaginary knot under his left ear, and jerking his head over on the right shoulder; a piece of dumb show which the Jew appeared to understand perfectly" (Dickens 1960: 77–78).

Also common in many kinds of criminal justice narratives is the motif of the double or multiple identity, such as the disguised detective or the hypocritical villain. Such a character's identity will be presented as a fusion or alloy of two selves—one that is private, mysterious, and possibly criminal and the other that is public and respectable such as Tom Driscoll's in Twain's (Clemens') *Pudd'nhead Wilson*, Norman Bates in Alfred Hitchcock's *Psycho*, or Jekyll and Hyde in Stevenson's tale. These dualistic characters may have one or more secret names like Vautrin (née Jacques Collin, alias Trompe-la Mort or Death Dodger) in *Père Goriot* and Dave Boyle (alias the Boy Who'd Escaped from Wolves) in *Mystic River* (Lehane 2000: 321). Such multiple names may also—as in the cases of Vautrin and Tom Driscoll in *Pudd'nhead Wilson*—indicate that the character inhabits conflicting identities and communities. In fact, in his divided identity as a changeling, Tom is both publicly a slave owner and secretly a slave at the same time. Or in the case of Dave Boyle, Dave seen by daylight is a harmless, rather pathetic victim of predatory child abuse, while by night he is "the Boy," who identifies with vampires and is himself, potentially, a sexual predator: one who is capable of committing homicide as a way of avenging what he suffered when he was eleven. Some of these dualistic characters, particularly Vautrin, are able to control their second, "criminal" selves, whereas others—Norman Bates, Dave Boyle, Edgar Allen Poe's William Wilson—have only sporadic, unreliable control.

A second set of carnivalistic motifs, emphasizing the duality and instability of groups more than individuals, may be grouped under the heading of what Bakhtin calls saturnalias, carnival feasts, and "scandal" scenes in which persons or "things which were once self-enclosed ... are drawn into carnivalistic contacts and combinations ... combin[ing] the sacred with the profane, the lofty with the low, the great with the significant, the wise with the stupid" (Bakhtin 1988: 123–24). Scandal scenes may begin in places and times when different classes or groups in a society meet and a certain kind of discursive decorum is supposed to prevail. A "reasonable" viewpoint or a familiar ritual is expected to control the behavior of the persons who arrive or speak. But these expectations are disrupted by new voices, parodies, eccentric, absurd, or "scandalous" behavior, and "bad" or enigmatic language. Discursive hierarchies may be disrupted, inverted, or become ambivalent. New or strange voices—obscene, irreverent, or "low" ones—accompanied by laughter and profanity—may crowd into the narrative and "decrown" authoritative, decorous voices (Bakhtin 1988: 117, 123) and the institutions they represent such as the family, religion, and judicial or political power. A dinner, a party, a courtroom, or a funeral may be disrupted; bizarre or eccentric behavior may displace anticipated social forms. Rebels, outcasts, criminals, drunks, and marginalized individuals may articulate their viewpoints while more "serious," authoritative persons are silenced or ridiculed. Conflicts and viewpoints that have been suppressed and animosities that have been concealed may flare into the open. Examples of such scenes would include Fernando Prats spitting on Pinochet, the Christmas dinner in Chapter 1 of Joyce's *Portrait of the Artist*, the scenes in the dining room of the Maison Vacquer in Balzac's *Père Goriot* that are dominated by Vautrin, the meeting of the Karamazov family at Father Zosima's monastery in Dostoevsky's *The Brothers Karamazov*, the temperance debate that turns into a riot in *Pudd'nhead Wilson*, and the horrific Du Toit family Christmas dinner in *A Dry White Season*. Moreover, because of their insistence on order and decorum, trials and legal proceedings are excellent targets for scandal scenes in which highly placed but unjust individuals can be defeated or unmasked. Examples would include Justice Harbottle's discomfiture when a ghost appears in Old Bailey in Chapter 4 of Le Fanu's novella "Mr. Justice Harbottle," Tom Driscoll's fainting when his secret identity is revealed by *Pudd'nhead Wilson*, and the collapse of the Anglo-Indians' case against Aziz in Chapter 24 of *A Passage to India*, and the near riot at Aziz's hospital that follows it.

Saturnalias, which are an overlapping category, may also be scandalous, but what is notable about them is that—as their name suggests—they have a seasonal element or a relationship to the solar cycle. This gives them a mythical or ritual resonance that contributes to their complexity and power. Thus, whereas legality is deeply related to the Newtonian worldview we associate with the Enlightenment, the Saturnalian elements of carnival can be related to what Northrop Frye describes as the archetypal "dialectic of desire and repugnance" that causes us to have a "desire for fertility or victory" and a fear or "repugnance for drought or enemies. [Therefore] we have rituals of social integration, and we have rituals of expulsion, execution, and punishment." This kind of ritual, says Frye, "is pre-logical, pre-verbal, and in a sense pre-human. Its attachment to the calendar seems to link human life to the natural cycle" (Frye 1957: 106)—a logical linkage since Saturn was the Roman god of fertility and agriculture. Since the natural cycle is such a complex trope, when carnivalistic motifs of this sort (including ones related to Halloween and Mardi Gras as well as to the winter solstice) appear in justice narratives, they almost invariably involve a broad spectrum of issues related to fertility, generation, family, death, rebirth, survival, and renewal as well as those representing justice per se, such as verdicts, revenges, and the expulsions, executions, and punishments Frye speaks of.

Legality and carnival fusions: three cases—Sean Devine vs. Jimmy Marcus; Bob Ewell vs. Atticus Finch; The King of Spain vs. Augusto Pinochet Ugarte

Despite these differences, which are significant and substantial, the "voices" of legality and carnival can be compatible and can co-exist—or even supplement one another—in the same narratives. Both are inclusive discursive systems; legality and the rule of law are supposed to apply to everyone (i.e., no one is "above the law"), and no one is excluded from carnival, no matter how strange or outlandish his or her behavior. Returning to the meeting of Jimmy Marcus and Sean Devine, for example, at that moment in the film each has become the other's enemy and antithesis. Though haggard, disheveled, and hung-over, Sean is still the alumnus of the Boston Latin School who has a college education and is well on his way to becoming a young urban professional "super cop" who can close cases faster than anyone else. His adversary, Marcus, who spent his late adolescence in prison before going straight and owning a neighborhood grocery store, may very well return to criminality. In his leather trench coat and gloves, his face and feelings masked by black sunglasses by the end of the novel, he is already considering becoming a "benevolent" neighborhood crime boss—the kind of discrete semi-legitimate criminal who dispenses extralegal justice in his territory and who sometimes may be indicted but rarely convicted, even by super cops like Sean Devine. Yet in the Epilogue and final scene Sean and Jimmy meet again during a neighborhood street parade and carnival. The cop and the gangster—carnival can contain both.

Moreover, hearing the "deep, steady tom-tom" beat of the parade drums (Lehane 2000: 436) revitalizes them both. Reunited with his estranged wife and celebrating the birth of his infant daughter, Sean is, for the first time, a happy man. Marcus, absolved from the guilt he felt for killing Dave Boyle by his wife Annabeth's sexual power, has begun to overcome the grief and depression that followed his daughter's death. Both men are reintegrated with their families and community by carnival, not by the strict legal justice that the Commonwealth of Massachusetts would prefer.

Despite Atticus Finch's commitment to legality, it is carnival, not the law, that saves his family from a squalid disaster. Bob Ewell, the narrative's redneck villain, is not content with perjuring himself and indirectly causing Tom Robinson's death (Tom is shot by a deputy while trying to escape). Ewell is also determined to punish Finch for making him look like a fool and a liar on the witness stand. Too cowardly to attack Finch directly, though he does spit in Finch's face in public, Ewell later tries to kill his children instead. Finch, incapable of being that evil or vindictive himself, dismisses Ewell as someone who will "settle down when the weather changes" and takes no precautions (Lee 1960: 287). Ewell waits until Halloween for an opportunity to attack, which is appropriate, since, like other seasonal festivals and carnivals, Halloween has its sinister side expressed through its iconography of witches, demons, and goblins. Another carnival motif, feasting, and a touch of grotesque humor are provided by Finch's daughter's costume. Ordered to appear in a school pageant about her region's products, she is dressed as a ham, one that Ewell plans to "carve."

Unfortunately for Ewell, he is not the only demon or goblin afoot that Halloween night. For years the town's children have treated a young man called Boo Radley as a bogeyman and outcast. Thought by the townsfolk to be mute and possibly mentally handicapped, Boo is actually a gentle recluse who secretly watches over the Finch children, without their knowing it. Despite his negligible social skills, he is shrewd enough to carry a butcher knife with him on

Halloween; presumably it is a sharp one since it ends up firmly embedded between two of Ewell's ribs. Finch, ever the lawyer, thinks the facts of Ewell's death will have to be presented to a Grand Jury, but the county Sheriff, Heck Tate, thinks otherwise. Boo's vigilante act performed several helpful community services, so why subject him to a community interest that he would not enjoy? To use carnival terminology, the Sheriff has become, like Boo Radley, a wise fool who behaves more intelligently than Finch does with his legalistic qualms. "Bob Ewell fell on his knife," the Sheriff announces in the film version of the story.

> "He killed himself. There's a black man dead for no reason. Now the man responsible for it is dead. Let the dead bury the dead this time, Mr. Finch. I never heard tell it was against the law for any citizen ... to do his utmost to prevent a crime from being committed, which is exactly what [Boo Radley] did. But maybe you'll tell me it's my duty to tell the town all about it, not to hush it up. You know what'll happen then. ... takin' one man, who done you and this town a big service, and draggin' him with his shy ways into the limelight ... To me, that's a sin. It's a sin. And I'm not about to have it on my head. I may not be much, Mr. Finch, but I'm still Sheriff of Maycomb County, and [I say] Bob Ewell fell on his knife."
>
> (Script, *To Kill a Mockingbird*, 1962)

Legality, as embodied in Finch, insists on accuracy, truth, due process, and transparency as means for achieving justice. Carnival, speaking through the Sheriff, is less scrupulous, quite willing to mask the truth, if it is necessary to do so, or to present in symbols, such as Isabelle Allende's portrait of Pinochet as a pig in a Presidential sash and uniform in *Of Love and Shadows* (1988).

Considered in this context, the Pinochet narrative is an excellent example of how legalism can co-habit with carnival as the two discourses reinforced one another when the dictator's numerous enemies sought to hold him accountable for his crimes and the suffering he and his armed forces had inflicted. With at least 3,000 Chileans and citizens of other nations killed and a further 1,200 "disappeared"; with an estimated 180,000 detained during the first year of his regime (90% of whom had been tortured); and with approximately a million Chileans living in exile (Dorfman 2002: 20), there obviously were going to be demands for some kind of justice, revenge, or retribution when Pinochet stopped being President and Army Commander in the 1990s. The dictator and his associates began protecting themselves against this threat as early as 1978 when they rewrote the Chilean constitution to provide amnesties for themselves. As an additional precaution an office was created, Senator for Life, that was immune from prosecution and to be occupied by Pinochet himself, and of course he and his associates also could count on the statutes of limitations expiring on many of their crimes.

Yet another obstacle to justice was created by the Chilean junta's proclivity to "disappear" the corpses of their victims, usually by throwing them from helicopters far out to sea or by burying them in abandoned mine shafts. Incriminating causes of death, mutilation, marks left by torture, all were conveniently eliminated, along with the *desaparecidos* themselves.

Much to everyone's surprise, however, the aging ex-dictator became a major character in a legal thriller that began in October 1998 when he went to England for surgery. While still in the hospital, he was arrested and put under house arrest for seventeen months while the British government and the English legal system struggled with a Spanish demand that he be extradited to Spain and put on trial for genocide, torture, murder, and other crimes committed against Spanish citizens residing in Chile during his dictatorship. The other major actor in this thriller was Pinochet's nemesis, a Spanish Investigating Magistrate, Judge Balthazar Garzon. A judicial celebrity in Spain, Garzon's reputation is based not only on his legal skills but also his willingness to take on high-profile, high-risk cases against dangerous adversaries such as drug traffickers, terrorists, and arms dealers. In the legal battle that followed Pinochet's arrest, Garzon and his allies had to display a considerable amount of legalistic creativity. To deal with the statutes of limitations issue, for example, Garzon charged Pinochet "with 'crimes against humanity,' as defined by the 1946 Nuremberg Principles," which describes them as "'universal crimes against basic human standards' (which include systematized torture, killings, disappearance[s], etc.) that have no statute of limitations and can be tried at any time in any nation" (Feitlowitz 2000a). Not once but twice the case went to the Law Lords, Britain's equivalent of the US Supreme Court, and Garzon won both judgments by votes of 3–2 and 6–1 (on November 25, 1998 and March 24, 1999, respectively). More nations such as France, Belgium, and Switzerland indicated that they too might wish to extradite Pinochet and put him on trial. Legally, it was a considerable achievement against heavy odds; when Pinochet did return to Chile, in late March 2000, it was due to a political—not a legal—decision by the British government based on a controversial "medical report" supposedly containing the results of tests claiming he was mentally and physically unfit to stand trial.

While these intricate legal battles were being waged by elite lawyers, judges, and Law Lords arguing arcane technicalities, other Chileans and their supporters were using other means to express their opinions during the late 1990s. During a trip to his native Chile in 1998, Ariel Dorfman was in a neighborhood in central Santiago when he heard drums and saw red banners waving. He thought it must be another march to demand that General Pinochet be extradited to Spain. Instead, "it was about 100 university students dressed like medieval fools, their faces painted with many colours, some advancing on stilts, others jumping about in a happy caravan that daringly invited the public to a theatre festival. It was a carnival celebration of arts, full of tricks and good humour." Following close behind this group, Dorfman said, was an "association" made up of "relatives of those murdered for politics, members of a movement against torture. Here were the women who—for more than 25 years—had fed the fire of memory, refusing to forget their loved ones who had succumbed in some dark and sordid cellar in this very city" (Dorfman 1999).

In Dorfman's encounter, politics and carnival are divided discourses, separated by generations and life experiences, but elsewhere other Chileans—either in Chile itself or in the exile communities that existed in Europe—began to unite them. In political demonstrations held in London's Trafalgar Square and Madrid's Plaza del Sol, for example, the exiles added a spooky Halloween/Carnival motif: besides the usual drums, flags, and banners ("EXTRADITE PINOCHET" in London), they also wore blank, white paper carnival masks. The masks, they told BBC, symbolized the *desaparecidos*. By doing this they reintegrated—in symbolic terms—the same individuals that Pinochet had tried totally to obliterate, first by torturing and murdering them, then by disappearing them so they could not be used as evidence or given proper burials from their families. On a more prosaic level, the masks were an excellent device for attracting the media such as television, which is highly dependent on images, and for reminding the public of how cruel and bloody the Pinochet regime had been in its heyday. An additional practical consideration was that the masks protected the identities of demonstrators who had relatives and friends living in Chile.

When the English government caved in and sent Pinochet back to Chile in 2000, the lawsuits and carnivals continued and so did important political and social changes. During the seventeen months he spent in England, Pinochet had become a marginal figure politically who no longer controlled the Army or was able to terrify his nation's judges, lawyers, editors, and ordinary citizens, as he had in the 1970s and 1980s. Starting in 2000, Chileans elected Socialist governments, though more moderate than Allende's, and the changes in the Chilean Army and its attitudes—achieved after years of delicate compromises and negotiations—were especially significant. In November 2004 its Chief of Staff, General Juan Emilio Cheyre, gave a speech and published a report acknowledging the Army's "institutional" culpability for crimes committed during Pinochet's dictatorship; for good measure he also disbanded an Army unit notorious for its human rights abuses. Two months earlier he had presided over "an official military commemoration" honoring one of Pinochet's most prominent victims, General Carlos Prats (Rohter 2004). In another significant ceremony in early December Cheyre "used the graduation of an Army cadet class as a well-publicized forum to disavow the atrocities of the Pinochet era, inviting victims and their families to sit in the front row and hear speeches from leading activists and lawyers—and Cheyre himself—on respect for human rights" (Kornbluh 2005). These gestures of reconciliation and repentance were also signals that, as Chile's Defense Minister commented, "the new army ... will work to lawful ends and use legitimate methods" (Rohter 2004).

Some members of the Chilean judicial system had also become bolder and more independent. Led by an Appeals Court Judge, Juan Guzman, they began chipping away the immunities and amnesties that had protected Pinochet and other officers from prosecutions. By a particularly creative piece of legalistic reasoning they even changed the *desaparecidos* from a legal problem into a judicial resource. By indicting the officers who had disappeared these victims for the crime of "aggravated kidnapping," rather than murder, the prosecutors nullified the statute of limitations and surmounted "an amnesty law decreed by the military government. ... Since the fact of death could not be established, the court held, it was impossible to know" whether the victims had been killed within the period covered by the amnesty (Tiede 2004: 21). Like Sheriff Tate's story about Ewell and his knife, it was a blatant legal fiction, but it was one that served the cause of justice even better than the truth.

By applying this kind of adroit legalistic reasoning, Chilean prosecutors were able, by May 2007, six months after Pinochet's death, to claim that 148 individuals (including almost 50 military officers) had been convicted of human rights violations during his seventeen-year dictatorship. Nearly 400 more persons, mostly military, had been indicted or were being investigated ("Slaking a Thirst for Justice" Economist 2007a). As for Pinochet himself, by the time he arrived back in Chile, he faced more than sixty criminal complaints made by relatives of victims, trade unions, and professional groups. Besides the earlier charges of crimes such as murder and kidnapping, he began to be accused of tawdry misdeeds, including stealing public funds, tax evasion, and falsifying passports. As his legal immunity eroded, he was again forced, as he had been in England, to fall back on his immunity of last resort, his age and his poor mental and physical health. When Guzman ordered him to take pretrial mental tests, a satirical tabloid summed up what many Chileans had concluded about the decrepit dictator: "WHY BOTHER WITH THE TESTS?" said the headline, "ONLY A PSYCHOPATH WOULD TOSS BODIES INTO THE SEA" (Shah 2001). For these Chileans Pinochet will probably become their nation's collective ogre: Jack the Ripper, and Ivan the Terrible, a bloodthirsty killer with no redeeming qualities. For them his death was an event to be celebrated when it occurred in December 2006. In Madrid they wore masks, blew whistles, waved Chilean flags, and chanted anti-Pinochet slogans. In Santiago what the BBC called a "carnival atmosphere" prevailed as crowds sang, danced, beat drums, and drank wine and champagne.

This ending to what the BBC called the "Pinochet legal saga" may be interpreted in two ways. From a strictly legalistic standpoint it is a disappointing outcome. The Chilean, British, and Spanish legal systems had spent years trying to resolve his case; they had been led by two exceptionally courageous and capable prosecutors, Garzon and Guzman, and there had been an enormous range of crimes for them to choose from—250 pages listing crimes and tortures in the dossier Garzon presented to the British courts (Dorfman 2002: 91–94). Yet at the rather messy and inconclusive end of this saga, when Pinochet died, he had suffered nothing worse than house arrest, and only one of the thousands of Chileans whose lives had been destroyed or damaged by Pinochet, Francisco Prats, was able to attain a modicum of revenge through a very extralegal act, spitting on Pinochet's corpse. On the other hand, the legal stalemate that kept Pinochet out of jail can also be considered a historical and political quagmire: a steady source of toxic information about Pinochet and his regime that included new details of old crimes (such as the murder of General Prats) or revelations of new ones (stealing $27 million and hiding it in North American banks).

Seen from a carnival perspective, the parties in Santiago and Madrid celebrating Pinochet's death were a more positive phenomena. Some of the Santiago crowds clashed with Pinochet's supporters in brawls that resulted in 100 arrests and 43 injured police officers—an extremely mild outcome, with no one dead or "disappeared," compared to what probably would have occurred if Pinochet's dictatorship had still been in power. The fear and terror of himself, the Army, and the police that Pinochet had sought to instill had been dispelled by what Ariel Dorfman had described earlier, in a related context, as expressing a "collective joy," felt by people who were "ceasing to hide" and finding their voices "after so many decades of silence and shame" (Dorfman 2002: 83). This kind of joy, especially when expressed in public, represents a kind of de facto verdict, as do the tabloid's "PSYCHOPATH" headline, General Juan Cheyre's statements and ceremonies, the reports by the human rights commission and non-governmental organizations, and the six-volume Rettig report on torture and human rights violations commissioned by the Chilean government in 1990 and published in 1991. In each case the verdict was an implicit or explicit "guilty." As for the argument by Pinochet and his supporters that the violations were justified because they prevented a Communist takeover, Cheyre's answer was emphatic: "Was that political scenario an excuse for the human rights violations that occurred in Chile? My answer is singular and clear: no" (Rohter 2004).

History, revenge, and national security

As our discussion of Pinochet and his legal problems implies, the history and the contexts they create are often crucial components of justice narratives. Like Banquo's ghost in *Macbeth*, they demand their seats at the carnival feast and the legal trial so they can reveal what they know about present crimes, revenges, and retributions. This past information may be public or secret, limited or extensive. It may be from a character's back-story or it may be from a nation's, a society's, or an empire's history. But whatever its source or its scope may be in justice narratives it is never safe to believe, like Henry Ford, that history is "bunk." The reason for the revenge, the motive for the murder, the injury that produced the injustice—virtually all of them begin in the past and influence the present.

We cannot fully understand *Mystic River* without having some knowledge of the social and ethnic history of South Boston and nearby communities (what Lehane calls, "the Flats"). Analogously, key events in *To Kill a Mockingbird*—such as the jury verdict—seem absurd or irrational if one does not know the racial mores of Jim Crow Alabama, circa the 1930s, which is the novel's and film's setting. Nor can we comprehend the nervous panic that grips the colonial officials when Aziz is accused of attempted rape in *A Passage to India* if we do not know the rudiments of the history of the Raj, the British Empire, as it existed in what are now India and Pakistan. Or in classic detective tales of the Sherlock Holmes variety the clue for solving a crime frequently involves information from a victim's or a perpetrator's past. The consequences of a crime or a treachery committed in some godforsaken part of Utah or India years earlier will be a corpse in an empty house in London and the word "RACHE"—German for "Revenge"—scrawled in blood on one of the walls (Doyle 1930: 31).

Once that past information interacts with the narrative present—as evidence in an investigation or a trial, for example—there may be many kinds of endings. Three of these types are especially significant and are therefore emphasized.

"Just Closures," as their title suggests, are narratives with endings—usually in the form of arrests or verdicts—that are perceived as just. Successful detective story writers, such as Conan Doyle, Agatha Christie, and Georges Simenon, are experts at producing narratives with this kind of ending in which the innocent are exonerated and the guilty are apprehended. The evidence is adequate, their detectives' reasoning is persuasive, the perpetrators' motives and confessions are believable, and the punishments are fair. Moreover, all of this information is packaged at the story's conclusion in a smoothly functioning linear narrative with no obvious loose ends or nonsequiters. Violence and punishment are depicted as controlled and legitimatized, and even when the ending is an extralegal form of revenge—such as Boo Radley's stabbing of Bob Ewell—it is still recognized as a just conclusion by authority figurers in the narrative (Sheriff Tate in the case of *To Kill a Mocking Bird*).

"Redemptive Violence," to adopt the term as used by theologian Walter Wink, flourishes in popular culture media, such as cartoons, spy thrillers, westerns, and cop shows in which justice, violence, and closure are often represented as virtually synonymous (Wink 1999: 48–49). Seen positively, this kind of scenario redeems violence by portraying it as a crude but "effective" way of achieving a desirable goal, defeating evil and restoring order: the good gunman shoots the bad one and rides off into the sunset. James Bond blows up the villain and his lair and flies into the sunset with a beautiful woman. This kind of violence is also redemptive because it is often performed by flawed individuals—rogue cops, alcoholic gunmen—who redeem themselves by risking their lives. Seen more skeptically, this kind of narrative may seem problematical, because extralegal and vigilante revenges are not only tolerated but condoned since they can be even bloodier than official, legal forms of punishment. Retribution, revenge, and justice are equated with physical, emotional, or psychological violence. This is victor's justice in which the losers are silenced and humiliated. Its goal is not merely to identify and punish the guilty, but to destroy them either physically or psychologically so that they are incapable of retaliating. This is the kind of justice practiced by the Special Branch police in *A Dry White Season*, by Pinochet's torturers in Chile, by Clint Eastwood in his *Dirty Harry* films, by 007 James Bond, and by Sheriff Little Bill Daggett in *Unforgiven*. In the case of Little Bill, when anyone challenges his authority, he never hesitates or negotiates; instead he beats them to a bloody pulp: a tactic that works very well until he encounters William Munny, a man with an even greater and speedier capacity for violence.

As for Munny, even though he might have redeemed himself personally by killing his friend Ned's killers, it is significant that he immediately returns to his pig farm and children in Nebraska instead of trying to restore order to Big Whisky. Nor does he wait for anyone from Wyoming to try to avenge Little Bill. Instead, according to a scroll at the end of the film, he "disappeared with [his] children ... some said to San Francisco where it was rumored he prospered in dry goods." In non-fictional cases, however, the process is likely to be more complicated. Many of Pinochet's torturers are now fighting lawsuits, and many of the historical equivalents of Brink's Special Branch police had to testify before South Africa's Truth and Reconciliation Commission to receive amnesty. But this occurred after their efforts to achieve redemptive violence had become something else.

"Cyclical Revenge" from a social and political standpoint is the worst kind of ending, one that may not bring closure or redemption for decades or generations. Instead it can trigger new injustices and injuries, create new cycles of revenges and retributions that cause nations and communities to split along ethnic, sectarian or racial fault lines. This process creates a "politics of vengeance" (Kiss 2000: 87) in which insurgency and repression, state and anti-state terrorism, martial law, attacks and reprisals become the favored or only means to achieve what is considered "justice."

Trapped in cycles of retribution and vengeance, both sides in such conflicts become participants in melodramatic histories documenting the other side's conspiracies, betrayals, and atrocities and their side's innocence. "Both sides [are] cursed by near-absolute self-righteousness" and swear they are "the victims—never the cause of any harm," as Amos Elon (Elon 2001: 11) says of Israelis and Palestinians in terms that apply to combatants in places such as Ulster, Sri Lanka, the former Yugoslavia, Rwanda, and apartheid South

Africa. Such situations are not hopeless, but they can be lengthy, expensive, and literally bloody. Political solutions are difficult, and political leaders able and willing to negotiate and implement them are a rare species. It took 26 years after Bloody Sunday for Ulster to achieve the 1998 Good Friday agreement ending sectarian violence and another nine years more before Ian Paisley, Martin McGuiness, and Gerry Adams implemented that agreement. It took more than 30 years after the Sharpeville massacre before F.W. DeKlerk, Nelson Mandela, and Thabo Mbeki negotiated the end of apartheid in South Africa.

What will happen with present-day Iraq? How will post-9/11 United States conduct itself in the future? As the final chapter indicates, many portions of the most important strategic decisions made by the American government after 9/11 were dictated less by rational self-interest and more by desires to avenge previous attacks and injuries. One side, the military, supported an attack on nation states that supported al Qaeda, such as Afghanistan, which had actually harbored bin Laden and his training camps. But, through a campaign of innuendo and intimation, the American government implied and many Americans believed (70% in August 2003) that Iraq also was somehow responsible for the 9/11 attacks (USA Today 2003). In May 2003, for example, President Bush claimed:

> The liberation of Iraq is a crucial advance in the campaign against terror. We've removed an ally of al Qaeda, and cut off a source of terrorist funding. And this much is certain: No terrorist network will gain weapons of mass destruction from the Iraqi regime, because the regime is no more. ... We have not forgotten the victims of September the 11th—the last phone calls, the cold murder of children, the searches in the rubble.
>
> (Milbank and Deane 2003: a1)

Saddam Hussein was depicted as not only an odious dictator who might have weapons of mass destruction, he was also a patron of terrorists, and so deposing him would avenge Americans killed in the World Trade Center, the Pentagon and on the flights held hostage by the terrorists. But the attack on Iraq produced an insurgency that resisted the American "occupiers," leaving thousands of Americans and many thousands of Iraqis dead, and it exacerbated tribal, ethnic, and sectarian hostilities. In February 2003 a report by the American War College's Strategic Studies Institute warned that Saddam Hussein, the Baath Party, and the regime they had established was "the culmination of a violent political culture," and if Hussein were deposed, "Ethnic, tribal, and religious schisms could produce civil war or fracture the state. ... many internal grievances exist among the various factions. ... Some of these differences are centuries old and cannot be resolved by any third party," and American efforts to do this "could fuel mass action or even an uprising" (Crane and Terrill 2003: 45). The American government adopted a radically more optimistic scenario in which the violence of an invasion and occupation would be ultimately redemptive and positive, since it would enable the United States to create a "free, stable and democratic Iraq that will serve as an inspiration to its neighbors" (Dobbs 2003: A17). Its main author was a Pentagon official, Paul Wolfowitz, but the rest of the Bush administration, especially the President, enthusiastically adopted its main tenets. Citing Germany and Japan after World War II as past examples of this process in a February 2003 speech, President Bush declared that Iraq was just as "capable of moving toward democracy and living in freedom" and thus becoming an "inspiring example of freedom for other nations in the region" (The White House 2003).

This scenario turned out to be dangerously naïve and deeply flawed. When many Iraqis responded to their new freedom by looting everything not nailed down, when Sunni insurgents allied themselves with al Qaeda and began attacking their Shia countrymen as well as American troops, and when Shia militias and death squads responded in kind, it quickly became clear that there was no American Plan B for bringing order to Iraq except by becoming embroiled in a semi-declared sectarian civil war. Thus, elements in the Shia-dominated government, democratically elected in January 2005, began tacitly allowing forces from the Interior Ministry to be "likely responsible" for targeting and killing Sunnis. This set off a "wave of retaliatory killings" by both Sunni and Shia militias, and eventually the Americans began arming and paying Sunni militias to protect Sunni areas and "operate beyond the control of the central government"—even though many of the Sunnis being recruited were former insurgents (Rosen 2006). Yet at the same time the American government continued to support and subsidize the same central government.

Thus, American military forces had to struggle to protect themselves against insurgent attacks whilst simultaneously trying to avoid an all-out civil war by supporting both Sunni and Shia factions at the same time. Only in this way could they try to prevent the Iraqis from avenging old and new grievances by attacking one another's mosques, exploding car bombs, assassinating clerics, and murdering their fellow citizens because they live in the wrong neighborhoods (Rosen 2006). What further fueled the Iraqis' grievances and hostilities against Americans were tactics like the ones that led to the photos showing US guards humiliating and torturing Iraqi prisoners at Abu Ghraib. Either way, it was the Americans who became incorporated into the Iraqis' "politics of vengeance," the patterns of revenges and retaliations that govern interactions between tribes, ethnic groups, and religious sects.

As for the side of the "War on Terror" focused on the past and present leaders of al Qaeda, efforts to achieve closure by bringing them to justice, obtaining verdicts, and punishing them have devolved into a political and legal quagmire. In an interview on September 16, 2001, in which he was asked how the United States was going to "pay back big time" for the 9/11 attacks, Vice President Cheney said governments like Afghanistan's that harbored terrorists would feel the "full wrath" of the United States, and he added later that in dealing with terrorists like Osama bin Laden, "We also have to work, though, sort of the dark side, if you will. ... to spend time in the shadows" (The White House 2001). By February of 2002, bin Laden still had not been found, but Secretary of Defense Donald Rumsfield announced that President Bush had informed him that the Geneva Conventions did not apply to "terrorist detainees" (i.e., prisoners) from Afghanistan, but all would be treated "humanely" (Abu Ghraib Timeline 2004). Gradually rumors and scandals began to leak out about the military and the CIA, but sometimes from more obscure agencies, that they were allegedly performing all kinds of ugly semi-legal, extralegal, or downright criminal acts as their contributions to the War on Terror. All of these allegations became more credible in April 2004 when CBS showed the Abu Ghraib images on a *60 Minutes* news cast, and lawyers, journalists, human rights organizations, and other interested parties began investigating more aggressively. What they found, besides instances of cruelty and abuse, was a pervasive pattern of duplicity and a blurring of the boundaries between facts and fictions.

Acts were being committed that might or might not be torture—depending on who was defining that word. There were secret meetings at places that did not officially exist—but some of them could be photographed if you had a camera with a very long lens. There were 81-page memos authorizing certain kinds of interrogations that were kept secret—though their contents were known for years through rumors. There were secret videotapes of CIA tortures that were hastily destroyed when their existence became known. There were disturbing revelations about living conditions and interrogation tactics at the Guantanamo Naval Base. There were fleets of airplanes owned by bogus companies used to transport prisoners to secret locations for interrogations—hence their nickname, "torture taxis"—even though outwardly they were just mundane Boeing 737s sitting on runways in regional airports. It was Cheney's "dark side" hiding in plain sight, disguised as the ordinary. Abu Ghraib might be rationalized by arguing that most of the culprits were low-ranking, poorly trained guards and that the US Army had itself begun the tardy process of punishing the guilty and vastly improving conditions at the prison (Taguba Report 2004). But Guantanamo, "torture taxis," and the other "dark side" activities were different. They had been funded from "black budgets" and initiated or approved by high officials, so the culpability is much higher in the chain of command, and the rebukes can be correspondingly more severe.

It is difficult for many Americans to understand this, since they are educated to equate torture with dictatorships and to presume that their own government would never violate anyone's human rights or the Geneva

Conventions. But this presumption may become another casualty of the "War on Terror." Thus Lord Steyn, one of the Law Lords who voted to extradite Pinochet, described "the detention of prisoners at Guantanamo" as having "one single object: the United States administration wanted to place them beyond the protection of the rule of law. They created a hellhole of utter lawlessness" where the prisoners are "at the mercy of the American Army, [and its] commander in chief" (Rozenberg 2004). John Gibbons, a retired federal Appeals Court judge who argued one of the Guantanamo prisoners' cases before the US Supreme Court was less moralistic, but just as harsh. "These guys," he said of the Bush administration, "have been reading too much James Bond" (Gibbons 2006).

We would describe this pattern as a vigilante mentality disguised as legality, Dirty Harry pretending to be Atticus Finch, James Bond disguised as an Attorney General. The vigilante mentality has its virtues, but they are romantic virtues, the charismatic loner obeying his own code rather than the law. As enunciated by a character like Balzac's Vautrin, Sean Connery as Bond, or Sean Penn as Jimmy Marcus, it's an attractive role, but one ill-suited to heads of state who are expected to enforce laws, not circumvent or subvert them. When they do that they are likely to harm their own reputations and that of their nation, and to deserve the verdicts we have quoted from Judge Gibbons and Lord Steyn.

Revenge and the detective tradition

When dogs don't bark and detectives don't tell

"Great is information, and she shall prevail."

(E. M. Forster, *A Passage to India*, 1952: 211)

As its critics are quick to point out, one defect of vigilante justice is its tendency to prefer speedy punishments to the more rational and tedious process of obtaining the best possible information that may be admissible as evidence in a court trial. Consequently, as Jimmy Marcus (in the film *Mystic River*) discovers the morning after he has killed Dave Boyle, sometimes the wrong man dies for the wrong crime. Pauline Kael summed this problem up in her comments on Clint Eastwood's *Dirty Harry* films. "What makes Harry the sharpshooter a great cop," Kael says sarcastically,

> is he knows the guilty from the innocent, and in this action world there's only one thing to be done with the guilty—kill them. Alternatives to violence are automatically excluded. If we talk to Harry, if after he dispatches his thirty-fifth or eightieth criminal one of us says 'Harry, could you maybe ask the guy's name before you shoot to make sure you got the right man?' Harry's answer has to be 'all criminals are liars anyway,' as he pulls the trigger. Because that's what he wants to do, pull the trigger.

> (Kael, *Reeling*, 1976: 256)

In the detective tradition, on the other hand, the emphasis is upon exact information instead of passionate action. As embodied in Sherlock Holmes and his successors, the detective mindset prizes logic, rational analysis and hard evidence—but without the formality, the time-consuming procedures and judicial loopholes that can occur in legal trials. Thus, the detective narrative can be considered a moderate compromise between official legalism as enforced by courts, and the individuality of vigilante justice. Detectives' goals usually are the same as those of judges and courts in many cases, to identify and punish the guilty and to exonerate the innocent, but they accomplish these ends in a freelance, individual way—preferably with a touch of the exotic, mysterious, or eccentric—rather than through some type of police or legal standard operating procedures. Nevertheless, they resemble the courts in that they relieve individuals of the need to seek revenge or punish crime on their own behalf.

Classical and "Golden Age" detectives, such as those created by Doyle and Christie, are distinctly orderly in a Newtonian way. They scrutinize space and crime scenes to find clues that will yield good circumstantial evidence: fingerprints, soil samples from a suspect's boots, tobacco ashes from a specific brand of tobacco, and other tiny details can be as revealing to the detective as smoking guns and bloody hand prints are to the less observant. They scrutinize time with equal precision; the private lives and histories of victims and suspects can be mined to yield motives, grudges, and old injuries or insults that can be motives for crimes committed years later. Family secrets are often the most problematic. A not untypical "Golden Age" detective mystery, for example, might begin with the rich but unpopular Lady Deadstone being found deceased in her bedroom with the doors locked and the windows bolted. Was she poisoned with a shot of arsenic added to her nightly snifter of brandy, perhaps by her niece or nephew, Arlene or Bert, who long ago squandered their shares of the family fortune on, respectively, fast cars and slow horses? Or was it her deceased husband's erstwhile business partner, the shady Major Malefactor, or perhaps it was her former gardener whom she sacked for having an affair with her maid Francine? All or any of the above may be guilty, and that detail, plus their secrets, will be revealed by Geraldine, the vicar's eccentric daughter who solves the County's homicides as easily as other people solve crossword puzzles—as soon as she investigates the grease stain on the carpet and the missing pound of gouda cheese.

Above all, these detectives have the talent for perceiving the significance in what normal people perceive as insignificant. In the Sherlock Holmes' case we mention in the first half of this Chapter's title, "Silver Blaze," one of the most significant events in this story is one that does not occur. The dog does not bark, even though a horse is being stolen. And of course no one but Holmes realizes the significance of that non-event, that the crime was committed by someone who knew the dog. Similarly, detectives are able to connect disparate facts and seemingly unrelated events so that they become parts of a meaningful narrative. This process often culminates in a final speech by the detective in which he or she explains the story's mysteries, identifies the guilty person, and then lets the police take over. But not always—as the following cases demonstrate.

Sir Arthur Conan Doyle's "Charles Augustus Milverton"

Sir Arthur Conan Doyle, the creator of Sherlock Holmes, took topics such as loyalty and treachery, trust and distrust, seriously. In 1927 he gave his readers a list of his twelve favorite stories, divided into two groups of six each. Five of the first group of six deal with these subjects, and their main characters include a treacherous stepfather in "The Speckled Band," a disloyal employee in "The Red-headed League," a royal but unreliable lover in "A Scandal in Bohemia," and a homicidal colonel who also cheats at cards in "The Empty House."[1] Other important examples would include the disloyal servants in "Silver Blaze" and "The Musgrave Ritual" and Stapleton, the villain of *The Hound of the Baskervilles,* who pretends to be a friendly neighbor when he is actually trying to murder his cousin to gain control of the Baskerville estate. The Sherlock Holmes story that deals most directly with this theme, "Charles Augustus Milverton," is in other respects something of an anomaly among the Holmes stories. It does not really contain any mysteries or intellectual puzzles for Holmes to solve. Instead it is largely focused upon ethical problems. The story's villain is identified at the outset, and he provides ample evidence of his own wickedness that will justify his eventual downfall. As Holmes tells Watson on the first page of the story, Milverton is "the worst man in London," a cunning and relentless blackmailer who preys on the rich and the foolish by collecting evidence of their indiscretions and then charging them large sums of money to destroy that evidence. Thus, Milverton is not only treacherous and dangerous in his own right, he actively encourages disloyalty in others, since his chief source of incriminating information about his victims is their own servants. He is able to break the law with impunity because his victims fear exposure so much, and the legal penalties for Milverton's particular crime are so mild. "What would it profit a woman, for example," Holmes explains, to get Milverton "a few months imprisonment if her own ruin must immediately follow? His victims dare not hit back. If ever he blackmailed an innocent person, then, indeed we should have him, but he is as cunning as the Evil One" (Doyle 1994: 272–73).

The Evil One? It is also notable that the Milverton story is probably the most melodramatic of the Holmes tales, and the one in which Holmes himself is portrayed as being highly emotional rather than rational and detached. In stories such as "The Speckled Band" and "The Red-Headed

League" Holmes confronts cold-blooded killers and bank robbers with aloof arrogance, the Victorian equivalent of Dirty Harry's, "Go ahead. Make my day." But in "Milverton" he becomes far more emotionally involved for a variety of reasons. Hired by one of Milverton's victims to bargain with the blackmailer, Holmes fails so miserably that he actually loses his temper and tries to seize the incriminating letters. Milverton eludes his grasp, shows him he has a revolver, and says he is "armed to the teeth, and ... perfectly prepared to use my weapon, *knowing that the law will support me*" (Doyle 1994: 276; emphasis added).

Reading between the lines of Holmes' rage, one discovers a portrait of the English upper classes that reveals a substantial cultural anxiety related to the late Victorian social order. As depicted by Doyle, the English upper classes are ruled by a code in which sexual snobbery is mixed with acute social insecurity. Apparently even the slightest appearance of a misalliance with a member of the lower or middle classes, or even the lesser nobility, is enough to "ruin" an upper-class woman and her reputation. In the case of Holmes' client, the woman is a beautiful debutante, the fiancée of the Earl of Devonshire. But this marriage will not occur if Milverton sends the letters to the Earl and his family, and, therefore, the desperate woman has gone to Holmes in the hopes that he will persuade Milverton to moderate his severe financial demands.

What makes this code so powerful and the women so vulnerable is that it conforms to what might be called the Jekyll and Hyde doctrine of human duality that flourished in the nineteenth century. According to this doctrine, which Peter Brooks calls "the melodramatic imagination," there are no operative moral middle grounds or moderate compromises between opposites. Instead the world is "built on irreducible manichaeism, [and] the conflict of good and evil" is all-or-nothing because "the middle ground and the middle condition are excluded" (Brooks 1976: 36). In actuality, existing privately on a "middle ground" might be possible and even enjoyable. However, as Robert Louis Stevenson's Dr. Jekyll and Holmes' client discover, since any deviation from the ideal is considered "evil," individuals' public personas must be immaculate, or they will lose control over their lives to a Mr. Hyde or a Milverton.

Another dualism in the Milverton story is that which exists between Milverton and Holmes himself. For in certain respects Milverton is a kind of mirror image of Holmes, an evil detective who uses that profession's skills for selfish, illegal purposes. Thus, Holmes uses the histories of characters, such as Stapleton in *The Hound of the Baskervilles*, to solve crimes and mysteries, whereas Milverton uses his victims' histories to break the law and make his victims' lives miserable until they pay him off. In addition, Holmes protects the social order in stories like "Silver Blaze" and "The Musgrave Ritual" by solving mysteries involving disloyal or treacherous servants; in contrast Milverton does the opposite: he erodes the social order by systematically corrupting servants to sell him incriminating notes and letters that he will use to blackmail their employers.

The mirror analogy applies to Holmes as well as to Milverton as he adopts the blackmailer's *modus operandi*. By disguising himself as a working-class plumber, he courts Milverton's housemaid to learn his house's floor plan and the location of his safe. When Watson is shocked by this breach of professional ethics, Holmes blithely replies, "I wanted information ... you can't help it ... You must play your cards as best you can when such a stake is on the table. However, I rejoice to say that I have a hated rival who will certainly cut me out the moment that my back is turned" (Doyle 1994: 277). Clearly, Holmes has no qualms about living on the middle ground morally in which good intentions excuse bad or unethical behavior. Nor for that matter does Watson have any deep qualms about their illegal course of action, for he is delighted by the opportunity to participate in a burglary, and he insists that he must be allowed to accompany Holmes. The adventure turns out to be more exciting than either of them had expected.

Thanks to coincidence, always a welcome participant in melodrama, they are interrupted during their burglary of Milverton's study and hide behind curtains where they are able to see the blackmailer welcome a veiled woman. Milverton thinks the woman is a servant who is going to sell him incriminating letters, but he is very wrong. She is one of his former victims, one whose husband has died of shame because Milverton revealed her indiscretions to the public. Now she has invaded Milverton's privacy seeking revenge that Doyle describes in vivid detail. In fact, the details are so vivid that the passages sound like a murder from a 1920s or 1930s American "hard-boiled" detective magazine. "You will ruin no more lives as you ruined mine," the woman cries, as she draws a revolver; "you will wring no more hearts as you wrung mine. I will free the world of a poisonous thing. Take that, you hound, and that!—and that! And that!" She then grinds her heel into the dying man's up-turned face and leaves (Doyle 1994: 283–84). Thanks to an additional coincidence, a fire is burning in the fireplace, and Holmes quickly dashes to Milverton's safe, pulls out the packets and bundles of letters, and throws them into the flames before he and Watson flee with the police literally at their heels.

The next day the police come to Holmes and ask his help to solve the murder of Milverton. Naturally he refuses and gives his reasons in the cool rationalistic manner that we expect from him: "I think there are certain crimes which the law cannot touch, and which therefore, to some extent, justify private revenge." But this is not the final word in the story. Later Holmes takes Watson to a shop that sells photographs of celebrities, and there in the shop window is a photograph of the woman they saw kill Milverton. "Then I caught my breath," Watson recalls, "as I read the time honored title of the great nobleman and statesman whose wife she had been. My eyes met those of Holmes, and he put his finger to his lips as we turned away from the window" (Doyle 1994: 286). Normally of course the final words in the Sherlock Holmes stories are those by Holmes explaining the case and identifying the criminal, followed by additional words of explanation by Watson. But this story is different. Revenge rules and speaks in its own voice when Milverton is killed, and Holmes and Watson accept silence as their part of the justice process.

Agatha Christie's *Murder on the Orient Express*

Structurally, Agatha Christie's *Murder on the Orient Express* seems quite different from Doyle's tale because it is a 1930s "Golden Age" detective novel. That is, it has multiple suspects and a variety of mysteries rather than a single criminal or puzzle that characterizes the detective tale as perfected by Doyle and Poe. Given that difference, however, certain other, more significant similarities are present. First, both works have a heavy element of Carnival motifs, which is to be anticipated in works that rely on extralegal forms of revenge or retribution. In particular, masking and concealed or inverted identities are important in both narratives. In the Milverton story the veiled noblewoman pretends temporarily to be a disloyal servant so that she can gain access to the blackmailer and achieve her revenge. Holmes and Watson wear masks when they are doing their burglary and function temporarily as criminals to destroy Milverton's information rather than support the state's effort to identify his killer. In *Murder on the Orient Express*, the masquerades and false identities are even more elaborate, but readers could trust that justice would prevail from the novel's title and its first few pages.

For in 1933 when the novel was written, the Orient Express was one of the great corporations of continental Europe, a powerful institution incorporating the culture and technology of modernism. Even though it traveled through picturesque but desolate areas of what had been the old Ottoman Empire, it still maintained its high standards of luxury and service in its Wagon Lits sleeping cars. Moreover, by the second page of the novel readers would learn that one of the passengers would be Hercule Poirot, who was boarding the train at Aleppo after solving a difficult case involving the honor of the French Army and the future of the French empire in Syria. Poirot had become by that time a celebrity detective, like Sherlock Holmes before him, and one could trust that he would solve any mysteries that would occur. For good measure M. Bouc, a director of the Orient Express's parent company was on board and would do whatever was needed to assist Poirot. In addition, another, later passenger, conveniently enough, would be a Greek physician, and therefore expert medical testimony would be available.

By the second chapter the Express has a passenger, who calls himself Ratchett, who is clearly some kind of villain. Poirot introduces him with the same kind of lurid, melodramatic language that Holmes used to describe Milverton. Thus, though Ratchett has "the bland aspect of a philanthropist" that "seemed to speak of a benevolent personality," his "eyes ... were small, deep set and crafty," and a page later Poirot tells Bouc that Ratchet is a "wild animal—an animal savage." Being near the man, he says, "I could not rid myself of the impression that evil had passed me by very close" (Christie 1960: 21, 22). A nervous man, who admits he has enemies, Ratchett tries in vain to hire Poirot, but the detective refuses adamantly, and when Ratchett demands a reason, Poirot tells him, "forgive me for being personal—I do not like your face" (Christie 1960: 34).

The other passengers seem harmless and diverse. "All around us are people of all classes, all nationalities, all ages," M. Bouc tells Poirot, "for three days the people, these strangers to one another, are brought together ... they cannot get away from each other" (Christie 1960: 27). Judging from their external identities and their resemblances to national stereotypes the passengers do seem to fit Bouc's claim. There is a crusty British colonel from India traveling through the Middle East to reach home, an English governess from Baghdad, named Mary, who is doing the same, and Masterman, another Brit, who is Ratchett's valet, plus a voluble, emotional Italian, a haughty Russian princess, a Hungarian count and his wife, and a contingent of Americans. There is a vulgar "loud" one named Hardman who chews gum, speaks vintage slang, and says he is a private detective hired to protect Ratchett. Balancing him is a more likeable American, MacQueen, who is Ratchett's Secretary, plus the elderly Mrs. Hubbard who supplies a touch of comic relief with her gauche opinions.

As any reader of mystery novels knows, one or more of these people will be capable of homicide, and sure enough, two chapters later Ratchett is discovered dead, stabbed to death in his sleeping compartment. Adding to the suspense is the fact that the train is stalled in a snow bank somewhere north of Belgrade during a blizzard, and, therefore, the killer must be one of the persons on board the train. For even though the window of Ratchett's compartment is open there are no footprints on the snow outside indicating that the murderer has left. No one, especially Bouc, is enthusiastic about entrusting the investigation to the Yugoslavian police when and if they arrive on the scene (Christie 1960: 203), so Bouc deputizes Poirot to begin an investigation immediately. Poirot begins logically enough by interviewing MacQueen, Ratchett's secretary, and the young man discloses that the dead man had been receiving "threatening letters," that he shows to Poirot. Written in the style of American gangster or detective thrillers, they include phrases like "we're going to take you for a ride," and "we're out to get you" (Christie 1960: 55). According to the rules of detective fiction, information like this—that is freely volunteered—is likely to be worthless. And sure enough when Poirot investigates the crime scene, he quickly finds evidence that the murder was much too strange and messy to have been performed by professional gangsters. As the Greek doctor points out there is a great variety to the wounds. Some were clearly struck by a strong man or woman and had forcibly torn through muscle and caused Ratchett's death—but others were scarcely more than scratches or mild flesh wounds. Moreover, several of the wounds, including some deep ones, were made after the victim was dead. From the position of the corpse and the placement of some of the wounds, it is also clear that several of them must have been made by a left-handed person—but that others could only have been made by a right-handed person. The plot thickens.

But the clue in the compartment that really launches Poirot's investigation is an insignificant piece of charred burnt paper in Ratchett's ashtray. Delicately prying apart the gnarled paper Poirot discovers four words still visible, "member little Daisy Armstrong" (Christie 1960: 68).

Daisy Armstrong was the child of a rich and presumably happy Anglo-American family that was destroyed by Ratchett in his earlier identity as Cassetti, the leader of a notorious gang of kidnappers that abducted and killed Armstrong's daughter. Due to the frailties of the American legal system, Cassetti was able to escape any punishment. He might have been lynched "by the populace had he not been clever enough to give them the slip ... he changed his name and left America. Since then he has been a gentleman of leisure, traveling abroad," Poirot tells Bouc (Christie 1960: 72). The effect upon the Armstrong family was devastating. The mother who was pregnant at the time of Daisy's kidnapping died in childbirth and the second child was stillborn. The father, who had been a colonel in the English Army in World War I, was so devastated that he killed himself. A French or Swiss nurse-maid falsely accused of complicity with the kidnappers also killed herself.

By ignoring this information, the detective is able to produce a clearly inadequate theory, that we would call Theory A, at the beginning of Part III of the novel (Christie 1960: 189). In this theory, the killer is an "intruder" wearing a conductor's uniform he has somehow obtained and using a master key is able to elude observation by going from compartment to compartment and then murdering Ratchett. Also in the beginning of Part III Poirot makes up a list of all the passengers on the train accompanied by comments on their alibis and their motivations. Without considering the Armstrong factors, most of the passengers have weak or no motivation to harm Ratchett, and virtually all of them have solid alibis.

Therefore, switching to Theory B, experienced mystery readers and Poirot will reason that the killer will be someone among the train passengers who has a weak alibi and a strong connection to the Armstrong family or court case. This person has killed Ratchett to avenge Daisy and the other Armstrongs. However, when Poirot tries to identify the killer by asking leading or trick questions he is able to discover that a surprising number of the passengers did have connections with the Armstrong family as servants, friends, or relatives—but their alibis remain as strong as ever. The presence of so many members of the Armstrong ménage on the same train, in which Ratchett is murdered, cannot be a coincidence. It must be part of a plan or conspiracy, and this encourages skepticism toward the passengers' alibis. Seen more critically the alibis are almost entirely circular in the sense that the different passengers are simply claiming that they saw other passengers at certain times, but there is no outside agency guaranteeing that these encounters really did occur. At that point Poirot makes his imaginative leap to Theory C by realizing that not one, or two, or six of the passengers are acting in complicity with one another but that the whole group, including the conductor, were cooperating to kill Ratchett and are now cooperating to deceive him.

In the climatic final scene in the novel when Poirot brings all the suspects together to reveal which of them is guilty, he instead proposes two solutions to the question of who killed Ratchett. Bouc and the doctor must choose between them. Theory A is his old "intruder" theory that he offers despite its obvious limitations. The second option, Theory C, is a more elaborate and complicated narrative in which everyone except for Poirot, Bouc and the Greek doctor is involved in the killing. The Italian was the Armstrongs' chauffer, and Masterman was Colonel Armstrong's batman during the war, for example; Hardman and the train conductor were, respectively, the French nursemaid's fiancé and father. The passenger who responds and is the killers' spokesperson is the woman who called herself Mrs. Hubbard, but was Daisy Armstrong's grandmother, a famous actress named Linda Arden. No longer speaking in Hubbard's naïve, provincial voice, she is articulate, passionate, and persuasive. What she tells Poirot in a factual sense is a confession, but in a moral sense it is the justification for what she and the other passengers have done as a group: execute the man responsible for the Armstrong family's deaths. Now that he knows everything she tells Poirot, what is he going to do about it?

> "I would have stabbed that man twelve times willingly. It wasn't only that he was responsible for my daughter's death and her child's, and the other child who might have been alive and happy now. It was more than that. There had been other children before Daisy—there might be others in the future. Society had condemned him; we were only carrying out the sentence. ... and Mary and Colonel Arbuthnot they love each other ... "
>
> (Christie 1960: 253)

Instead of responding to her, Poirot simply looks at his friend Bouc and asks him for his verdict. "In my opinion," Bouc responds, "the first theory [Theory A] you put forward was the correct one – decidedly so. I suggest that that is the solution we offer to the Yugoslavian police when they arrive." The Greek doctor agrees and withdraws his earlier medical testimony, and Poirot informs the group that he has the "honour" to withdraw from the case (Christie 1960: 253–54). Like Holmes in the Milverton case, Poirot's part in the narrative given to the police will be a silent one. Revenge and homicide—for the right reasons—will be just, and truth and the law will be ignored.

Despite this important thematic similarity there are also significant differences between the two narratives. Christopher Clausen, writing about Sherlock Holmes in terms that also apply to Christie's detective in *Murder on the Orient Express* points out that in Doyle's tales "order, if not always law, is upheld, and in those cases where Holmes allows the criminal to escape, it is either because the victim represents a greater threat to society than the criminal ... or because the crime was a pardonable act of revenge" that the law could not redress (Clausen 1984: 113). The villains/victims in both narratives cause disorder and disrupt society, but they do this in different ways.

In the Milverton tale, the actual murder is highly melodramatic, but the rest of the story is almost entirely set in a rational framework that we associate with Holmes and his allegiance to reason and cool, logical thinking. In fact, Milverton's crime, blackmail, is a highly rational one, and he can be seen as a cold, hardheaded businessman striking tough bargains even if he ruins his victims. Holmes' response is also cold and calculating—to court the housemaid and then destroy the source of Milverton's power, the documents he uses for blackmail. In contrast, Christie's novel is far more melodramatic, and its carnival motifs are more significant. Ratchett in particular is the sort of villain that readers and audiences love to hate: one whose crimes are outrageous and despicable, but who is wealthy and powerful and therefore able to escape punishment. Noah Cross in Roman Polanski's *Chinatown* (1974), Keyser Soze in Bryan Singer's *The Usual Suspects* (1995), and many of the villains in the James Bond films are in this category, and so is Ratchett. For as Poirot tells Bouc when the gangster was arrested for the Armstrong kidnapping, "by means of his enormous wealth he had piled up and by the secret hold he had over various persons, he was acquitted on some technical inaccuracy" (Christie 1960: 71).

Orient Express also possesses the dynamic dualisms that are an important feature of the Carnival approach to life and justice. It develops by the end of the novel with Ratchett's dualistic opposite in Mrs. Hubbard, alias the actress Linda Arden. He is the evil, dangerous male destructive force, the destroyer of families and a murderer of children. As her name from a nursery rhyme, "old Mother Hubbard," indicates, she is his female opposite and antagonist. Though she is no longer fertile herself, she still represents the power of fertility and a matriarchal commitment to nurturing her clan or community. And her real name, Arden, is the name of a forest in central England that was seen as a natural haven. It was she presumably who has provided the leadership that the Armstrong ménage needed to survive the devastating series of events which destroyed Daisy, her parents, and the nursemaid, Suzanne. By organizing men as part of her revenge "team," whose capabilities are indicated by their names—Hardman, Masterman— she has been able to track Ratchett down, infiltrate his domestic life, and provide the revenge that the American courts failed to achieve. Her reference at the end of her speech to the love which exists between Mary and the Colonel implies that Ratchett's death has restored fertility and vitality to her tribe or clan. Once again children will be born and the "old mother" will triumph. The only things that almost defeated her were coincidences: the snowstorm which stopped the train so that the crime could not be blamed on an outsider, and the fact that a famous detective would just happen to be traveling on that particular train. However, the latter coincidence turns out to be harmless. At the beginning of the novel Poirot had demonstrated his respect for male, patriarchal authority by putting his talents in the service of the French Army and Empire; he now shows he can be equally respectful toward matriarchal authority. Through his silence, like Holmes in the Milverton story, crime has been punished and a revenge achieved, but only after a premeditated—justified—homicide.

Despite the well-deserved popularity of Doyle and Christie and their detectives, there may be some twentieth- or twenty-first-century readers who feel that their vision of crime and justice is perhaps a little exclusive, even a little snobbish. What about the people who no one would ever bother to blackmail because they couldn't have paid even a penny for their letters, no matter how incriminating? What about poor, lonely, isolated people who barely can afford bus fare to commute to work, and are clearly never going to be able to be able to ride on the Orient Express? Don't these people have injuries to revenge? They do, and one of the great classics of revenge literature is this work by Susan Glaspell.

Susan Glaspell's "A Jury of Her Peers"

> The American Correctional Association recently conducted a national survey of women in prison ... Of the few women convicted of serious offenses, most had been involved in abusive relationships and had lashed back at their batterer ... most women convicted of murder or manslaughter had killed men in their lives who repeatedly and violently abused them.
>
> (Donziger 1966: 150)

Presumably all of the women in the cases Donziger cites in his 1996 study received trials, or opportunities to plea-bargain, in which they were able to tell their stories about how the "men in their lives" had abused them. In Susan Glaspell's story, "A Jury of Her Peers," on the other hand, an abused wife, Minnie Wright (née Minnie Foster), does not directly speak or appear in the story itself after she has murdered her husband. Her few words that are heard in the narrative—and in Glaspell's one-act play, *Trifles* (1916), written a year earlier—are quoted secondhand by other characters: a neighboring farmer and his son who discovered her sitting in her kitchen the previous morning, while her husband was dead in their bed upstairs with a rope knotted around his neck. When asked, "Who did this?" Minnie replies, "I don't know," then explains that she did not wake up when her husband was being strangled because, "I sleep sound."[2] This scarcely credible explanation is her final and only testimony in the story that takes place the next day when five persons arrive at the Wright farm to investigate the homicide: the neighbor, Lewis Hale, and his wife, Martha; the sheriff, Peters, and his wife; and the County Attorney, Henderson. This is the early twentieth century when discovering truth and achieving justice in the public sphere were tasks reserved almost exclusively for men, and, therefore, in the course of "A Jury," the sheriff and Henderson, accompanied by Hale, act as the official, legal investigators of the crime. But Peters and Henderson are not good detectives, and they discover nothing that would incriminate Mrs. Wright or reveal her motive for killing her husband. In the meantime Mrs. Peters and Martha Hale, who have been relegated to dealing with "trifles" in the private, domestic sphere of the Wright's kitchen, do find the clues revealing why John Wright died. But—acting as a judge and jury as well as unofficial detectives—they conceal this evidence so that, in effect, Minnie Wright is acquitted, because they consider the homicide justified.

What is notable about "A Jury of Her Peers" as a justice narrative is how much is kept secret and not said, or at least not said directly. In most narratives on this theme there is a high priority on achieving justice through conclusive, articulate storytelling by dominant characters who reveal the narrative's secrets, and by detectives such as Dave Wilson in *Pudd'nhead* and Holmes in Doyle's stories. In contrast, Minnie Wright is silenced in the sense that she never tells the story of her dismal marriage and John Wright's abusive behavior toward her; that story has to be reconstructed by Mrs. Peters and Mrs. Hale from the clues they find in her kitchen: bad stitching in a quilt, a bird cage with a broken door, and a dead canary. Moreover, after the two women make these discoveries they too are, in effect, silenced since only the readers of Glaspell's story (or the audiences of *Trifles*) learn from them what caused Minnie Wright to kill her husband, and the reason she performed that act with a rope in such a "funny way" when there was a gun in the house. In other words, even though they are successful detectives who "solve" a murder case, the two women do not announce their solution in a public, dramatic way before an audience composed of a judge, jury, and spectators to enhance their standing in the public sphere as Dave Wilson does. Nor do they have an admiring chronicler of their exploits like Dr. Watson. Nevertheless, as Glaspell's narrative implies strongly, justice is achieved, and this is almost certainly because of, not in spite of, the two women's decision to conceal the truths they learn about Wright's marriage and John Wright's death.

Despite "A Jury's" brevity and its lack of eloquent speeches, Glaspell's story nevertheless conveys a great deal of information about those characters and the kind of society that has shaped their lives. Written and published in 1917, "A Jury" is a canonical example of the kind of populist realism that flourished during the Progressive era in American literature and politics during the nineteenth and the early twentieth century when editors, journalists, and creative writers sought to alleviate or correct social problems by, as one editor wrote, "depicting life's everyday tragedies" and encouraging people to "frankly face conditions as we find them."[3] This was a minimalist, bare-bones realism whose authors eschewed such charismatic vestiges of Romanticism as pseudo-supernatural hounds and "superman" detectives. Nor were they much interested in giving their readers the kind of entertaining realism exemplified by Twain's *Pudd'nhead Wilson* and *Huckleberry Finn* with clever knaves such as Tom Driscoll, the Duke, and the King or lively characters such as Roxy, Jim, and Huck Finn. What narratives by populist, Progressive-era realists offered instead were earnest, pragmatic social and political messages that could be learned from the lives and problems of fictional but definitely "ordinary" people. "The old time artists thought they served humanity by painting saints and madonnas and angels from the myths they conjured in their brains," wrote attorney Clarence Darrow in his essay, *Realism in Literature*, but realist artists create pictures "so true" that everyone seeing them knows they are likenesses

> of the world that they have seen; they know these are men and women and little children that they meet upon the streets ... and the moral of the picture sinks deep into their minds ... The artists of the realist school have a sense so fine that they cannot help catching the inspiration that is filling all the world's best minds with the hope of great justice and more equal social life ... The greatest artists of the world today are telling facts and painting scenes that cause humanity to stop, and think, and ask why one should be a master and another be a serf, why a portion of the world should toil and spin ... that the rest should live in idleness and ease.
>
> (Darrow 1963: 368, 370)

Within that genre, "A Jury" can also be considered a good example of a sub-genre called "prairie realism": a bleak, factual evocation of life as it was lived by "average" farmers and their families on isolated homesteads and small towns in the Midwest and prairie states. Like other successful realist writers in that genre, such as Hamlin Garland, Glaspell's forte was her ability to take factual details from the rural environment where she had grown up—in her case, Iowa—and give them a charged significance in her narrative.

Virtually every detail of "A Jury"—its setting, the characters' names, the weather, the Wright's farmhouse and its domestic furnishings—possesses a symbolic or ironic meaning that readers can decode to discover why Minnie Wright killed her husband and to approve of Mrs. Hale's and Mrs. Peters' decision to conceal the crime.

The setting of "A Jury" is the type of seemingly conventional, isolated place that conceals evil in the way that Sherlock Holmes claimed in *The Copper Beeches* when he told Watson that the "lonely houses, each in its own fields" that they saw in the countryside through their train window might contain "deeds of hellish cruelty ... hidden wickedness which may go on, year in, year out ... and none the wiser" (Doyle 1930: 323). Set on a bleak prairie somewhere in the Midwest, the Wrights' farmhouse is even lonelier than the houses Holmes observed and far more isolated. As Martha Hale and her companions approach it, she sees the "Wright place" as "looking lonesome" and as being a "lonesome-looking place" surrounded by "lonesome looking trees," all in one paragraph. This physical isolation, and the house's location "down in a hollow [where] you don't see the road," is intensified by the Wright's social isolation; later in the story Martha Hale reproaches herself for not visiting Minnie Wright because, "I stayed away because it wasn't cheerful—and that's why I ought to have come." Nevertheless, there is nothing Gothic or overtly frightening about the farmhouse; it is an ordinary place in which an extraordinary event has occurred so that the Wright's isolated, private lives have become subject to public scrutiny.

Similarly, the characters' names are ordinary ones—the kind of plain, Anglo-Saxon surnames that readers would expect in a rural, Midwest milieu in the early twentieth century. Yet all of them possess significantly symbolic qualities. That power in the community is situated in patriarchy is implied not only by the way the men take charge of the investigation but also by the name of the county where the story takes place, "Dickson" (not the more common Dixon), and, in another sly pun, by the name of the Sheriff, Peters, who is described as a "heavy man with a big voice." The frigidity and sterility of the Wright's childless marriage is suggested by the extremely cold weather—even though it is March the temperature still goes well below zero at night—and by the name of their neighbors, Hale, since hail storms are a threat in the Midwest because they can damage crops in the spring and early summer. As for John Wright, his name is heavily ironic since he turned out to be the wrong man for Minnie or anyone else to marry. Everything readers learn about him from Martha Hale and evidence in the story reveals that he was stingy, dour, and silent. Before her marriage, says Mrs. Hale, Minnie Foster was a lively girl who wore pretty clothes, "a white dress with blue ribbons [when she] stood up there in the choir and sang" (Glaspell 1993: 303). But it appears that Minnie, like her name, has been diminished in many ways. When the two women collect Minnie Wright's clothing so they can bring it to her in the county jail, they discover it is drab and shabby, because Wright was "close" and "maybe that's why she kept so much to herself ... you don't enjoy things when you feel shabby." As for Wright's temperament, Mrs. Hale's husband comments that he did not talk much and that he refused to cooperate with his neighbors to have telephones installed because Wright "put me off, saying folks talked too much anyway, and all he wanted was peace and quiet." Later in the story Martha Hale adds that Wright "was a hard man ... Just to pass the time of day with him" was like facing "a raw wind that gets to the bone" (Glaspell 1993: 291, 299).

Just as names are significant in "A Jury," so are the details of the Wright's domestic existence that Mrs. Hale and Mrs. Peters observe in the kitchen. Minnie Wright's rocker sags, has a missing rung, and is painted a "dingy red"; her cupboard is a "peculiar, ungainly structure," and her stove barely functions. An even more significant detail is the pattern of the quilt she is making just before the murder. It is, the other women recognize, a log cabin quilt which is composed of repetitions of a basic block made up of over-lapping strips, symbolizing logs. Symbolically and emotionally, the quilt's structure can be considered Minnie Wright's pathetic effort to bring some order, physical and emotional, into her home with its bad stove and a husband with a personality like a "raw wind."

However, none of these details of the Wright's life would have been considered significant if John Wright had not been murdered. Like Tom Driscoll, Wright is an example of what might be called realist evil, a bad man who is able to conceal his destructiveness behind a façade of conven-tional behavior and respectability. Midway through "A Jury" Martha Hale agrees with Mrs. Peters that people in the community say John Wright was a "good man," but this was because, "He didn't drink, and kept his word as well as most, I guess, and paid his debts." Because of this public respect-ability and reliability, and because of the Wright's isolation, his cruelty toward his wife and the conflicts within their marriage had remained con-cealed for years—until his violent death made the community realize there was something very wrong about the Wrights. In this respect Minnie Wright's act can be considered a typically realist crime. In Romantic justice narratives, crimes that violate the social order violently are usually depicted as expressions of evil or rebellious personalities, and therefore these narratives often contain climatic revelations of those personalities—for example, Vautrin's defiant tirade in *Père Goriot* or Dr. Jekyll's full statement about how he became Edward Hyde who was "pure evil." In contrast, in realist justice narratives, such crimes are more likely to be represented as symptoms of social conflicts, tensions, and malaises that would otherwise be concealed behind the façade of normalcy; therefore, the climatic revelations that occur in these narratives may imply the kind of "moral" lessons about society and its inequalities and injustices that Darrow spoke of. In *Pudd'nhead*, for example, Roxy switching the identities of the two babies and Tom murder-ing Judge Driscoll express the inequalities and racial conflicts that are concealed behind the Dawson's Landing façade of "comfortable," "slave-holding" prosperity. Analogously, in "A Jury" John Wright's violent death reveals the gender conflicts and inequities that exist beneath the surface order of a community that considers him a "good man" because he pays his bills and does not drink alcohol.

However, since "A Jury" is basically a detective story, not a sociological tract, these revelations are made in the form of clues and evidence that show why Minnie Wright finally rebelled against her cold, abusive husband and committed homicide. To discover that, the main characters in Glaspell's narrative, like those in Doyle's and Twain's, need to construct a "story" of their own: the clear, linear narrative, well stocked with clues and evidence, which is the denouement of so many detective stories and police investigations, telling who committed a crime and why he or she did it. Early on in "A Jury," Glaspell implies that the men in the story are certain that they— and not the women—are the ones qualified to do this. Looking around the kitchen, Henderson, the county attorney asks the sheriff if there was anything "important here," something that will "point up any motive," and the sheriff replies that the room contains only "kitchen things ... with a little laugh for the insignificance of kitchen things" (Glaspell 1993: 287). In other words, since he considers kitchens to be the domain of women, one would scarcely expect to find anything significant there. Women, the men think, can be expected to concern themselves with "kitchen things" and other "trifles"—such as quilts and whether or not Minnie Wright's canned fruit has frozen—whereas they have the responsibility to decide upon questions of justice, guilt, and innocence. Arrogant and self-confident, the men proceed to examine the bedroom where the murder took place and then the Wright's barn. Nevertheless, Henderson does encourage Mrs. Peters—presumably because she is "married to the law"—to "keep your eye out ... for anything [in the kitchen] that might be of use. No telling: you women might come upon a clue to the motive—and that's the thing we need." But this condescending delegation of male authority is promptly negated by Hale's contemptuous question, "But would the women know a clue if they did come upon it?" (Glaspell 1993: 289).

The women respond to most of these insults and condescending remarks in the same way—with silent resistance—so that they seem unwilling to challenge the men's dominance openly. For example, Glaspell's narrative persona comments that, "The two women moved a little closer together." After Hale sneered at his wife and Mrs. Peters for "worrying over trifles," then "neither of them spoke." But these repeated silences turns out to be a mask, presumably a self-protective one, since the two women quickly reveal that they are far more capable detectives than the men are—but only when the men are conveniently out of the kitchen. Given the opportunity to examine that room by themselves, they quickly discover that "kitchen things" can be extremely significant. Seeing a half-filled bag of sugar by a sugar bucket, Martha Hale realizes that these "[t]hings begun—and not finished" are signs of a crisis, of some kind of interruption in Minnie Wright's life, a perception that is confirmed when she and Mrs. Peters examine the unfinished quilt and see that one of its squares has wildly erratic stitching, whereas the others are "nice and even." A few minutes later Mrs. Peters finds the bird cage with a broken door hinge, and after that Mrs. Hale discovers, hidden in a sewing basket, a dead canary with its neck broken. Earlier Mrs. Peters said she had heard the county attorney remark, "what was needed for the case was a motive. Something to show anger—or sudden feeling" (Glaspell 1993: 293). The badly stitched quilt and the canary are exactly that kind of evidence, circumstantial but powerful clues revealing both why Minnie Wright killed her husband and why she killed him with a rope, so that he would die in the same way that he had killed her bird.

By using these clues to reveal what happened on the day before John Wright's murder, Glaspell has fulfilled the realist criteria that justice issues should be resolved by recourse to emphatic facts, by evidence that conforms to the rational norms of the public sphere, not fanciful theories or Romantic eloquence. However, what is also notable about the detection process in "A Jury" is not only the obvious irony that the women prove to be better detectives than the men, but that their process of detection occurs in a way that is significantly different from the typical realist detective story. In most narratives in that genre, revelations of the criminal's identity emphasize the distance and difference between the detective and the criminal who can be considered polarized representations of legality and illegality. In a story like Doyle's *The Speckled Band* (Doyle 1930: 257–272), to give only one example, each detail of the life history of the murderer Dr. Grimesby Roylott is a clue not only to his criminality but also evidence of how little he has in common with Holmes, Watson, and the narrative's presumably law-abiding readers, and how alien his values are to theirs.

In contrast, each new revelation about Minnie Wright and her marriage that tells why she finally killed her abusive husband is accompanied by an increasing sense of empathy and solidarity between her and Martha Hale and Mrs. Peters. Looking at the Wright's stove, says Glaspell's narrative persona, Mrs. Hale was "swept into her own thoughts, thinking of what it would mean, year after year, to have that stove to wrestle with," and Mrs. Peters supplements that insight with the comment, "A person gets discouraged— and loses heart" (Glaspell 1993: 294). Or when Martha Hale sees the bad stitching in Minnie Wright's quilt, she "felt queer, as if the distracted thoughts of the woman who had perhaps turned to it to try and quiet herself were communicating themselves to her." The most powerful moment of empathy with Minnie Wright occurs after they discover the dead canary. Mrs. Peters, who had wavered between her sympathy for Minnie Wright and her responsibility to what she calls "the law," suddenly remembers and tells a story from her own past about a kitten that tips the balance to empathy. Then she and Martha Hale begin to speak, in effect, for the woman who is not there to speak for herself as they understand the terrible isolation and feel the capacity for anger within themselves that made that woman kill. "When I was a girl," says Mrs. Peters,

> "my kitten—there was a boy took a hatchet, and before my eyes—before I could get there—" She covered her face an instant. "If they hadn't held me back I would have"—she caught herself looking upstairs where the footsteps were heard, and finished weakly—"hurt him."
> They sat without speaking or moving.
> "I wonder how it would seem," Mrs. Hale began, as if feeling her way over strange ground—"never to have any children around?—No, Wright wouldn't like the bird, ... a thing that sang. She [Minnie] used to sing. He killed that too."
> Mrs. Hale had not moved. "If there had been years and years of nothing, then a bird to sing to you, it would be awful—still—after the bird was still."
> It was if something within her not herself had spoken, and it found in Mrs. Peters something she did not know as herself.
> "I know what stillness is," she said in a queer monotonous voice. "When we homesteaded in Dakota, and my first baby died—after he was two years old—and me with no other then—"
> (Glaspell 1993: 302–3)

Like other realist justice narratives, "A Jury" places a priority on certainty, on clues and material evidence, but in Glaspell's case this evidence becomes meaningful not through the application of logic, as it does in Doyle's tales, or through the intervention of science, as it does in *Pudd'nhead Wilson*. Instead, it occurs through the creation of an empathic relationship between the person who committed the crime and the persons who "read" the clues that reveal her identity. That is, Martha Hale and Mrs. Peters temporarily become Minnie Wright, by experiencing what she must have felt hearing the "stillness" after her bird was killed—instead of merely discovering information about her from clues as more conventional, male detectives do. Through these acts of empathy they are able to construct their own narrative of events in which Minnie is the victim, not the perpetrator, of crimes. First and most obviously, she is the victim of her husband who made her life miserable and then killed her canary. However, as Martha Hale realizes, she and the other women of the community also contributed to Minnie's loneliness by ignoring her. "Oh, I *wish* I'd come over here once in a while!" she tells Mrs. Peters; "That was a crime! That was a crime! Who's going to punish that? ... I might've *known* she needed help" (Glaspell 1993: 303; emphasis in original).

The two women's sense of empathy with Minnie Wright comes too late to save her from her isolation, bad marriage, and abusive husband. However, it does enable them to save her from the gallows and the kind of legalistic justice that would be imposed on her by the men who are busily hunting for "evidence" above them in the Wright's bedroom. As Martha Hales and Mrs. Peters make their discoveries they instinctively realize that they cannot share what they have learned with the men, since the information would almost certainly lead to Minnie's conviction for premeditated murder. Mrs. Peters expresses this realization as a nervous joke that is complemented by Martha Hale's grimly laconic answer:

> "My!" [Mrs. Peters] began, in a high, false voice, "it's a good thing the men couldn't hear us! Getting all stirred up over a little thing like a dead canary." She hurried over that. "As if that could have anything to do with—with—My, wouldn't they *laugh*?"
> Footsteps were heard on the stairs.
> "Maybe they would," muttered Mrs. Hale—"maybe they wouldn't."
> (Glaspell 1993: 304; emphasis in original)

Hale reaches this conclusion quickly because of her memories of Minnie Foster before she was married and because of what she knows about John Wright. Mrs. Peters is more reluctant. She is a sheriff's wife and during part of the story she shares the men's conception of justice that "the law is the law" and "[t]he law has got to punish crime" (Glaspell 1993: 294, 303). But gradually, as she listens to Martha Hale and achieves a sense of empathy with Minnie Wright, she too achieves an understanding of Minnie's situation that Glaspell's narrative persona describes as a "look of peering into something," a "Look of seeing into things, of seeing through a thing to something else." Having done this, Mrs. Peters collaborates with the other woman by helping her lie to the county attorney about why the bird cage is empty and, in the story's final, climatic scene, to hide the box containing the dead canary. At that moment, says Glaspell's narrative persona, the two women's eyes "held each other in a steady burning look in which there was no evasion or flinching"; Martha Hale's look "pointed the way to the basket in which was hidden the thing [the box with the canary] that would make certain the conviction of the other woman—that woman who was not there." Mrs. Peter's responds by giving Hale the box so she can hide it in her coat pocket so that the men never see that crucial clue (Glaspell 1993: 306).

By concealing the bird, Martha Hale and Mrs. Peters subvert the official, male-dominated legal system, act conclusively as a "jury" of Minnie Wright's peers, and acquit her on the basis of the extenuating circumstances they have discovered. Once again silence allows a "just" revenge.

Chapter 3

Some like it wild

Supernatural revenge in Sheridan Le Fanu's "Mr. Justice Harbottle"

"Judges are people of violence."

(Robert Cover, 1988: 53)

Idealistic lawyers like Atticus Finch may believe "courts are the great levelers" (Lee 1960: 218), and this may be true of plaintiffs and defendants. However, it is difficult to apply it to judges, since they have so much power over courts and their procedures. Therefore, not only the legal skills and training, but also the personal qualities of judges may affect the quality of justice that is achieved in courts. In particular, qualities such as fairness and impartiality are considered crucial, for as Aristotle said in the "Nicomachean Ethics", a "judge is intended to be a sort of a living embodiment of what is just" (Aristotle 1990: 45). And one of the most common iconic representations of justice is that of a blindfolded woman holding scales to symbolize that judges and courts are supposed to make balanced decisions without knowing or caring whether plaintiffs and defendants are rich or poor, powerful or weak. Moreover, in modern legal systems if judges make unfair decisions, those decisions are supposed to be reversed by higher courts and more powerful judges. Yet the media often contain stories about court rulings by or about judges that definitely seem unjust when they are measured by any standard of fairness.

In the fall of 1993, for example, a federal judge sentenced a man named Sol Wachtler to a prison term of fifteen months after he had confessed that he had harassed a former lover for months with threatening letters, conspired to extort $200,000 from her, and made telephone calls to her in which he threatened to kidnap her daughter. The mildness of his sentence was perhaps explained by the information that Wachtler was not a typical spurned lover but the former chief judge of the New York Court of Appeals, that he had been represented in court by a team of three excellent lawyers, and that he had been so widely respected that he had considered running for governor in 1994. When Wachtler's lawyers claimed that his behavior was due to mental illness, a prosecutor retorted that this case was not a replay of *The Exorcist*. Wachtler "wasn't possessed by an evil spirit. He wasn't in the grip of forces beyond his control" (Schemo 1993: B1).

That Judge Wachtler's "case" is not a new but a perennial problem is suggested by the popularity of the "magical justice" folktales that are found in many cultures. In these tales, it is assumed that even kings, queens, and emperors must be fair and compassionate when judging their subjects. If they are cruel, unjust, or wicked, they can be punished by "evil spirits" and powers acting as avengers whose "penalties [are] harsh, ranging from public humiliation to agonizing death" and eternal damnation. For even though these "tales of retribution" may seem chilling to modern readers, "they provided their own consolation, for within their ambit cruelty was always punished, and tyrants were never let off scot-free. If such justice could not be guaranteed in the mundane world, it was, at least, a certainty in the enchanted one" (Le Fanu 1986: 8–9). Sheridan Le Fanu's 1872 novella, "Mr. Justice Harbottle," shows how a writer, steeped in the Gothic and Romantic tradition, could apply this folktale motif in a more sophisticated literary and cultural context. In addition, Le Fanu also approaches this theme so it fuses a sacralized, "enchanted" vision of revenge with the more secular, psychological perspective that characterizes modern societies starting in the late Enlightenment and Romantic eras.

Because Le Fanu's narratives are not well known except among connoisseurs of ghost stories, a brief summary of his novella is helpful. In the mid-eighteenth century a Shrewsbury grocer named Lewis Pyneweck steals his wife Flora's fortune, spoons, and earrings and otherwise mistreats her. She runs away to London with the title character, Elijah Harbottle, a corrupt and bad-tempered "hanging judge," changes her name to Carwell, and becomes his "housekeeper." Several years later, Pyneweck is accused of forging a bill of exchange, and Flora Pyneweck tries to persuade the Judge to be merciful to her husband. A fictional counterpart of actual hanging judges like George Jeffreys and Sir Thomas Page, Harbottle enjoys seeing defendants convicted, and he enjoys sending them to the gallows even more. However, he takes special pains to make sure he is assigned to Pyneweck's case when he goes on circuit to Shrewsbury, so he can personally preside over the grocer's trial and sentence him to be executed: "Did he not, as a lawyer, know that to bring a man [like Pyneweck] from his shop to the dock, the chances must be at least ninety-nine out of hundred that he is guilty? ... In hanging that fellow he could not be wrong" (Le Fanu 1993: 95). Afterwards, instead of feeling any remorse, Harbottle "laughed, and coaxed, and bullied away [Mrs. Pyneweck's] faint upbraidings, and in a little time Lewis Pyneweck troubled her no more; and the Judge secretly chuckled over the perfectly fair removal of a bore, who might have grown little by little into something very like a tyrant" (Le Fanu 1993: 100). Nevertheless, during the month following Pyneweck's trial and execution, the Judge is troubled by nightmares and the "blue devils" of depression until at the end of the novella he commits suicide by hanging himself.

Like Nathaniel Hawthorne's Judge Pyncheon in *The House of Seven Gables* and Gérard de Villeforte in Alexandre Dumas's *The Count of Monte Christo*, Harbottle is an unjust magistrate, a cunning schemer who uses his position in a judicial system to further his own nefarious interests. In each text judicial power is held by a clever but wicked man who conceals his private crimes by performing them within the legal system. Since none of the narratives suggests a political remedy—such as reforms or revolution—they all raise the issue of how justice can prevail or how revenge be attained when the legal system is itself corrupted by chicanery and—in Harbottle's case—by cruelty as well. Hawthorne relies on a fantastic coincidence, that Judge Pyncheon should die of a stroke at an opportune moment. Dumas depends on a fantastically rich, talented, dedicated avenger, the Count of Monte Christo, who revenges himself for his own unjust imprisonment by destroying Villeforte's life and driving him insane. Le Fanu relies on yet another, more wildly carnivalistic form of retribution: the Gothic fantastic blended with the psychological.

After a Prologue mentioning several "reports" and "accounts," the events of Harbottle's story begin with a ghostly appearance recounted by the tenant of a house in the Westminister section of nineteenth-century London. The tenant is reading late at night when the closet door of his bedroom opens, and

> a slight dark man, particularly sinister, and somewhere about fifty, dressed in mourning of a very antique fashion, such a suit as we see in Hogarth, entered the room on tip-toe. He was followed by an elder man, stout, and blotched with scurvy, and whose features, fixed as a corpse's, were stamped with dreadful force with a character of sensuality and villainy.
>
> (Le Fanu 1993: 85–86)

The tenant's story about the dualistic appearance of the two ghosts—one slight and presumably middle-class in "mourning" dress and the other stout and wealthy—is followed by a description of the haunted house, the information that it was once owned by Harbottle, who died there under "extraordinary" circumstances, and a description of Harbottle himself. The

Judge—like many Romantic and Victorian Gothic villains—makes no efforts to conceal his wickedness. He is a "burly," hard-living man who looks like a Hogarth caricature of vice and cruelty with his "great mulberry-colored face, a big, carbuncled nose, fierce eyes, and a grim and brutal mouth. ... His voice was loud and harsh, and gave effect to the sarcasm which was his habitual weapon on the bench" (Le Fanu 1993: 88). In addition, he is an aristocrat, has his place in the House of Lords, travels in carriages and sedan chairs, and entertains himself by carousing at "dubious jollifcations" (Le Fanu 1993: 90). Harbottle, in other words, is one of those full-blooded villains, very popular with nineteenth-century readers and authors, whose ruthlessness and egoism is exceeded only by his lack of scruples.

> The old gentleman had the reputation of being about the wickedest man in England. *Even on the bench he now and then showed his scorn of opinion.* He had carried cases in his own way ... in spite of counsel, authorities, and even of juries, by a sort of cajolery, violence, and bamboozling, that somehow confused and overpowered resistance. He had never actually committed himself; he was too cunning to do that. He had the character [reputation] of being, however, a dangerous and unscrupulous judge; but his character did not trouble him. The associates he chose for his hours of relaxation cared as little as he did about it.
>
> (Le Fanu 1993: 88; emphasis added)

As for legality and the enlightened publicity and fairness it supposedly insures to protect defendants and their rights, these safeguards do not deter Harbottle, since he is still able to carry "cases in his own way" because of his scorn for public opinion and despite his bad reputation.

The events of the novella are set in the 1740s and reflect the Victorian conception of the eighteenth century as a more brutal and licentious age than the nineteenth century: a time when English law, says Le Fanu, was "a rather pharisaical, bloody and heinous system of justice" (Le Fanu 1993: 95). As for Harbottle, he is the kind of cruel, vindictive hanging judge that existed in some seventeenth- and eighteenth-century courts and continued to haunt the British imagination long afterward. Twentieth-century historians like Douglas Hays and Lawrence Stone may cite statistics to point out how the harshness of the eighteenth-century British judicial system was tempered by pardons and clemency, the precise application of legal rules, and the willingness of juries to acquit defendants on flimsy pretexts.[1] Despite these caveats, however, eighteenth-century British justice was still literally a "bloody" business and one which had a powerful class bias (Gay 1977: 426–27).

During that century parliament increased the number of capital offenses from fifty to over two hundred, and many of these capital crimes were offenses against property clearly designed to protect the interests of aristocrats, the rich, and the well-to-do by terrorizing England's poorer or more lower-middle-class citizens with the threat of death for such offenses as house-breaking, burglary, poaching deer, stealing live stock, and forging documents (Gay 1977: 426–27; Stone 1987: 243; Jacoby 1994: 257). During the early nineteenth century, parliament rapidly lowered the number of capital crimes, to fifteen by 1837, but the memory of a time when a "dangerous and unscrupulous" judge could sentence a poor man or woman to death for stealing a few shillings—or commute the sentence to "transportation" to the wilds of Georgia—persisted and influenced the British conception of justice as a process that could easily be tainted by the personal and class interests of judges. It is significant in "Mr. Justice Harbottle" that the Judge himself is portrayed as being ostentatiously wealthy. He has a mansion, many servants, and a coach—whereas his defendant and victim, Pyneweck, is clearly of a lower social class and the Judge's dualistic opposite: a mere "grocer with a demure look, a soft step, and a lean face," who must beg his estranged wife for a fee for a counselor when he is accused of forgery.

Compared to Harbottle, Pyneweck does indeed seem (as the pun on his name suggests) "weak" and therefore unable to challenge Harbottle's injustice. Early on in the story, however, it is implied that though Pyneweck may not be powerful in the material world he may still have dangerous associates from another realm to avenge him. This conflict between the Judge and Pyneweck is developed through a series of increasingly sinister and carnivalistic masquerades and confrontations. In Chapters II and III of the novella,[2] even before Pyneweck goes on trial at Shrewsbury, Harbottle encounters a mysterious, seemingly "infirm" old man with a "quavering" voice who calls himself Hugh Peters, pretends to be an informer, and tells the Judge he should not try Pyneweck's case. A secret cabal is being formed by anonymous men, says Peters, who call themselves the High Court of Appeal, "the object of which is to take cognizance of the conduct of the judges; and first, of *your* conduct my lord" (Le Fanu 1999: 92, 91; emphasis in original). When Peters leaves, the Judge orders his "stalwart" footman to follow the feeble old man. But when the servant catches up with Peters, Peters pretends to drop a guinea and, while the footman is searching for it, fells him with two heavy blows, and runs "like a lamplighter down a lane to the right, and was gone" (Le Fanu 1993: 94). This event initiates a pattern in the narrative in which the weak confront the strong and unexpectedly defeat them by turning out to be much more powerful than their appearances would suggest. What is even stranger is that—though the Judge had earlier thought that Peters had a suspiciously "chalky" face—he now decides that "allowing for change of tints and such disguises as the playhouse affords every night, the features of this false old man ... were identical with those of Lewis Pyneweck" (Le Fanu 1993: 97). Indeed, the Judge is so certain Peters and

Pyneweck are the same that he makes inquiries to be sure that Pyneweck has not escaped from Shrewsbury jail. Nevertheless, the Judge assumes Peters is a material being, a footpad hired to frighten him.

At this point in the text, Chapter 3, readers will have noted some of the dualisms in "Mr. Justice Harbottle": two ghosts in Chapter 1, one of them middle-aged, lean, and dark (Pyneweck), the other stout and elderly (Harbottle); two main characters in Chapter II (the "burly" Harbottle and the supposedly "feeble" Peters), and two courts of justice (Harbottle's and the High Court of Appeal). One of these courts is mysterious and concealed (the High Court of Appeals), whereas the other (Harbottle's) is material and will meet on schedule in Shrewsbury and convict Pyneweck. Thus, two realms of existence are beginning to converge and mix with one another. In Balzac's *Père Goriot* this carnivalistic eliding or blurring of boundaries occurs on a social plane in the mingling of social classes in Madame Vauquer's boardinghouse. In Le Fanu's novella, it is the boundaries that separate the living and the dead that are becoming porous. Considered from this perspective, the name "Peters" has symbolic overtones, since St. Peter is the heavenly gatekeeper who stands between this world and the afterlife and carries keys that can open one realm to the other.

Though it is fairly short, Chapter IV of "Mr. Justice Harbottle" contains three significant events. First, there is the court trial in Shrewsbury, even though none of its details are reported since Le Fanu's narrator does not follow the Judge to Shrewsbury to tell the jury's verdict, and the execution that follows. Instead, Le Fanu's narrator stays back in London with Pyneweck's wife and recounts her growing anxiety as she waits for news of the outcome of her husband's trial. When that information does come, it arrives in the most minimal form: a list in a newspaper of the names and offenses of seven persons executed at Shrewsbury with "Lewis Pyneweck—forgery," last on the list. The second event in Chapter IV occurs when Le Fanu recounts the grief of Pyneweck's widow. Because her relationship to her executed husband is a secret, there is no one in the household she can tell about his death, including their daughter who had been told her father was dead years earlier. Though she sheds "tears of horror," the widow Pyneweck's fury does not last long. She was a "person who lived not upon sentiment but upon beef and pudding; … she did not trouble herself long even with resentments," and the Judge soon bullies away her "weak upbraidings" (Le Fanu 1993: 99–100). Harbottle has become an especially grasping patriarchal villain, since now he has not only taken his rival's life and wife—he has also, in effect, stolen his daughter and thus deprived Pyneweck of his paternity.

We would interpret these two developments—Le Fanu's omission of the Shrewsbury trial and Mrs. Pyneweck's inability to speak to her daughter—as signaling the failure of earthly justice in the story. The trial was omitted because its outcome was so predetermined that its details were irrelevant. As for Mrs. Pyneweck not telling her daughter about Pyneweck's death, this insures that no living person can bring Harbottle to justice or avenge Pyneweck since she was the only person alive who knew why the Judge sentenced him to death. Like many crimes committed by persons working within a judicial system, Harbottle's is concealed by the system itself, because it appears that Pyneweck was condemned by a jury's verdict rather than by the Judge's personal animus.

The third event, in the final part of Chapter IV, indicates that another form of authority—one not composed of the living—may be interested in the Judge's case. The next time he tries a case of forgery at the Old Bailey, Harbottle begins his usual charge to the jury, "thundering dead against the prisoner, with many a hard aggravation and cynical gibe," when suddenly the "eloquent Judge" stops short to stare at a lean, dark, "small mean figure" who is standing among "the persons of small importance" at the side of the courtroom and has just handed a letter to a court official. The lean man says nothing, but he has Pyneweck's features, plus Pyneweck's unpleasant smile as he stretches his cravat so Harbottle can "see distinctly a stripe of swollen blue round his neck, which indicated, he thought, the grip of the rope" (Le Fanu 1993: 101). Suddenly and significantly the Judge loses his eloquence that he had earlier used to bamboozle juries, lawyers, and court officials: "His lordship signed energetically with his hand in the direction in which the man had vanished. He turned to the tipstaff. His first effort to speak ended in a gasp. He cleared his throat, and told the astounded official to arrest that man who had interrupted the court" (Le Fanu 1993: 101). Once again the dualistic pattern of the weak vanquishing the strong is repeated when the powerful, "eloquent Judge," who was dominating the courtroom, is silenced and "decrowned," to use Bakhtin's terminology, by a person "of small importance," who says nothing out loud.

Needless to say, no one else has seen a disturbance, and clearly Pyneweck dead is going to be more troublesome to the Judge than he was when he was alive. This assumption is quickly justified by the events of Chapters V through VII. In Chapter V the Judge reads the letter that Pyneweck's ghost (or double) brought to Old Bailey and discovers it is an indictment ordering him to prepare himself for trial before "the High Court of Appeal ... for the murder of Lewis Pyneweck ... wrongfully executed for forgery ... by reason of the willful perversion of the evidence, and the undue pressure put upon the jury, together with the illegal admission of evidence" (Le Fanu 1993: 102). Written in quasi-legal language and signed by "Caleb Searcher, Officer of the Crown Solicitor in the Kingdom of Life and Death," it concludes with the announcement that Harbottle will be tried by a "Lord Chief Justice Twofold." And, if he receives a death sentence, he will be executed one month later, on March 10th. This document signals the beginning of the invasion of the Judge's private life and mind by the procedures of a High Court that has begun to judge him.

The Judge tries to believe that he is being threatened by a "conspiracy" of material enemies. But in the next chapter, as he is waiting outside the Drury Lane theater in his carriage, Harbottle has a carnivalistic nightmare or hallucination in which he is "arrested" (the title of Chapter VI) by two armed, evil-looking strangers dressed as Bow Street officers, and he discovers that his coachman has become one of his deceased servants, one who had died of jail-fever after the Judge had indicted him for stealing a spoon. The boundaries between life and death and between reality and fantasy disappear as the Judge's coach glides through a Halloween-Gothic waste land filled with rotting trees whose fantastically shaped branches destroy the boundary between the human and the natural, "standing here and there in groups, as if they held up their arms and twigs like fingers, in horrible glee" (Le Fanu 1993: 105). After passing a gigantic gallows, the Judge is taken to a monstrous, prison-like building where he is arraigned at the High Court of Appeal. In this court Harbottle's position in the justice system is inverted according to the "peculiar logic" of the "carnival sense of the world" that Bakhtin describes in which events become turnabouts and shiftings "from top to bottom, from front to rear ... travesties, humiliations, profanations, comic crownings, and uncrownings" (Bakhtin 1984: 11).

In Twofold's court, Harbottle's position is ruthlessly reversed as he is transformed from a hanging judge, who condemns others to death with sneers and gibes, to a victim-defendant who is condemned by his own sneering alter ego and ridiculed by the "deafening" laughter of demonic courtroom spectators. But otherwise the system is a supernatural, symmetrical travesty of the earthly justice system. This symmetry is completed with grim precision when the Judge reaches the courtroom. Unlike the earlier dualistic confrontations in which he encountered persons looking like Pyneweck, the Judge faces an even more dangerous enemy: Chief-Justice Twofold, his own malevolent, supernatural double. All the rage, malice, and bias that Harbottle had to conceal from public opinion at least partially in his earthly courtroom can be expressed openly by his monstrous counterpart in this infernal courtroom. And since in this court there are no human, civil restraints upon judicial power, Twofold has a voice so powerful that even Harbottle's cannot compete with it.

Le Fanu's narration of the proceedings of Twofold's court is one of the most brilliant carnivalistic visions of justice in literature. It combines the paranoia of Kafka, the gusto of Dickens, and the imagery of Goya's Black Paintings. All the sadism, rage, and unfairness that can be achieved in the course of a court trial are dramatized by Le Fanu in two ferocious pages.

> "Is the appellant Lewis Pyneweck in court?" asked Chief-Justice Twofold, in a voice of thunder, that shook the woodwork of the court, and boomed down the corridors.
> Up stood Pyneweck from his place at the table.

"Arraign the prisoner!" roared the Chief [Justice]: and Judge
Harbottle felt the panels of the dock round him, and the floor ... quiver
in the vibrations of that tremendous voice.

The prisoner, *in limine* (at the bar), objected to this pretended court, as
being a sham, and non-existent in point of law. ...

Whereupon the chief-justice laughed suddenly, and every one in the
court, turning round upon the prisoner, laughed also, till the laugh
grew and roared all round like a deafening acclamation; he saw nothing
but glittering eyes and teeth, a universal stare and grin. ...

... ...

One thing could not fail to strike even him. This Chief-Justice
Twofold, who was knocking him about at every turn with sneer and
gibe, and roaring him down with his tremendous voice, was a dilated
effigy of himself; an image of Mr. Justice Harbottle, at least double his
size, and with all his fierce colouring, and his ferocity of eye and visage,
enhanced awfully.

Nothing the prisoner could argue, cite, or state, was permitted to
retard for a moment, the march of the case towards its catastrophe.

(Le Fanu 1993: 108)

Besides being a ferocious satire on the justice process, this scene is also a
brilliant example of what Bakhtin would describe as a carnivalistic
"decrowning" with its "ritual laughter" and parody, aimed at Harbottle.
For such laughter, says Bakhtin, is "directed at something higher—towards a
shift of authorities and truths, a shift of world orders" through the parodic
"creation of a *decrowning double*" who turns the world upside-down or
inside-out (Bakhtin 1988: 127; emphasis in original).

The verdict of such a court is, of course, guilty; and Harbottle is sentenced
to die on the tenth of March. He is taken to a smithy in which two monstrous men fasten a red-hot fetter around his ankle—which causes the Judge
to awaken back in his carriage suffering from a bad attack of the gout. By
returning to the mundane world of gout and carriages, Le Fanu's narrative
implies that the supernatural personages of Justice Twofold's court may be
only a "dream" and that they cannot intervene directly in the justice process
as they might have done in a tale told in a more religious age. Instead, the
forces of justice must intervene indirectly through the Judge's psyche. For
after Harbottle awakens from his nightmare and recovers from the gout, his
"ferocious joviality did not return. He could not get this dream, as he chose
to call it out of his head" (Le Fanu 1993: 111). He becomes increasingly
disturbed and depressed until he commits suicide some time during the
night of March 9–10 after a series of bizarre events disrupt his household.

During that night Flora Pyneweck's daughter sees a strange man in the
Judge's sedan chair, who resembles the deceased grocer, since he is thin and
dressed in black, with "sharp dark features" (Le Fanu 1993: 113). The thin

man disappears, but Mrs. Pyneweck herself sees an odd-looking stranger leaning over the railing above a stairwell and holding a coil of rope. A scullery maid hears heavy strokes from a back kitchen at midnight and, going there, sees a "monstrous" smith standing over what looks like a dead body and hammering on the rivets of a chain—a repetition of the Judge's nightmare on the night he went to the theater. The other servants, alarmed by the maid's hysterics, go to their master's bedroom where they find Harbottle awake and as bad-tempered as ever as he threatens to discharge anyone who dares disturb him. Nevertheless, the next morning the Judge is discovered hanging from the banister at the top of the staircase.

> There was not the smallest sign of any struggle or resistance. ... There was medical evidence to show that, in his atrabilious [depressed] state, it was quite in the cards that he might have made away with himself. The jury found accordingly that it was a case of suicide. But to those who were acquainted with the strange story which Judge Harbottle had related to at least two persons, the fact that the catastrophe occurred on the morning of March 10th seemed a startling coincidence.
>
> (Le Fanu 1993: 117–18)

From the standpoint of justice, however, this outcome is not coincidental at all, particularly if one favors justice of the *lex talonis* variety: the "eye for an eye, tooth for a tooth," kind of retribution proscribed by the Bible.

Le Fanu hints strongly at another aspect of this retribution when, at the very end of the tale, he refers to Harbottle's funeral in Biblical language: "A few days after the pomp of a great funeral attended him to the grave; and so, in the language of Scripture, 'the rich man, died, and was buried'" (Le Fanu 1993: 118). Alert readers will recognize this as a reference to Luke 16:19, the parable about the rich man and the poor beggar, Lazarus. In Luke's parable, when the two die, the rich man is sent to Hell and Lazarus goes to heaven, thus reversing their earthly conditions. In Le Fanu's story Harbottle and Pyneweck do not go to heaven or hell; they seem condemned to a kind of limbo in which they haunt the Judge's house together. But during the course of the story, the power relationship that existed between them is reversed in a way analogous to the rich man and Lazarus story after the Judge is "decrowned" in Chief-Justice Twofold's court. In the beginning Harbottle was rich and "feasted sumptuously everyday" (Luke 16:19), while Pyneweck was languishing in prison, unable to defend himself. In the material world Harbottle was able to persecute Pyneweck and use his status in the earthly court system to destroy the grocer. But after Pyneweck was executed, he becomes the one with power, the supernatural power to persecute Harbottle through the High Court of Appeal. Thus the Biblical reference to Luke also resolves the dualism of the implied class difference between Harbottle and Pyneweck by reminding readers that the rich and the powerful in this world are still subject to a higher law that may punish them if they are wicked.

But where or what is the High Court of Appeal? Only one of the series of occult events in the story, Harbottle's appearance before his malign alter-ego, Chief-Justice Twofold, is explicitly explained as being a nightmare. Most of the other mysterious events seem to be, in varying degrees, mixtures of the supernatural and the psychological. Parallel to the novella's overt story of Judge Harbottle and the retribution he receives there is a parallel, less explicit, contextual story that deals with the conflict between the super-natural and the rational in a de-sacralized universe in which many readers might consider the events in Le Fanu's narrative as being at best incredible and at worst ridiculous. What this contextual story asks, in effect, is how seriously and under what conditions can readers—including skeptical readers—respond to the kind of justice that is portrayed in "Mr. Justice Harbottle"?

Even at the height of the popularity of Gothic Romanticism, in the late eighteenth and the early nineteenth centuries, the genre's practitioners had an ambivalent attitude toward their narratives' spooks and occult events, since they could not entirely ignore the rationalistic side of Enlightenment culture, even while they were subverting it. The problem they confronted was explained by Sir Walter Scott in the 1820s in two essays on Gothic fiction in which he warns that the "management of such [fictional] machin-ery" as ghosts and witches was a "task of a most delicate nature," since it was but one step

> betwixt the sublime and the ridiculous, and in an age of universal incredulity, we must own it would require, at the present day, the sup-port of the highest powers, to save the supernatural from slipping into the ludicrous. ... [T]he belief in prodigies and supernatural events has gradually declined in proportion to the advancement of human knowl-edge; and that since the age has become enlightened, the occurrence of tolerably well attested anecdotes of the supernatural characters are so few, as to render it more probable that the witnesses have laboured under some strange and temporary delusion, rather than that the laws of nature have been altered or suspended. ... A sense that the [aesthetic] effect of the supernatural in its more obvious application is easily exhausted, has occasioned the efforts of modern authors to cut new walks and avenues through the enchanted wood, and to revive, if possible, by some means or other the fading impression of its horrors.
>
> (Scott 1990: 61, 66, 68)

Le Fanu, who published his first ghost story in 1839 and his last ones in the early 1870s, was one of the Gothic writers who sought, as Scott says, to find "new walks and avenues" for this genre of Romantic fiction. For him and a number of other writers of ghost stories during the nineteenth century, the solution to the problem of how to represent irrational events and grotesque images—without descending to the ridiculous—was to create ambivalent alliances between carnivalistic Gothic Romanticism, the medical sciences, and what would now be called psychiatry or psychoanalysis.[3]

In the five stories that appear in Le Fanu's collection, *In a Glass Darkly*, which includes "Mr. Justice Harbottle," he accomplished this, in part, by manipulating the stories' viewpoints so that they are set in multiple narrative frames and often refer to a bewildering number of narrators, witnesses, and informants. He did this by prefacing his stories with Prologues ostensibly written by an anonymous physician and surgeon who says he is the Editor of assorted documents, tracts, essays, and other texts written or collected by a deceased German physician named Dr. Martin Hesselius: a "wanderer" and "genius" who traveled through Europe collecting strange tales from patients whom he had seen either "to the light of day, or through the gates of darkness, to the caverns of the dead" (Le Fanu 1993: 5). Except for one story, "Green Tea," in which Hesselius actually appears as a character and is the first-person narrator, the stories are based on accounts, supposedly taken from Hesselius' files, by persons who have heard about the events they describe from other persons who witnessed them.

The beauty of these frame narratives with their references to informants about whom we can know nothing but their names (and sometimes the Editor's assertions that they are reliable) is that they make it impossible for skeptical readers to be sure exactly where the fantastic elements in the tale are coming from. Are they actually present in the events described? Have they been added by credulous narrators? By Hesselius? It is impossible to be sure. Yet the story contains some language and a few comments that imply that its viewpoint is also that of a medical physician, and these comments make it difficult to know whether Harbottle is being persecuted by Pyneweck and other ghosts or by the "blue devils" of his own "atrabilious state."[4]

It is possible, for example, that the mysterious disruption of the Judge's court by the lean man with marks on his neck, might well have been a hallucination induced by the Judge's repressed but guilty conscience since he was trying a forgery case, the same offense that had sent Pyneweck to the gallows. Yet the silent man does give a court official the letter, signed by Caleb Searcher, telling Harbottle he will be prosecuted by the High Court of Appeal. However, in a parenthetical note that follows this event someone, perhaps Hesselius, comments: "What of the paper I have cited? No one saw it during his [Harbottle's] life; no one, after his death. He spoke of it to Dr. Hedstone; and what purported to be a 'copy', in the old Judge's handwriting was found. The original was nowhere. Was it a copy of an illusion, incident to brain disease? Such is my belief" (Le Fanu 1993: 104). In similar comments Le Fanu's narrative persona, who is presumably Hessiliuz, says that just before the Judge killed himself his "spirits were very low; he was frightened about himself. ... He was sinking into that state of nervous dejection in which men lose their faith in orthodox advice, and in despair consult quacks, astrologers, and nursery storytellers. Could such a dream mean that he was to have a fit, and so die on the 10th?" (Le Fanu 1993: 111–12).

Comments like these—that only the Judge saw the document from Caleb Searcher or that he was in a state of "nervous dejection"—could reassure skeptical readers that they are not being asked to take all of the story's ghostly machinations too seriously, since the narrative itself interprets them skeptically and suggests they might have been produced by the Judge's demented brain. In passages like this in *In a Glass Darkly*, Hesselius functions as a mediator between the mystical and the rational, the scientific and the supernatural, as he eliminates the opposition between them by combining their respective viewpoints and speaking like a kind of psychiatrist or psychoanalyst.[5] In this way readers can enjoy the fearful effects of Le Fanu's Gothic events and images without feeling that they are, as Sir Walter Scott warned, giving credence to the "ridiculous." Through Hesselius, as Nelson Browne argues, Le Fanu is able to present "readers with two interpretations of events in these narratives—one rational, or scientific, the other, supernatural. He leaves us free to reject or accept whichever we please" (Browne 1951: 78). In other words, applying Bakhtin's and Habermas' terminologies, Le Fanu can show justice as being achieved through Gothic/carnivalistic decrownings, dualisms, and images—but without offending the rationality of the public sphere enough to make his tales seem ridiculous as well as Gothic.

But of course, from the perspective of the characters in "Mr. Justice Harbottle" and several of the other stories in *In a Glass Darkly*, this choice of interpretations is irrelevant, and this freedom does not exist. For them, the "difference between psychological ghosts and real ghosts is eliminated because the story forces us to glimpse a world in which such nice distinctions do not have any relevance. Skulking through that world—and breaking through into ours—are unearthly energies which are neither material nor spiritual but a hideous synthesis" (Sullivan 1978: 51–52). And, considered in this context, this grim synthesis may be an advantage in justice narratives about revenge and retribution.

Secular, procedural justice may seem very certain and comprehensive, but sometimes it is actually rather limited. It often does not demonstrate, in particular, that it has much power to punish the rich and the powerful, such as hanging judges who are able to bamboozle juries, counsel, and legal authorities through cajolery and sarcasm (Le Fanu 1993: 88). But skulking, "unearthly energies" that combine the material and the spiritual can be more formidable furies than a material legal system, furies so powerful that they can hunt down and destroy even a Harbottle.

Moreover, in a supposedly more secularized and modernized society, such as twenty-first-century America, it may be easy for someone, like the prosecutor in Judge Wachtler's case, to assume that the boundary lines separating the normal from the abnormal and the sane from the insane are fixed and secure; therefore, he can confidently assert that Wachtler has no "evil spirits" troubling him. In Le Fanu's domain one cannot have such assurance.

For as Captain Barton, the guilty victim/protagonist of "The Familiar," another story in *In a Glass Darkly*, explains to the sympathetic but ineffectual clergyman who tries to help him:

> whatever may be my uncertainty as to the authenticity of what we are taught to call revelation ... I am deeply and horribly convinced, that there does exist beyond this [material world] a spiritual world. ... a system which may be, and which is sometimes partially and terribly revealed. I am sure—I *know*. ... that there is a God—a dreadful God—and that retribution follows guilt, in ways the most mysterious and stupendous—by agencies the most inexplicable and terrific ... a system malignant and implacable.
>
> (Le Fanu 1993: 60; emphasis in original)

For Barton, like Harbottle, the origin or exact location of this "spiritual world" does not matter. What matters is that its agents have sought him out to exact justice in the form of retribution, and no earthly persons or powers can give him any refuge from them or their effects on his mind.

Chapter 4

Law and the romantic ego

Conspiracy and justice in Honoré de Balzac's *Le Père Goriot*

"There are two kinds of history: official history, all lies, the history which is taught in schools. ... Then there's secret history, which explains how things really happened: a scandalous kind of history. ... set yourself a splendid goal, but don't let anyone see what means you adopt and the steps you take to reach it. You have been acting like a child: be a man. Do what a hunter does. Lie in wait, lie in ambush. ... "[1]

(Vautrin speaking to Lucien de Rubempré in *Lost Illusions*, Balzac 1971: 641, 648)

In *Père Goriot* and other novels in Balzac's *Comédie humaine*, readers enter a significantly different world than they encounter in Le Fanu's Gothic narratives: a world that is, culturally speaking, considerably more modern in the sense that it is much more secular in its vision of justice and how it may be attained. Le Fanu's crime and ghost stories are derived from the eighteenth- and early nineteenth-century Gothic mode of Romanticism in which nightmares, spooks, and midnight horrors may punish characters like Harbottle. In contrast, Balzac is one of the great transitional novelists linking Romanticism with the realism of later nineteenth-century literature, and he was one of the writers who secularized Romanticism by creating human equivalents for the ghosts and supernatural paraphernalia that had fascinated the Gothic imagination. At one of the climatic moments of *Goriot*, Eugène de Rastignac exclaims, "It's divine justice" (Balzac 1998: 149), believing that some form of supernatural retribution has punished the arch-criminal Vautrin for his crimes. But Rastignac is wrong. There are no supernatural powers dispensing justice or causing injustices in *Père Goriot*—only human criminals, policemen, spies, ordinary citizens, and informers, almost all of whom are living by the predatory, ruthless code Vautrin outlines first to Rastignac in *Père Goriot* and later to Lucien de Rubempré in *Lost Illusions*.

Vautrin's allusions to a secret, "scandalous kind of history" refers to a kind of political *modus operandi*, based on conspiracy theories, that flourished in the late eighteenth and the early nineteenth centuries. That was when the Bastille as a symbol of injustice, secrecy, and illegitimate power was replaced, says Marilyn Butler, "by the even more ghastly image of the guillotine," and it was believed that nations could succumb to secret societies led by bands "of dedicated fanatics bent on drawing the innocent into their clutches" (Butler 1975: 115). France during the Napoleanic era and afterwards—a period that coincided with the beginning of Balzac's writing career in the 1820s—was especially fertile ground for conspiracies and conspiracy theorizing. Bontapartists, revolutionaries, republicans, aristocrats, and opportunists all engaged in shady plots and strange alliances with or against each other as they tried to gain power through assassinations, revolts, and *coups d'état* (Hunt 1972: 10–16). Meanwhile, shady financiers and swindlers schemed and conspired to get rich by defrauding or stealing from their fellow citizens so that there were financial as well as political "secret" histories and scandals.

For Balzac, such conspiracies (or rumors about them) were both sources for his novels' plots and one of the chief ways he was able to make the transition from Gothicism toward a more "realistic" kind of Romanticism. He explained his rationale for this process explicitly in his "Preface" to *The History of the Thirteen,* a novel he published in 1833, just before *Père Goriot* (1835). In a previous novel, *The Fatal Skin* or, *The Magic Skin* (*La Peau de chagrin*), published in 1831, his main character relied on magic to achieve his desires, an ass's skin inscribed with Sanskrit letters that gives its owner whatever he wishes. But in the *History of the Thirteen* Balzac wanted to depict characters who used their own extraordinary but human powers to achieve success. As Balzac describes it, that novel was supposed to portray a band of ruthless conspirators and Romantic rebels who were "impervious to fear; and [had never] trembled before public authority, [or] the public hangman ... they were undoubtedly criminals, but undeniably remarkable for certain qualities which go to the making of great men. ... they were the very incarnations of ideas suggested to the imagination by the fantastic powers attributed in fiction to the Manfreds, Fausts and Melmoths of literature."[2] In other words, political conspiracies and paranoia would replace the Gothic occult as the locus for "fantastic powers."

Instead of depending on an ass's skin with magic powers, Balzac's band of "outstanding people" would rely on their pacts with one another and on their own extraordinary abilities, which would be quite enough for them to dominate a "petty society" when they combined "their natural intelligence, their acquired knowledge and their financial resources" (Balzac 1974: 26). "Living in society but apart from it and hostile to it, accepting none of its principles, recognizing no laws or only submitting to them out of sheer necessity," he says, these conspirators would rule society in a manner that "was at once horrible and sublime." Therefore, the author of their history would not need to rely on the supernatural or on tricks, trap-doors, and other crude Gothic devices. Such an author would, Balzac said,

> disdain to convert his story ... into a sort of toy with a secret spring and, as some novelists do, drag his reader through four volumes from one subterranean chamber to another, merely to show him a dried-up skeleton and tell him by way of conclusion that his bogey effects have been obtained by means of a door hidden behind a tapestry. ... *the power wielded by this organization* [the Thirteen], *though acquired by natural means, alone can explain the apparently supernatural agencies at work.*
>
> (Balzac 1974: 26, 23; emphasis added)

Despite Balzac's intentions and this resounding "Preface," however, only one of the thirteen conspirators, Ferragus, actually appears in *The History*, and Balzac seems to have forgotten about the other twelve since, as Italo Calvino notes, "he showed them only in the distance as decorative 'extras' at a splendidly pompous funeral Mass" (Calvino 1987: 184).

In later novels like *A Murky Business* and *A Harlot High and Low*, Balzac deals mainly with political and financial conspiracies. The conspiracy in *Père Goriot* is chiefly a criminal one, and in that novel Balzac distilled his idea that conspiracy was a substitute for the "apparently supernatural" into his characterization of Vautrin who appears first in *Goriot*, reappears at the end of *Lost Illusions*, and then dominates *A Harlot High and Low* in which, at the end of that novel, he changes sides and becomes the head of the Secret Police.[3] In *Goriot*, the Vautrin plot (as we shall call it) is only one of three main plots that Balzac weaves together. Vautrin's conspiracy and the other two plots—Goriot's obsessive patriarchal love for his ungrateful daughters and the *Bildungsroman* of Eugène de Rastignac's introduction into the Parisian *haute monde*—are connected by the coincidence that Vautrin, Goriot, and Rastignac all live at the same boarding house, the Maison Vauquer.

Each of these plots has its own dynamic protagonist whose ambitions or obsessive passion sets him against the values of the "false and petty society" that prevails in Balzac's Paris and is centered in the Maison Vauquer itself. Balzac the realist describes the urban geography and domestic interiors of Paris with a meticulous precision whether he recounts the tawdry, petite bourgeois banalities of the Maison's furnishings, the glitzy luxuries of Delphine Nucingen's *nouveau riche* mansion, or the squalid poverty of Père Goriot's lodgings after he becomes destitute. At the same time, Balzac the

Romantic depicts his main characters as moving through the city and its interior spaces impelled by their passions and desires that set them apart from their social environments and make them (in varying degrees) opposed to those environments. It is also Balzac the Romantic and his narrative person who repeatedly describes his characters' behavior and their appearances in the "exaggerated and overcharged" style[4]—which would be condemned by his negative critics—so that they reveal their inner drives and motivations visually as well as verbally in an intensified, highly dramatic, and often melodramatic manner. It is Balzac the Romantic, whom the poet Baudelaire called a "passionate visionary," who heightens the significance of these characters with metaphors, allusions, and hyperbole. "A man like you is a god," Vautrin tells Rastignac. Goriot is described as "exalted," "sublime," and a "Paternal Christ." Vautrin is spoken of as being a "bull," a "demon of a man," and "the Tempter"; when he is captured by the police, "his eyes gleamed like some savage cat's."[5]

Goriot is driven by his obsessive paternal love for his daughters. Even though he has provided them with generous dowries so that one has married a count and the other a baron, the two women are so extravagant that Goriot dies like a pauper so they can live in luxury. If their husbands or lovers ignore them or treat them badly, Goriot is eager to arrange an assignation for one of them with Rastignac who is young and handsome. But even though Rastignac may consider Goriot "sublime" and Balzac's narrative persona may say his paternal sufferings are Christ-like (Balzac 1998: 62, 164), the other characters in the novel have little or no respect for his patriarchal obsessions or his bourgeois social standing. While his fortune is still intact, Madame Vauquer, the widowed landlady, sees him as a potential spouse, who "is a fine flower of the bourgeoisie." But when he displays no interest in her and (even worse) his money disappears, she and the other boarders, a petite bourgeois lot, decide he is a "libertine with queer tastes" whose " self-indulgence had turned him into a snail, a human mollusk" (Balzac 1998: 23, 30, 34). Led by Vautrin, they ridicule and decrown him in the saturnalia scenes in the Maison's dining room where he is the butt of jokes because he is too slow-witted to respond to their word games and insults (Balzac 1998: 42). The novel's aristocrats are even more contemptuous of Goriot as a nouveau social climber. The haughty, cynical Duchess of Langeais sneers that he has become, by the beginning of the novel, an embarrassment to his daughters and an annoyance to his sons-in-law who treat him "like a dirty stain on the carpet" (Balzac 1998: 61, 62).

As for Rastignac, he is extremely ambitious both because he wants to enjoy all the prestige and pleasures of the *haute monde* (including a love affair with Goriot's daughter Delphine) and because he is well aware that his family in the provinces, noble but poor, must struggle to provide him with the money he needs to study law in Paris (Balzac 1998: 27). His determination to become wealthy and a success increases as he becomes acquainted with the luxury and style of his Parisian cousin, Madame de Beauséant, and he begins to find the squalor of the Maison Vauquer "utterly ghastly" (Balzac 1998: 64). But as Rastignac's ambitions increase, his scruples diminish, and he becomes the kind of man who, though he might not commit crimes himself, becomes an "ambitious man of the world, who wants to reach his goal but still preserve appearances, [and] manages to get round his conscience" (Balzac 1998: 101).

On the other hand, Vautrin (née Jacques Collin, alias Trompe-la Mort) has no qualms about breaking laws and his ambitions are so elaborate they must be described in detail. Unlike most of the main characters in Balzac's *Comédie humaine*—who are well endowed with parents, children, spouses, and other relatives—Collin has virtually no family except for an aunt mentioned in other novels, and his past and his origins are very unclear. One of the definite things readers do learn about his background in *Père Goriot* is that he once was convicted of forgery to save a friend from prison, but as Félicien Marceau points out "everything about [Vautrin], his behavior as well as his reputation, indicates that he is not the sort of man to have limited his career to that one crime" (Marceau 1966: 290). This life history, such as it is, is gradually revealed during the course of *Père Goriot*, and one of the functions of the novel's plot is to reveal Vautrin's identity and some of his secrets gradually: that he wears a wig and dyes his whiskers, that he is an ex-convict who escaped from prison, that he is a homosexual, that he is a kind of "banker" who keeps and invests money for other convicts while they are in prison, and that he is so adept at eluding the police that he has earned his nickname of "Trompe-la Mort" or "Death-Dodger".

No matter how obscure Vautrin's past may be, there is nothing secret in *Père Goriot* about his values or his plans for the future. He shares that information, in eloquent detail, with Rastignac and the novel's readers in his speech in the Maison Vauquer's linden-tree arbor. Society is a "mud pit," he insists, and its laws and morals are frauds designed to protect the rich and cunning and to exploit the poor and foolish (Balzac 1998: 39). Therefore, for a person with any spirit, there are only two alternatives— "stupid obedience" or "mutiny" (Balzac 1998: 82). Vautrin has chosen mutiny, and he urges Rastignac do the same—but it is not open, political revolution that he has in mind but covert, conspiratorial revolt. Thousands of ambitious young men are competing for fortunes in Paris, desperately devouring "each other, like spiders in a chamber pot" (Balzac 1998: 85), but Rastignac can have a fortune merely by following Vautrin's directions.

One of the other lodgers in the Maison Vauquer is a shy, pretty young woman, Victorine Taillefer, whose father—a millionaire banker—doles out a pittance to her and refuses to recognize her as his legal daughter because he wants to leave all his wealth to his only son. Vautrin seizes the opportunity to avenge this injustice: "I don't like to see anyone playing unfair like that.

I'm a regular Don Quijote [*sic*], I like defending the weak against the strong," Vautrin tells Rastignac; " ... should God in his wisdom deprive old Taillefer of his son, he'd take up his daughter again" (Balzac 1998: 88). In the event that God does not punish the male Taillefers' "unfair" behavior in a timely fashion, Vautrin has an alternative plan, one that would horrify the Don Quijote who was created by Cervantes. A devoted friend of Vautrin's— a colonel in the Royal Guards who "would put Jesus Christ back on the Cross if I told him to"—will arrange to quarrel and have a duel with Taillefer's son. Since the colonel is an expert swordsman, he will almost certainly kill young Taillefer, and the banker will then accept Victorine as his heir. In the meantime, Rastignac will court Victorine and marry her for the Taillefer millions.

"You see? I play the role of Fate [for you], our good Lord's wishes are in my hands," Vautrin tells Rastignac in a cynical parody of providential reasoning (Balzac 1998: 88). In return for this "fateful" aid, Rastignac will later reward his benefactor and mentor Vautrin with enough francs from the Taillefer fortune, so Vautrin can fulfill *his* great dream, which is to

> live like a patriarch on some great estate ... in the United States, down in the South ... living like a king, doing what I feel like, leading the kind of life you can't even imagine here. ... I've got fifty thousand francs, which wouldn't buy me more than forty Negroes. I've got to have two hundred thousand francs ... [so I can own] two hundred Negroes. These Negroes, you know what I mean? They're like little children, you can make them do whatever you want, without some nosy district attorney snooping around.
>
> (Balzac 1998: 86)

If one is as amoral and ruthless as Vautrin is, it is an excellent plan: Taillefer *père* and his son will be punished for being "unfair"; Victorine will have a handsome husband; Rastignac will become rich, and Vautrin will have his life of "patriarchal" bliss somewhere in Alabama or Virginia. Unfortunately for the Taillefers, Rastignac eventually refuses Vautrin's offer, but is too afraid of him to tell anyone else, and he is not cunning enough to prevent the ex-convict from carrying out his part of the conspiracy. A few weeks later the colonel kills young Taillefer as per Vautrin's scenario, and Victorine rushes off to console her father. It is at this point that Vautrin mysteriously collapses, apparently stricken by a stroke, and—as we said earlier—Rastignac wrongly thinks that "divine justice" has punished his "Tempter" (Balzac 1998: 149, 123).

However, seeing Vautrin chiefly as the instigator of a conspiracy that is a "perfect crime," does not do justice to his cultural significance or to the complexity of Balzac's characterization of him. First of all, as Italo Calvino has commented, Vautrin is one of the first and most important embodiments of a major nineteenth- and twentieth-century archetype in both high and popular culture: the "single individual on the fringes of society" who possesses a "mysterious omnipotence." "The myths destined to mold both popular and cultural fiction for over a century all pass through Balzac," Calvino writes.

> The Superman who takes his revenge on the society that has outlawed him by transforming himself into a totally elusive demiurge features throughout all the volumes of *La Comédie humaine* in the manifold guises of Vautrin, and was later reincarnated in all the Counts of Monte Christo, the phantoms of the Opera, and even the Godfathers whom best-selling novelists are now [1973] putting into circulation.
>
> (Calvino 1987: 183)

On the level of popular culture, says Marceau, Vautrin is a personage like Fantomas or Buffalo Bill who can be considered "a myth more than a mere character" (Marceau 1966: 299). He is one of the ancestors of the arch-criminals in crime and detective stories, such as Doyle's Professor Moriarty whom Sherlock Holmes describes as being the "Napoleon of crime" (Doyle 1930: 471). On a more sophisticated level, and in a more ominous ethical context, Vautrin can be related to the assorted fictional and non-fictional Nietzschean Supermen, "men of destiny." Joseph Conrad's Kurtz, Francis Ford Coppola's Colonel Walter Kurtz, and charismatic political leaders whose eloquence, opportunism, and "genius" causes them to proclaim themselves, their goals, and the acts of their followers as being above conventional morality, laws, and conceptions of justice. "Heavens! how that man could talk!" says one of Mister Kurtz's admirers in Conrad's *Heart of Darkness*, " ... He had the faith—don't you see—he had the faith. He could get himself to believe in anything—anything. He would have been a splendid leader of an extreme party."[6] Moreover, Vautrin's vision of patriarchy, a plantation of slaves who will be like "children" and over whom he will have total power, contains ominous similarities to Kurtz's racism in *Heart of Darkness* (1902) in which he claims that white imperialists can "approach [Africans] with the might as of a deity" (Conrad 2002: 181, 155).

In addition, within the novel itself Vautrin is considerably more than the "Godfather" Calvino describes or the Conradian Kurtz to whom we have compared him. As Vautrin himself remarks obliquely at one point in the novel, "I am anything and everything" (Balzac 1998: 148). Besides being a criminal and a conspirator with grandiose ambitions, Vautrin is also an entertaining middle-class *bon vivant*, the "life of the party" at the Maison Vauquer with his "good-natured, easygoing manners" (Balzac 1998: 15). He sings popular songs from the music halls, plays word games, and takes Madame Vauquer to the theater. He knows the glamour and the costs of living in the *haute monde* so he can tell Rastignac how many thousands of francs per year he will need to afford a carriage and a valet. In the *Bildungs-roman* part of the novel he acts not only as Rastignac's tempter, but also as his mentor, a cynical, worldly surrogate father who sometimes seems genu-inely affectionate as he offers his "son" the advice he needs to see behind the puppet shows of society (Balzac 1998: 65).

Above all, Vautrin has an extraordinary verbal prowess, energy, and charisma that enable him, when he has the stage to himself, to define "fate," justice, and morality in his own terms, to create a vision of society that is far more persuasive than the windy rhetoric espoused by most of the Romantic outlaws and rebels who were his nineteenth-century cousins in crime and rebellion. He demonstrates this prowess most impressively in the scene in the linden arbor when he outlines his conspiracy to Rastignac and also narrates Rastignac's past and future life. In the process of doing that he inverts not only the morality but also the narrative processes of what would become, later in the nineteenth century, the crime and detective genre. In classics of that genre—such as Doyle's Sherlock Holmes tales—the detec-tive shows his verbal prowess by discovering and revealing criminals' life histories as linear narratives, showing how selected secrets from their past lives deviated from the moral or legal code and thus proves they are wrong-doers. In contrast, in *Père Goriot* it is Vautrin who is the criminal, but he is able to read the secrets of other people's minds: "Like a stern judge, his glance seemed to pierce to the bottom of every issue, every conscience, every emotion" (Balzac 1998: 15). He is able to know, for example, immediately that Victorine Taillefer may be in love with Rastignac (Balzac 1998: 80). But what is even more impressive in the scene in the arbor is his ability to tell Rastignac all about his own ambitions and his family back in the provinces, including their exact social and economic status. Despite their aristocratic standing, says Vautrin, Rastignac's "family eats more chestnut porridge than good white bread ... [their] little place brings in three thousand a year and they send you twelve hundred. ... . we want to be rich but we haven't got a cent, we eat boiled stews at Momma Vauquer's but we prefer fine dinners at the Faubourg Saint-Germaine" (Balzac 1998: 82–83). As for Rastignac's future, if he decides to be vir-tuous, completes his law studies, and attempts to succeed on the basis of merit, Vautrin sneers, after suffering years of

> boredom and deprivation that would drive a dog mad [you may be] appointed assistant to some odd fish, off in some hole of a town where the government generously lets you have a salary of a thousand francs a year, the way you toss a soup bone to a butcher's watchdog. ... you argue cases for the rich, you send people who have anything in them to the guillotine. ... If there's no one looking out for you, they'll leave you in your provincial courthouse until you rot.
>
> (Balzac 1998: 83)

To do better than that, Vautrin argues, Rastignac will have to accept graft and sordid deals until he is no better morally than the criminals he sends to prison or the guillotine. He will never realize his grand ambitions; his sisters will have become nuns (no dowries), and he will be competing for promotions against "jokers who'd sell their grandmothers to climb a single notch"—so much for the rewards of virtue and "stupid obedience" to society's laws and values (Balzac 1998: 84). For Vautrin, in other words, the public sphere is only a cynical game in which the corrupt deceive the naïve by disguising their private passions and ambitions.

Considered within the context of the ethics of Balzac's Paris in *Père Goriot*, however, Vautrin is not really very different from some of the other characters. They are just as ruthless and predatory in their behavior as he is, even though they may not use criminal means to achieve their goals. In a well-known passage in the novel, Rastignac's aristocratic cousin Madam de Beauséant, who is Rastignac's other mentor and whom Balzac characterizes as the epitome of the Parisian great lady, tells him to "treat the world exactly as it deserves! You want to succeed ... You'll learn what feminine corruption can sink to, you'll find out just how profound men's vanity can be. ... The more coldly you calculate, the farther you'll go. ... Think of men and women simply as post-horses to be discarded in a ditch" (Balzac 1998: 62). Contemplating this advice later, after he hears Vautrin's speech in the arbor, Rastignac decides that it is not much different than Vautrin's cruder cynicism: Madam de Beauséant has only stated the same ideas more "politely" (Balzac 1998: 90).

If the public sphere is as corrupt as Vautrin says it is, if he is as cunning as he appears to be, if Rastignac is as vulnerable as he seems to be, and if "divine justice" really does not exist, why then does Vautrine's conspiracy ultimately fail to succeed completely? The answer to that question lies in another force in the novel, the city of Paris itself. For Balzac, the social activities, mysteries, and institutions of the metropolis replace Le Fanu's haunted house as a "magic" environment in which contending forces can meet and at least a flawed kind of justice may prevail. In Italo Calvino's phrase, Balzac's city is a "protagonist" in its own right (Calvino 1987: 182), and not a mere *mise-en-scène* or stage set. Along with the people who inhabit it, the city has its own fabulas, its own secrets and enigmas, for as Cesare Pavese wrote in a diary entry:

> Balzac discovered the big city as a den of mysteries, and the sense he keeps ever-alert is that of curiosity. It is his Muse. He is never either tragic or comic; he is curious. He is always delving into a tangle of things with the air of a man who scents a mystery and promises one, and dismantles the machine piece by piece with biting, lively, triumphant gusto. Look at how he approaches new characters. ... His judgments, observations, harangues, and maxims are not psychological truths, but

the tricks of a suspicious examining magistrate with his hands on a mystery that must at all costs be solved.

(Cited in Calvino 1987: 188)

Unlike Edgar Allen Poe's vampirish "man of the crowd" or some kind of flaccid flaneur, however, Balzac and his characters like Rastignac do not confront the city in a passive way, recording its scandals and activities to titillate readers. Instead, they observe it like "suspicious examining magistrates."

Balzac's city energizes his novel in several ways. First, of course, there are the usual urban activities of visits and conversations with friends and acquaintances, dinners, balls, theaters, and business deals. But often, concealed just beneath the surfaces of these activities, there is the second, more paranoid Paris that contains its "secret history," its "mysteries" Pavese describes. This Paris is animated by lusts, rivalries, grudges, confidence games, and power plays, many of them involving laws and crimes, justice and injustice, that can radically alter an individual's life for better or worse almost overnight. For not only the major characters like Goriot and Vautrin have their secrets, but also some of the minor ones have their own mysteries in *Père Goriot*. Introducing Michonneau, the old woman who later acts as a police spy and informs on Vautrin, for example, Balzac says that though she is now an "angular" old woman, "What acid had eaten away this creature's feminine characteristics? Surely she had been pretty once ... Had it been vice, grief, greed? Had she fallen too deeply in love—had she been a peddler of used clothing—or had she simply been a whore?" (Balzac 1998: 12). In Michonneau's case, these questions are a red-herring, since almost nothing of her past is revealed. But they illustrate how Balzac encourages readers to be alert, to suggest how they must observe carefully, in fiction and in life, if they really want to understand a metropolis like Paris in which daily life is a carnival in the sense that any appearance can be a mask concealing a secret and anyone can rise or fall, be crowned or uncrowned, depending on luck, coincidence, and/or the success or failure of a plan or a conspiracy.

A second important way that Balzac's Paris animates his novel is by providing him with unlikely but helpful coincidences. Thanks to them, his Paris often seems to share the kind of "occult powers" that his conspirators and Romantic rebels also possess. Early in the novel Rastignac hears noises in Goriot's room, looks through the key-hole, and sees the old man bending a silver posset dish into ingots. The next morning Vautrin accidentally sees the old man in a goldsmith's shop selling the silver, and he reports this to the other boarders, including Rastignac. The next day when Rastignac is visiting the Countess de Restaud, he discovers that Goriot has been there when he chances to look out a window and sees him leaving by a back staircase. Only one of these Goriot "sightings," the first, is probable, since Rastignac and Goriot are neighbors in the Maison Vauquer. The other two are "fateful," at least for Balzac's narrative, since they enable Rastignac to discover within a few hours that one of Goriot's daughters is a countess and the old man is giving her money, but these facts must never be mentioned in front of the count who is much too snobbish to acknowledge that his father-in-law was a pasta-maker.

Coincidences also play an important part in the novel's Vautrin story which is constructed as two parallel narratives, each involving a conspiracy. Hints about Vautrin's conspiracy begin early in the novel when he first becomes interested in Victorine and implies that he will somehow help her: "What you need is a good friend to tell that old miser [her father] the brass tacks. ... Well, in a few days I'll stick my nose into your business, and it will all come out right" (Balzac 1998: 35). But only a few minutes and three pages earlier the reader learned that someone else was interested in Vautrin himself. Sylvie and Christophe, the servants at the Maison Vauquer, are talking, and Christophe mentions that he met "a man out on the street, and he asked me: 'Say, isn't there a big guy living at your place, a fellow with dyed side-whiskers?'" Sylvie adds that a stranger had stopped her in the market and asked if she had ever seen Vautrin with his shirt off (Balzac 1998: 32). Readers cannot know yet why exactly Vautrin is interested in Victorine's problems, nor can they know why strangers are questioning the servants about Vautrin; what is significant from a structural standpoint is the way in which these two incidents are so coincidental and yet nearly symmetrical in time.

After Vautrin has outlined his conspiracy to Rastignac in their conversation in the linden-tree arbor and volunteered to have Victorine's brother killed, Rastignac has a conversation with his friend Bianchon, a young medical student and another boarder at the Maison. He tells him he is troubled by a "temptation," which he explains by a cryptic reference to a parable: what would a man do if he could become rich, without leaving Paris, simply by "willing the death of some old Mandarin way off in China" (Balzac 1998: 106). Clearly Rastignac is referring indirectly to Vautrin and his conspiracy to kill young Taillefer. In the same conversation, just after they discuss this "temptation," Bianchon suddenly remarks that earlier he saw Michonneau and Poiret in the Jardin des Plantes "seated on a [park] bench and chatting with a man ... who looks to me like a policeman, trying to disguise himself as just another middle-class citizen."[7] Again the symmetry is subtle but distinct. Vautrin uses Rastignac as a pawn in his game against the Taillefers; the "policeman" is using Michonneau and Poiret, two elderly boarders at the Maison Vauquer, as his pawns to catch Vautrin.

The next stages of both conspiracies are crucial ones. Rastignac, uncertain of Delphine de Nucingen's love and short of cash, temporarily ignores his conscience and yields to Vautrin's plan part way by starting to court Victorine—though the next day he tells Vautrin, "I'm not your accomplice" (Balzac 1998: 126), a weak repudiation. After announcing it is "two days later," the text shifts immediately to Michonneau, Poiret, and the detective, once again meeting on a park bench in the Jardin des Plantes; and once again seen coincidentally by Bianchon. Now the text identifies the detective by name, Monsieur Gondureau,[8] and he in turn identifies Vautrin by both his given name, Jacques Collin, and by his convict nickname, "Trompe-la-Mort" (Balzac 1998: 127). Earlier in the novel it was Vautrin who boasted that he knew other men's "secrets" (Balzac 1998: 89). But now it is his secrets that are revealed as Gondureau explains Vautrin's/Collin's position and activities in the Paris underworld and claims his financial resources are so "immense" that he has *"established a kind of private police force,* a whole series of connections and interconnections wrapped around him like some impenetrable mystery. ... So both his money and his talents are constantly bolstering the forces of crime" (Balzac 1998: 130; emphasis added).

Just as there were two law and court systems in Le Fanu's "Mr. Justice Harbottle," one material and the other supernatural or psychological, so also there are two dualistic police systems/conspiracies in *Père Goriot*: Gondureau's legal one and Collin's underworld one. But though one is legal and the other is criminal, the operations of these two systems are quite similar. Vautrin tempts Rastignac with the Taillefer millions; Gondureau tempts Michonneau with a reward if she can verify that Vautrin is really Collin by drugging him and pulling off his shirt to see if the letters TF (*travaux forcés*—hard labor), identifying him as an ex-convict, are branded on his shoulder. An additional, ethical symmetry between the two conspiracies is suggested by some of the tactics of the Paris police that are not notably different from Vautrin's. Their main motive for capturing him, the novel implies, is to seize the money he "banks" for his fellow convicts, and therefore they plan to kill him while "resisting arrest," a development Gondureau blandly rationalizes as being an "immense" public service since it enables the police to "avoid all the legal fuss, the expense of watching over him, feeding him. ... and we stop a hundred crimes before they're committed." Squeamish people may not approve of such methods, Gondureau admits, but he justifies himself with reasoning that is similar to Vautrin's, though less candid: "a superior man needs to rise above prejudice, and a Christian needs to accept the evils that follow along in the wake of good, when it's effected in unconventional ways" (Balzac 1998: 146).

On the narrative level, another symmetry between the two conspiracies is created by the repeated coincidence that the medical student Bianchon yet again sees Michonneau and Poiret with the detective in the Jardin des Plantes, but this time he overhears a little of what they say.

> "Let me have three thousand francs if he is Death-Dodger. ... "
> "Fine," said Gondureau, "but on one condition: it's got to be done tomorrow."

. .... .

Bianchon, coming back from medical school, heard the strange name, "Death-Dodger," and was struck by it. ...

(Balzac 1998: 131–32)

At this point the Vautrin portion of the novel has become a kind of thriller, a race between the police and a criminal. Will Gondureau be able to arrest Vautrin before the duel? Will Rastignac resist Vautrin's lures and try to warn the Taillefers? Will Michonneau "sell" Vautrin to the police, or will she try to get a better deal by warning him? Vautrin puts the final pieces of his conspiracy into place by telling Rastignac, as they go into dinner at the Maison Vauquer, "Our pigeon has insulted my falcon. It's [the duel's] for tomorrow. ... By about eight-thirty in the morning Mademoiselle Taillefer will become heir to her father's love, and also to his fortune, even while she's sitting here and calmly dunking bits of freshly buttered bread in her coffee" (Balzac 1998: 134). In the chaotic evening that follows, both conspiracies flourish. Vautrin prevents Rastignac from warning the Taillefers by giving him and Goriot drugged wine. He also insults Michonneau—which helps her decide to betray him by drugging his coffee the next morning so she can see if he has TF branded on his shoulder. As Balzac's omniscient narrative persona points out, the outcomes of the two events are causally connected: "The little party which had enabled Vautrin to get both Père Goriot and Eugène to drink his opium-flavored wine was also the man's undoing. Bianchon, fairly tipsy, had forgotten to ask Mademoiselle Michonneau about Death-Dodger. Had he so much as pronounced that name, it would certainly have put Vautrin on guard" (Balzac 1998: 145). Retribution was achieved in "Harbottle" by the interventions of powers that were occult and inexplicable because they were supernatural (Justice Twofold) and/or psychological (the "blue devils" of the judge's depression) in origin, but in *Père Goriot* retribution or justice, such as it is, occurs because of coincidences and conflicts between forces that are eminently human.

Though Vautrin wins this part of the "race" between the two conspiracies, his victory is short-lived. The next day—minutes after the news arrives that young Taillefer is dying—he is drugged by Michonneau, and a few hours later he is arrested by the police. Just seconds before the arrest, however, coincidence again intervenes in the novel's events so that Michonneau and Poiret are, in effect, punished for *their* conspiracy. As Vautrin is boasting about how strong he is because he survived the "fit" that felled him, Bianchon is reminded of the nick-name he overheard the detective using in the conversation in the Jardin des Plantes a few days earlier, and he comments, "when Mademoiselle Michonneau was talking about someone called Death-Dodger, the other day, she used a name that fits you like a glove" (Balzac 1998: 152). Thanks to this revelation,

Michonneau's duplicity is revealed, and the boarders turn on her because they despise "stool pigeons" almost as much as they fear convicts. Led by Bianchon, they demand that Michonneau be evicted, so that she and Poiret (who leaves with her) are judged, ridiculed, and punished by a kind of communal justice.

Thus justice, as depicted in the conclusion of this part of *Père Goriot*, is flawed, ironic, and dependent on coincidences rather than on the actions of any higher, ethical authority. Vautrin is arrested—but not for the conspiratorial crime that he has just committed against the Tallifers since that remains concealed. The police and informers who capture him are almost as ruthless and criminal as he is; and as for the boarders at the Maison, they soon become more concerned with that night's stew, superficial news, and their own concerns than they are with subjects such as justice. At first, says the novel's narrative persona, though they were

> satisfied to discuss Vautrin and the day's events, they quickly yielded to sly, roundabout temptation, chattering on about duels, prisons, criminal justice, what laws needed amending, and what jail was like. They were soon a thousand miles distant from Jacques Collin, from Victorine and her dead brother. They may have been only ten of them, but they babbled and shouted like twenty ... [as the] casual indifference of this egotistic little world which, the next day, would need to have some new prey to devour, drawn just like this one from Paris's daily doings, inevitably took over.
>
> (Balzac 1998: 160)

Only the novel's readers, by implication, can properly appreciate how momentous these events were and how intimately they were secretly connected—but only because they have been initiated into the mysteries of Paris, the Maison Vauquer, and its "secret history" by Balzac's narrative persona—in much the same way that, analogously, Rastignac was initiated by Vautrin and his cousin, Madame de Beauséant, into the realities of Parisian society.

Besides providing Balzac with opportunities for the coincidences he needed to interweave his novel's plots and sub-plots together, Paris also gave him the linguistic energy and diversity—the babbling, shouting, and chattering—that help to make *Père Goriot* what Bakhtin might consider a modern, polyglot text. In language that is remarkably similar to Bakhtin's comments on carnival and heteroglossia decades later, Théophile Gautier said in 1858 that in order to "make all the voices of Paris sing together as in a symphony orchestra," to convey all of the city's sobs, cries, and sounds, and to "express this multiplicity of details, characters, [and] types" that made up "this modern Paris" that Balzac knew so well, he was "obliged to forge a special language for himself, composed of all the technical languages, of all the scientific jargons, all the argots of the artist's studio, the theater, and even the amphitheater. He welcomed every word that had something to say."[9] What these words had to "say," in Bakhtinian terms, were the attitudes and viewpoints of many of the individuals, classes, and groups of people that might be encountered in the streets and salons of Paris in the 1820s and 1830s, ranging from aristocrats to convicts, with the petite bourgeois boarders of the Maison Vauquer in the middle of this linguistic and social melange.

Balzac's fascination with the variety of Paris's languages is especially striking in the three main carnival events that occur in the dining room of the Maison Vauquer: the first dinner that is described in the novel (Balzac 1998: 40–43); the dinner that occurs the night before the colonel and young Taillefer fight their duel (Balzac 1998: 137–44), and the scene that occurs the next afternoon, first, when Vautrin is arrested and, following that, when Michonneau is reviled as a "stool pigeon" and forced to leave the Maison (Balzac 1998: 152–58). In each of these scenes, multiple languages are present because the Maison's boarders represent a spectrum that includes many (though not all) of the city's classes. Some of these scenes also contain conflicts between the individuals involved in the conspiracies we have described, and how these conflicts are resolved contributes to the outcomes of the conspiracies. Moreover, through their language and events these carnival scenes also imply the power shifts, social changes, and judgments that influence the ways in which these outcomes may be perceived as being fair or unfair, just or unjust, criminal or legal. In effect, therefore, justice is achieved through these carnivalistic coincidences and interactions more than through the rational operations of the public sphere's official agencies of justice such as courts or the police.

In the first of these scenes, the earliest dinner at the Maison (Balzac 1998: 40–43), the language is an excellent example of heteroglossia as the lodgers arrive and begin making jokes and puns with words with the suffix-rama, because the latest invention to fascinate the city is the diorama. Such "stupid" linguistic fads, says Balzac's narrative persona, "constitute a kind of droll humor ... whose principal virtue consists only in how the words are pronounced or what gestures accompany them. This sort of jargon is always changing. The jokes that underlie it never last a month, some political event, some lawsuit or trial, a street song, some actor's comic routine, all serve to keep this joke going" (Balzac 1998: 40). The boarders coin words like "coldarama" and "souparama". A dense fog is called a "Goriorama" of a fog because it looked as "lugubrious" as Goriot. Mixed in with these puns and slang are a quote (by Vautrin) from the seventeenth-century poet de Malherbe, plus a few words from Latin and the "scientific" jargon of Francis Gall's phrenology (by the medical student, Bianchon).

This carnivalistic linguistic instability of modern Paris is accompanied by an implied, analogous social instability as Goriot is ridiculed by the other

boarders and symbolically "decrowned" (to use Bakhtin's terminology) as the
boarders make jokes and puns about the old man's nose being a "horn":

> "A horny hoarary,"
>   "A horny hormone."
>   "A horny horehound."
>   "A hornarama."
> These ... responses, shot from all sides of the table as if fired from
> guns, seemed to them even funnier because poor Père Goriot was staring
> dumbfounded, like a man struggling to comprehend some utterly
> foreign language.
> "Horn?" he said to Vautrin, who was sitting next to him.
> "Like a horn on your foot, old boy!" said Vautrin, flattening Père
> Goriot's hat with a slap that drove it down on his head, all the way to
> his eyes.[10]

These jokes and Vautrin's insult reveal how completely Goriot has lost the
respect he would receive in a society in which patriarchal, bourgeois values
really were dominant. In such a society, Goriot's just deserts would be to
receive the gratitude he deserves from his daughters, because he lavished so
much paternal love on them,[11] and he would also presumably be respected
by the boarders because in his heyday he was an astute self-made businessman. Then he had known everything about wheat, flour, and pasta-making,
says Balzac's narrative persona, "how to obtain grains at a good price, lay in
stocks from Sicily, from the Ukraine. ... Had you seen him doing business,
explaining the laws governing the export trade. ... you might have thought
him capable of becoming a Government Minister" (Balzac 1998: 69). But
with his fortune gone, Goriot is judged as being no better than a "dirty stain
on the carpet" by aristocrats; he is ignored by his daughters as an embarrassment, and he is ridiculed by the boarders because he does not know the
"foreign language" of the latest slang.

The second, even wilder, carnival scene at the Maison Vauquer, which
occurs the night before young Taillefer fights his fatal duel, is orchestrated
by Vautrin as the pretext to give drugged wine to Rastignac and Goriot so
they cannot disrupt his conspiracy. Drunk on wine that is not drugged, the
other boarders imitate street language and animal noises as

> everyone grew lively, and the laughter sounded louder and louder. It was
> savage laughter, mixed with the cries of assorted wild animals. When
> the Museum employee emitted a well-known Parisian street cry, pat-
> terned on the meowing of an amorous tomcat, eight voices bellowed
> simultaneously:
>   "Knives sharpened!"
>   "Bird feed, bird feed!"

"Fix your china!"
"Fresh fish! Fresh fish!"
. ...

And then there was a wild, head-splitting racket, full of stuff and nonsense, a regular opera of an uproar which Vautrin conducted as if they'd been an orchestra.

(Balzac 1998: 139–40)

In the midst of this carnivalistic chaos, Vautrin, the master of his conspiracy, remains in command and in control as his power reaches its zenith. Rastignac is, metaphorically speaking, decrowned as—addled by opium—he is mute and cannot expose Vautrin while the latter whispers to him like a mocking, patriarchal mentor: "Young fellow, we're not sly enough ... for fighting with Papa Vautrin, and he loves you too much to let you do something stupid. When I've decided to do something, only God is strong enough to bar the door. ... Eugène could hear these words, but he could not reply: he felt his tongue sticking to the roof of his mouth ... " (Balzac 1998: 140).

In contrast to Rastignac, in the scene that follows Vautrin is at the height of his verbal prowess as he makes ironic, parodic speeches, filled with double entendres referring to his own conspiracy and mocking family, patriarchy, religion, and romance so cleverly, as we said earlier, that the others do not realize he is parodying the values of their society. "Stay and take care of him," he tells Victorine when she is concerned about the drugged, unconscious Rastignac; "After all ... it's your duty as a good wife. He adores you, this young fellow," and he declares that Eugène and Victorine will never be separated because, "God works his wonders in mysterious ways. ... God is just" (Balzac 1998: 141, 143)—at the same time that he knows that his friend the colonel will kill Victorine's brother early the next morning. Linguistically as well as ethically, "mutiny," conspiracy and revolt, as embodied in Vautrin, seem to have triumphed at this point in the novel since he seems able to impose his values, including his criminal and egotistical conception of "fate" and justice, upon the other characters and to parody the values of the society he despises. Yet at the same time Vautrin himself is still vulnerable to that society because of his status as an escaped convict. Thus, despite his clever planning and his disguise, he will still be arrested because he insulted Mademoiselle Michonneau by telling her she looks like "a lovely stone" Venus, like those in the cemetery. Insulted by this comparison, the old woman's revenge is to cooperate with the police and accept their bounty, rather than warning Vautrin and being paid off by him (Balzac 1998: 138).

The following afternoon the next carnival scene in the Maison's Vauquer dining room occurs in two stages. In the first, it is the ex-convict himself who is symbolically decrowned when he is arrested, his criminal name and identity are revealed, and his control over Rastignac and the other characters is destroyed by the arrival of the detective who goes "directly to where [Vautrin] stood, and swiftly punched Collin in the head with such force that his wig flew off, revealing the stark horror of his skull" (Balzac 1998: 153). The kind of criminal patriarchy represented by Vautrin turns out, thanks to Michonneau, to be as unstable as the bourgeois patriarchy of Goriot, just as subject to reversals of fortune and challenges from other forces in the social world of Paris. But though Vautrin can no longer control events and act as a kind of criminal demiurge through his conspiratorial skills, he continues to resist the "gangrenous" society he detests verbally. He silences everyone else, including the police, as he rages defiantly and shocks the petite bourgeois sensibilities of the Maison's boarders with a two-page tirade in which he harangues not only Michonneau but the rest of them as well for being "dumb animals," whereas he is willing to defy "the government and its whole pile of courts and cops, and its heaps of money, and I say screw them all" (Balzac 1998: 154, 155, 156). Instead of accepting society's judgment of him as an inferior being because he is a criminal, it is Vautrin, still the implacable "superior man" (Balzac 1998: 89) and Romantic rebel, who judges society and condemns it for its conformity and cowardice.

Because the Maison Vauquer is such a "respectable" boarding house (Balzac 1998: 5), merely seeing Vautrin's rage after the criminal part of his identity has been revealed makes the boarders cry out in "terror" as they hear his "prison language" and confront the ferocious energy of his "implacable ideas, his religion of self-indulgence. … he was no longer a man, but the embodied representative of a degraded people, a savage, logical nation, brutal, flexible. In an instant Collin had been transformed into a kind of hellish poem. … He looked the very image of the fallen archangel, forever militant" (Balzac 1998: 153, 154). No longer a mere human criminal, he has become a Miltonic Satan, a "hellish poem," whose language expresses his remorseless contempt for his society's conventional ideas of law, justice, and morality.

Earlier in the novel, Vautrin had challenged Rastignac by telling him he had to choose between "stupid obedience" or "mutiny," and he had proudly proclaimed himself the embodiment of mutiny, since "I obey nothing and no one" (Balzac 1998: 82). However, his arrest does not mean that the alternative, "obedience," is going to prevail. That response to the "social chain" was represented by Michonneau and even more by Poiret. A retired government clerk, dim-witted and inarticulate, Poiret is the epitome of conformity, and he is part of Michonneau's conspiracy to capture Vautrin because he worships authority. Thus it is significant that instead of being grateful to him and Michonneau for enabling the police to capture Vautrin, the boarders turn on them so that the "hellish," melodramatic sublimity of Vautrin's verbal defiance is followed by the comic melodrama of Michonneau's and

Poiret's expulsion from the Maison. The boarders use carnivalistic street language, parody, lines from a music hall song, and Latin poetry (by Bianchon from Virgil's *Eclogues*), plus a revival of diorama jokes to revile Michonneau as a "Judas" and to ridicule Poiret's attempts to defend her as the behavior of an "Apollo," a "Mars," or a "naughty boy" (Balzac 1998: 158–59).

> "Out, you stool pigeons!"
> "Out, both stool pigeons!"
> "Gentlemen," cried Poiret, standing up, suddenly infused with the courage love lends to a rutting ram, "show some respect for her sex!"
> "Stool pigeons don't have any sex," said the painter.
> "Celebrated sexorama!"
> "Out the doorarama!"
>
> (Balzac 1998: 158)

What these carnival scenes and events create in *Père Goriot* is a social milieu in which language and values are so unstable and changeable that they confirm Vautrin's criticism in his speech in the arbor to Rastignac that there are no "absolutes. ... there are no principles, just things that happen; there are no laws, either, just circumstances. ... If there really were fixed principles and absolute laws, people wouldn't go changing them the way we change our shirts" (Balzac 1998: 89). Nor are there any supernatural or psychological Chief-Justice Twofolds to intervene in the justice process in *Père Goriot*. By the end of the novel it is Rastignac, as his "education" becomes "complete," who has seen how the values and principles of many levels of Parisian society function—from the paltry concerns of the Maison Vauquer's boarders to the selfishness of Goriot's daughters and the aristocratic arrogance of their husbands. Learning how such people behave when they are motivated by these sordid but legal values, discovering "the horror [that exists] under all the gold and jewels" in "such a shabby society as ours, so petty, so superficial" (Balzac 1998: 198, 200), he decides that Vautrin's criminal values are not so evil after all. He reformulates the convict's early challenge to him to choose between revolt and "stupid obedience" (Balzac 1998: 82) so that it includes a third term that may apply to himself:

> He saw the world as an ocean of mud into which a man would fall, right up to the neck, if he ever stepped in at all.
> "It's one shabby crime after another!" he said to himself. "Vautrin's better than this."
> Now he knew society's three great foundations: Obedience, Struggle, and Revolt; or, put differently, The Family, the World, and Vautrin.
>
> (Balzac 1998: 192)

Since Rastignac believes that obedience to society's laws and principles is "boring" and revolt such as Vautrin's is "impossible," only struggle with "the World" is left, even though he recognizes that this conflict is "at best uncertain" (Balzac 1998: 192). At the end of the novel he witnesses Goriot's pauper's funeral that reveals the impotence of the old man's faith in bourgeois patriarchy as a source for values and justice. As the hearse is leaving for Père-Lachaise he sees the "fancy carriages" of Goriot's daughters arriving empty except for their coachmen to "attend" the dead man's internment—a gesture that symbolically reveals the emptiness and hypocrisy of the aristocratic society that the two women represent. Finally alone after the priest, gravediggers, and coachmen have departed, Rastignac stands alone, looks down at the lights of Paris, and utters his famous, duelist's challenge to Parisian society—which is followed by the wonderfully ambiguous commentary of Balzac's narrative persona:

> Left alone, Rastignac walks to the highest part of the cemetery and looked down at the heart of Paris. ... He looked at that swarming beehive, his very glance seemed to suck out its honey, and then declared grandly, "Now it's just the two of us!—I'm ready!"
>
> And then, for the first challenge he hurled at Society, Rastignac went to have dinner with Madame de Nucingen.
>
> (Balzac 1998: 217)

The lone individual's struggles to discover and apply his own principles of what is fair and just are heroic, challenging, and Romantic, the scene implies. However, in Rastignac's case such a struggle does not preclude the more immediate pleasures of an evening with Delphine de Nucingen—even though twenty five pages earlier Rastignac himself had judged her behavior toward her father as being "an elegant form of patricide" (Balzac 1998: 192). And with this equivocal irony, which is also an excellent example of what Bakhtin might consider muffled, "ambivalent laughter," Balzac leaves it to the reader to imagine how Rastignac's struggle with Parisian society will end.

Chapter 5

Justice, race, and revenge in Twain's *Pudd'nhead Wilson*

"The first thing I ever heard about Barack Obama was that he had a white mother and a black father. I heard this over and over again. ... Of course I am rather sensitive to all this because I, too, was born to a white mother and a black father. ... . Racist societies make race into a hard fate. So people who are the progeny of two races become curiosities. ... [But] we no longer live in an America that wants to make mixed-race people into pariahs. That was once done to keep firm the racial boundaries of American apartheid—the mulatto's tragic exile standing as a cautionary tale meant to keep people 'with their own kind.'"

(Shelby Steele, "The Identity Card," *Time*, November 30, 2007)

As Shelby Steele certainly knows, America relied on more than cautionary tales to maintain racial boundaries during its Jim Crow/apartheid era. In the Supreme Court's landmark 1896 decision in Plessy vs. Ferguson, near the beginning of that era, the Court not only created the "infamous" separate but equal doctrine, it also in effect declared that mixed-race people (such as Obama and Steele) did not, legally speaking, exist. In the 1890s they would have been "negroes" or "colored" or "black," and it would not have mattered how many white ancestors they had, or how many advanced degrees they had earned from Harvard Law (Obama) or the University of Utah (Steele). They still would have been arrested, like Homer Plessy on that June day in 1892, if they had tried to sit down in a railroad car designated for whites only. For Plessy, a New Orleans Creole, was seven-eights white, and his complexion was light enough for him to "pass" easily as a white man. By upholding his conviction for violating Louisiana's Separate Car Act, the Supreme Court gave a spurious constitutional legitimacy to a plethora of Jim Crow discriminatory laws passed by Louisiana and other states. It also tacitly legitimatized the so-called one drop rule that a single drop of Black blood (i.e., a single Black ancestor) was enough to relegate an individual to the "hard fate" of being a second- or third-class citizen of the United States.

Mark Twain's (Samuel Clemens') 1894 *Pudd'nhead Wilson* is an especially somber and problematical cautionary tale on this theme. Though set in the antebellum South between 1830 and 1850 when slavery was legal, Twain wrote and published it at the same time that Plessy vs. Ferguson was wending its way through the American legal system, and Jim Crow racism was becoming entrenched in much of the United States. Consequently, the novel can be read both as a critique of slavery and its injustices and as an expression of the fears and anxieties of the Jim Crow era as embodied in the bad character and dismal fate of its antihero protagonist, Tom Driscoll. Tom is a changeling: a man whose "true" name and identity are unknown to him for much of his life and whose "false" identity was constructed and foisted upon him by his slave mother, Roxy, when she switched him with her master's son when they were infants. Since Tom's dualistic identities are Black and White, a slave who is supposedly a white master and the son of one of his town's leading citizens, the novel is—as some critics have noted— one of the more brooding and disturbing fictional efforts to comprehend the psychological problems and social injustices that can be traced to racism as it was developing in the late nineteenth and early twentieth centuries.[1] In addition, the novel is structured as a crime or detective story, and the deadly detail that reveals Tom's "true" identity is his fingerprints. Since this is a method of identification that was only beginning to be used by police officials, *Pudd'nhead*, like Conan Doyle's tales, is also a harbinger of the twentieth-century's fascination with forensic science as a means to control criminality and resolve legal and social conflicts.

Twain's own persona throughout much of *Pudd'nhead* is very much that of the realist, either deadpan or openly scornful, who has set himself to the task of demolishing a society's Romantic illusions about itself and its values. However, in Twain's case the realist's harsh truths are sweetened and partially concealed by his "humor," with the jokes, gags and ironic mockery, that were his creative forte and had made him one of the most popular authors of his time. As he told the President of Yale when that University gave him an honorary M. A. in 1888, humorists practice a "useful trade," because humor, despite its "lightness and frivolity," had "one serious purpose, one aim, one specialty ... the deriding of shams, the exposure of pretentious falsities ... and who so is by instinct engaged in this sort of warfare is the natural enemy of royalties, nobilities, privileges and all kindred swindles, and the natural friend of human rights and liberties."[2] Injustice, royalty and privilege are to be "decrowned," to use Bakhtin's term, but this must be done with humor and also—as Twain emphasizes in the first sentence of his introduction to *Pudd'nhead*—with realist precision and verisimilitude. The climatic scene in the novel is a trial, and, as Twain warns his readers, a "person who is ignorant of legal matters is always liable to make mistakes when he tries to photograph a court scene with his pen." Therefore, he had given the "law-chapters in this book" to a friend who was a lawyer so they were subjected to "rigid and exhausting revision and correction" before they went to press (Berger 1980: 1). Photography, one of the nineteenth-century's arts and practices most associated with science and verisimilitude, not mere storytelling, was to be Twain's model. Equally significant, the book has been examined by a "trained barrister," a legal professional who will vouch for its accuracy.

The most visible subject of Twain's satiric humor and realism in *Pudd'nhead* is the constellation of attitudes and values that may be described as Southern chivalry, the belief that the way of life that prevailed in the South before the Civil War was based on a paternalistic slave system and a cavalier code of honor and valor that made Southern "civilization" superior to the culture of the more mercantile and mercenary North. Twain had attacked the same target a decade earlier when he had described the "sham castle" of the Louisiana state capitol in *Life on the Mississippi* and blamed its architecture on the pernicious influence of Sir Walter Scott's "medieval romances" with their "fantastic heroes ... and romantic juvenilities" (Clemens 1980: 235). In that book, Twain had debunked Southern chivalry by documenting—with quotations from newspapers he placed in footnotes—the violence that occurred when white Southern males of various classes set out to defend their honor for provocations that were often trivial and outcomes that were generally lethal: a General and a Major from Knoxville, one of them a bank President, who settled their differences with shotguns and revolvers; a "Professor" at a "Female College" in Somerville, Tennessee, who blew his brother-in-law's brains out in a local pool hall, a "course [of action that] met with pretty general approval in the community," according to a local newspaper.[3]

In *Pudd'nhead Wilson* the code duello and white paternalism are targets for a substantial share of Twain's satire. Even though Dawson's Landing, the novel's setting, has a rudimentary procedural justice system—a court and a police constable—the village is a conservative Missouri community that prefers to settle many disputes with simpler justice processes, ones that are more traditional and "Southern" in character. Disputes between masters and slaves are resolved by paternalistic, summary judgments meted out by the masters, usually in the form of harsh punishments. As for the masters and other members of the gentry, they still swear by dueling as the only way to resolve conflicts with their peers. With the exception of Tom Driscoll, virtually all of the other characters—judges, lawyers, foreigners, and even the slave Roxy—believe duels are preferable to law courts for settling differences between true gentlemen. Pembrooke Howard, a "lawyer and bachelor," one of the town's grandees and most popular citizens, for example, is "a fine, brave, majestic creature. ... a man always courteously ready to stand up before you in the field if any act or word of his had seemed doubtful ... and explain it with any weapon you might prefer, from brad-awls to artillery" (Berger 1980: 4). When the village does have a full-fledged, formal duel, its people are immensely proud of the event. Even though its outcome is inconsequential, it "was a glory to their town to have such a thing happen there. In their eyes the principals had reached the summit of human honor."[4]

However, Twain's major, more serious and subtle attacks are focused on the morally darker, more sensitive aspects of the region's culture, slavery and miscegenation, and much of *Pudd'nhead's* humor is correspondingly dark and sardonic. He depicts the community's duels as harmless exercises in male valor in which no one is injured, but the outcomes of its racial mixings are more ominous. The novel's first chapter begins with a lush, pastoral description of the village of Dawson's Landing as it existed in 1830 Missouri:

> a snug little collection of modest one- and two-story frame dwellings whose whitewashed exteriors were almost concealed by climbing tangles of rose vines, honeysuckles and morning-glories. ... All along the streets, on both sides, at the outer edge of the brick sidewalks, stood locust trees ... and these furnished shade for summer and a sweet fragrance in spring when the clusters of buds came forth ... The hamlet's front was washed by the clear waters of the great [Mississippi] river; its body stretched itself rearward up a gentle incline ... Dawson's Landing was a slave-holding town, with a rich slave-worked grain and pork country back of it. The town was sleepy, and comfortable, and contented.
>
> (Berger 1980: 3–4)

Gradually Twain will reveal the tensions and conflicts behind those "whitewashed exteriors," ones related to the slave system that produces the town's prosperity. But at this stage of the novel he is more concerned with introducing its slave-owning elite, a gentry class who are immensely proud of their adherence to the code duello and of their descent from the old Virginia aristocracy. Indeed, they are so proud of their ancestry that they are known as the F.F.V.'s (First Families of Virginia) for short and have absurdly anglophile names—thus implying their descent from the English aristocracy as well—Judge York Leicester Driscoll and his brother Percy, Cecil Burleigh Essex, and so forth. Despite their prestige and popularity, this class has certain implied limitations. Most males are either bachelors like Pembroke Howard or have childless marriages like that of Judge York Driscoll. When Percy Driscoll's wife gives birth to a son in February 1830, she dies "within a week," whereas the slave mother Roxy, who also gives birth to a son, is "up and around the same day, with her hands full, for she was tending both babies" (Berger 1980: 5). That the F.F.V.s may be lacking in artistic creativity and talent, as well as sexual vitality, at least with their white wives, is implied by the town's response to Counts Luigi and Angelo Capello, Italian twins who are aristocrats and musical prodigies. When the twins arrived in the town and give a piano concert, "the villagers were astonished and enchanted with the magnificence of their performance," says Twain; " ... They realized that for once in their lives they were hearing masters" (Berger 1980: 30).

A more covert and less reputable form of mastery is exercised by the male F.F.V.s with their female slaves. Since Roxy, in particular, is only one-sixteenth Black and has a white complexion and brown hair, it is clear that several generations of Dawson's Landing's male F.F.V.s have crossed the "color line" to sire Roxy and her ancestors, a kind of literal paternalism that is not easily acknowledged by white society even though its results can be very visible. Nevertheless, as Twain emphasizes, though Roxy might be for "all intents and purposes, as white as anybody ... the one-sixteenth of her which was black out-voted the other fifteen parts and made her a negro. She was a slave, and salable as such. Her son was thirty-one parts white, and he, too, was a slave, and, *by a fiction of law and custom a negro*"—despite his "blue eyes and flaxen curls" (Berger 1980: 8–9; emphasis added).

Dawson's Landing's sleepy, comfortable existence is disrupted over twenty years later by two events, both of them injustices, that occur in 1830 within several months of each other. The first of these events is the arrival in February of Dave Wilson, a young Easterner who has a college education and legal training. Because he makes a foolish joke on the day he arrives, the local wits decide he is a fool, a "pudd'nhead," and for two decades afterwards he is known by that nickname. Though Wilson is considerably more intelligent than the persons who mock him, they have unjustly decided he is a "perfect jackass" (Berger 1980: 6). Since no one wants a "pudd'nhead" for a lawyer, he must support himself by taking on jobs as a surveyor and accountant, and he spends his otherwise idle hours practicing palmistry and collecting the fingerprints of virtually everyone in Dawson's Landing—two avocations that Twain never bothers to explain beyond his casual comment that Wilson "interested himself in every new thing that was born into the universe of ideas" (Berger 1980: 7).

The second injustice occurs in September when Percy Driscoll—acting as judge, jury, and prosecuting attorney all at once—decides to dispense his kind of paternalistic justice to Roxy and his other slaves because one or more of them has pilfered small sums of money. If Driscoll's servants had been white he could have only fired them or tried to prosecute them in court. Because they are slaves, however, he can resort to a more fearful punishment. "Driscoll's patience was exhausted," says Twain sardonically; even though "he was a fairly humane man toward slaves and other animals." Calling his slaves before him, he threatens not only to sell them if they do not confess, but to sell them "DOWN THE RIVER!" Three of the slaves immediately confess; Driscoll promises to sell them in Missouri, and the

> culprits flung themselves prone, in an ecstasy of gratitude and kissed his feet, declaring that they would never forget his goodness ... for like a god he had stretched forth his mighty hand and closed the gates of hell against them. He knew, himself, that he had done a noble and gracious thing ... and that night he set the incident down in his diary so that his son might read it in after years and be thereby moved to deeds of gentleness and humanity himself.
>
> (Berger 1980: 11, 12)

Driscoll's son, Thomas à Becket Driscoll, never has the opportunity to read about his father's god-like "magnanimity." That night Roxy, horrified by the possibility that someday Percy Driscoll might sell her own son, Valet de Chambers, down the river, switches the two babies so that they become changelings—a change that Percy Driscoll is presumably too distracted to notice. Roxy's own son, the former Valet de Chambers, will be raised as a white person who will attend Yale and speak standard English; whereas Driscoll's son will become a slave, bearing Valet's name, who will be illiterate and whose "speech [will be] the basest dialect of the negro quarter" (Berger 1980: 114). (To avoid confusion, we refer to Roxy's "Black" son as Tom Driscoll hereafter in this study and to Percy Driscoll's white son as Chambers—the names Twain uses for them in the remainder of the novel.)

There is, *Pudd'nhead Wilson* suggests, a kind of rough justice in the form of revenge when Roxy appropriates the white social identity of Percy Driscoll's son and bestows it upon her own child. After all, Twain's persona argues, why shouldn't a slave steal a ham or a chicken from his master since "in taking this trifle from the man who daily robbed him of an inestimable treasure—his liberty—[the slave] was not committing any sin that God would remember against him in the Last Great Day" (Berger 1980: 12). Analogously, since Percy Driscoll and the other F.F.V.s have robbed Roxy's and her ancestors' freedom from them for generations, why shouldn't she take the freedom of one white male Driscoll and give it to her own son? To be sure, Roxy is almost as much of a racist and snob about her ancestry as the F.F.V.s themselves are. After she reveals Tom's origins to him, she boasts that they are descended from "Cap'n John Smith, de highes' blood dat Ole Virginny ever turned out" (Berger 1980: 70). Nevertheless, she bitterly hates Percy Driscoll after he threatens to sell her and his other slaves down the river (Berger 1980: 13), and as Tom is growing up she is "happy and proud" when she sees her son, "her nigger son, lording it among the whites and securely avenging their crimes against her race" (Berger 1980: 22). Later in the novel when she uses her knowledge of Tom's ancestry to blackmail him and force him to kneel in front of her, Twain's narrative persona comments that the

> heir [Roxy] of two centuries of unatoned insult and outrage looked down on [Tom] and seemed to drink in deep draughts of satisfaction. Then she said—
> "Fine nice young white gen'lman kneelin' down to a nigger wench! I's wanted to see dat jes' once befo' I's called. Now, Gabrel, blow dhawn, I's ready. ... "[5]

By switching babies, Roxy gives her son and Driscoll's not only very different social identities but also radically different lives and personalities. Thanks to the "nurture" Chambers (née Tom Driscoll) receives from Roxy and Percy Driscoll, he becomes a humble, compliant house slave. Roxy gives her son "all the petting," while "Chambers got none. Tom got all the delicacies. Chambers got mush and milk, and clabber without sugar. ... Tom was 'fractious,' as Roxy called it, and overbearing. Chambers was meek and docile." If Chambers dares to rebel against Tom's bullying, he quickly learns from Percy Driscoll that "under no provocation whatever was he privileged to lift his hand against his little master," and after several severe "canings from the man who was his father and didn't know it ... he took Tom's cruelties in all humility" (Berger 1980: 19). However, since Twain himself seems to have forgotten about Chambers for most of the novel, the development of his character is not significant.

Tom Driscoll, in contrast, virtually takes over the whole narrative as Twain chronicles his character defects and the ways he abuses the freedoms he enjoys as a member of the white gentry class. As Henry Nash Smith points out (Berger 1980: 253), Tom's personality combines some of the worst character traits of two negative racial stereotypes. Tom, the supposedly white member of Dawson's Landing's gentry, is the indolent, affected master's son who is arrogant toward his peers and cruel and overbearing rather than paternalistic toward his slaves. Tom, the nominally Black product of miscegenation, is cowardly and bitter and has "lax morals"—traits associated with the "Negro" character by *fin de siècle* racists (Smith cited in Berger 1980: 253). When Twain was creating Tom in the 1890s, the great nature versus nurture battle over whether genetics or environment determines "character" was raging with particular force in American culture. Unlike many of his peers, Twain took both sides in this debate since, in Tom's case, he strongly suggests that the forces that make Tom so despicable involve both nature *and* nurture. After he disgraces himself by going to court instead of fighting a duel over a public insult he has received from one of the Italian twins, a "titanic" kick in the buttocks before hundreds of people in the village's Market Hall, Roxy angrily blames Tom's cowardice on his Black "blood": "It's de nigger in you, dat's what it is. Thirty-one parts o' you is white, en on'y one part nigger, en dat po' little one part is yo' *soul*. 'T'aint worth savin; ... You has disgraced yo' birth" (Emphasis in original. Berger 1980: 70).

Elsewhere in the novel, however, Twain clearly suggests that Tom's early family and social environment, even more than his race, contributes to his cowardly and eventually criminal behavior. As we have indicated earlier, Tom is "spoiled" by Roxy when he is an infant, because she lavishes on him both the maternal love of a birth mother and the obsequious affection of a Black "mammy" toward her master's son—so that Tom becomes outrageously selfish (Berger 1980: 19). When he is an adolescent, his cowardice is nurtured because he can force Chambers to fight his battles with white boys who call him a "coward, liar, [and] sneak" (Berger 1980: 20, 21). As a master's "son," who becomes the ward of a rich "uncle," Judge Driscoll, after his supposed father dies, Tom never has to work or learn a trade. He is remarkably lazy, and when he becomes a young man he develops a gambling addiction that he practices (secretly) in St. Louis, upriver from Dawson's Landing—an addiction that eventually causes him to resort first to burglary and eventually murder to pay off his debts. Despite two years at Yale (before he flunks out), Tom is not especially intelligent. However, he is glib, clever, and articulate. Since most of Dawson's Landing's other inhabitants—with the partial exception of Dave Wilson—are less intelligent than he is, he is able to "pass" as a respectable, though not an especially popular, member of the gentry.

As various critics have commented, Twain's characterizations are highly deterministic in *Pudd'nhead*, particularly in the case of Tom.[6] Besides being dominated by the racial and environmental qualities described earlier, Tom's actions are also controlled by his own bad habits that he is powerless to change. Neither the shock of discovering he is Roxy's son nor his well-founded fear that Judge York Driscoll will disinherit him if he discovers his gambling debts is enough to make Tom change his "weak," wastrel ways. After Roxy tells him his parentage when she starts to blackmail him, for example, Tom suddenly understands the injustice of slavery as he asks himself, "'Why were niggers *and* whites made? What crime did the first nigger commit that the curse of birth was decreed for him? ... '" (Berger 1980: 44). For a few weeks he feels secretly like a "nigger" as he fears touching white people and "was ashamed to sit at the white folks' table" with his ostensible aunt and uncle. But even though some of Tom's "opinions" may have changed, emphasizes Twain's narrative persona, "the main structure of his character was not changed, and could not be changed." Therefore, he "dropped gradually back into his old frivolous and easy-going ways, and conditions of feeling, and manner of speech" (Berger 1980: 45). In the case of Roxy, her feelings and behavior are determined by the fact that she is a mother. Despite Tom's ingratitude toward her, his unreliability, and her own angry diatribes when he disappoints her, she continues to trust and help him. At one point in the novel, long after she has been freed as a slave, she voluntarily offers to let Tom sell her back into slavery, temporarily, so that he can pay his debts, because, she says, "Ain't you my chile? En does you know anything dat a mother won't do for her chile? ... In de inside, mothers is all de same. De good Lord He made 'em so" (Berger 1980: 80). Only after Tom repays her sacrifices by selling her "down the river"—after he had promised to sell her to a Missouri slave-owner—does she finally turn on him.

Because of this deterministic element, Tom is not a very interesting villain. Even though he has been called a "monster of meanness, cowardice, and ingratitude" by one critic (Parrott cited in Berger 1980: 218), he remains for much of the novel a rather dull monster, who deserves an 1895 critic's assessment that he is "a poor creature, as he is meant to be, but he does not arrest the reader with ... unmistakable reality" and his "conversations ... seem artificial and forced" (Anonymous cited in Berger 1980: 216).

However, driven by forces and habits beyond his control Tom becomes a destructive, destabilizing force in the community who survives by lying and producing fictional versions of himself and the other characters. In the community it is Tom who turns the anti-temperance rally at the village's Market Hall into a riot when he insults the twins and Luigi kicks him into the audience so that the Hall catches fire and is drenched by the village's overzealous firemen (Berger 1980: 56–57). Tom's response, to bring a lawsuit against Luigi instead of fighting a duel, leads to the duel between Luigi and Judge York Driscoll who disinherits Tom for being the "base son of a most noble father" (Berger 1980: 60). But Tom soon glibly lies his way back into the Judge's good graces, and his lies about Luigi create the bad feeling between the Judge and the twins that causes them to be considered guilty of the Judge's murder.

On a personal level, his identity, especially his social identity, is a complex mélange of fictions, lies, false appearances, disguises, and duplicities whose contradictions are exacerbated by his criminal behavior. In his social identity in the public sphere of Dawson's Landing, such as it is, he is—as Wilson describes him—"that fickle-tempered, dissipated young goose" (Berger 1980: 62) who is nevertheless a member of the town's white gentry class— even though he disgraces himself by initiating a law suit instead of fighting a duel with Count Luigi. As a member of that class, who is considered York Driscoll's nephew and Percy Driscoll's son, he is a master and property owner whose behavior toward his human "property" makes him a perpetrator of the cruelties and injustices of slavery. Moreover, since Tom is a member of the town's upper class, it is assumed that he is on the side of law and order, and Wilson and the village's constable talk about the burglaries that have been plaguing Dawson's Landing in front of him, an advantage that enables him to avoid arrest.

In his private, legal and racial identity in which he is Roxy's son, Tom *is* property because he is a slave. After Roxy's revelations he is very aware, at the beginning of Chapter 10, that as such he is a victim of the injustices of slavery as he laments, "'why is [there] this awful difference between white and black? ... How hard the nigger's fate seems'" (Berger 1980: 44). In his secret identity as gambler, thief, and murderer—even Roxy does not know he killed Judge Driscoll—Tom steals others' property and disrupts the order of the village by murdering an honored citizen and then escaping to St. Louis disguised first as a girl and then as a tramp. In order to commit these crimes, Tom not only lies; he also acts as a trickster, a one-man carnival who revels in his power to create duplicitous appearances and identities. Besides disguising himself twice as a girl (Berger 1980: 32, 46, 95), he also appears as a "stoop-shouldered old woman ... dressed in mourning" (Berger 1980: 65), and as a tramp (Berger 1980: 95), and he disguises himself as a Black man when he prepares to rob York Driscoll by putting burnt cork on his face. In his girl's disguise in particular, Tom raises his duplicity to the level of art. As he realizes that Pudd'nhead, who lives in the next house, is watching him, "he entertained Wilson with some airs and graces and attitudes for a while, then stepped out of sight and resumed the other disguise [as the old woman]" (Berger 1980: 46).

By the time he enters the courtroom to watch the trial at which he expects the Italian twins to be convicted of his ostensible uncle's murder, Tom has been both slave and free, Black and white, male and female, young and old, rich and tramp, a supposedly respectable member of the F.F.V. elite and a criminal. When contradictions between the assorted roles he plays do occur—most notably when he refuses to fight a duel and thus implicitly reveals that he is not a true member of the F.F.V. class—he cleverly lies his way out of these predicaments so that no one, except for Roxy, suspects the truth. Tom's deceptions are aided and abetted by the obtuseness of Dawson's Landing's inhabitants, including its would-be detective, Dave Wilson. Since Tom, disguised as a girl, was seen leaving the Driscoll house after the murder, Wilson spends fruitless hours comparing the fingerprints on the blood-stained dagger Tom left at the murder scene with the fingerprints of women in his collection (Berger 1980: 97), because he is too unimaginative to intuit that the supposed woman might be a man in disguise—until Tom supplies him with that insight by handing him a strip of glass with his fingerprints on it. In addition, Wilson is so duped by Tom's fatuous public identity that he cannot imagine that he could commit a homicide, since he thinks "Tom couldn't murder anyone—he hadn't character enough" (Berger 1980: 98).

Behind Tom's unpleasant but seemingly harmless social exterior he can also be described as being what Richard Weisberg describes as a "man of ressentiment": a vengeful and vindictive person who uses his verbal prowess and his "gifts" of observation, narration, and intellect to gain power and to disrupt others' lives. Such characters, as Weisberg points out, became especially significant in realist fiction starting in the 1860s and continuing well into the twentieth century.[7] Often very articulate, these characters are incapable of fulfilling their creative abilities in ways that are positive. Instead, they are motivated by a powerful sense of being inferior to others and having been insulted or humiliated in some way. They react cleverly but negatively—and sometimes violently—to people whom they envy and who have more "harmonious, positive [psychological] makeups," a strong sense of "absolute values," and a "genuine affection for other people" (Weisberg 1984: 13). What is important about these characters' negativity and violence is that they are almost always expressed in covert, clandestine ways—insidious insults and secret crimes, revenges, and betrayals rather than overt ones.

Though Weisberg does not include Twain or *Pudd'nhead Wilson* in his study, Tom Driscoll is an excellent example of this type of character, and ressentiment explains a great deal about his vindictive relationships with the other characters, starting when they are boys with Chambers who—thanks to his "slave" upbringing—is healthier, stronger, and a better fighter (Berger 1980: 19–20). The adult Tom is just as envious and vindictive but more subtle. He is the master of the snide insult and the hypocritical apology when he taunts Wilson by reminding him that he has never been able to practice his profession as a lawyer and by ridiculing his avocations of palmistry and collecting fingerprints. When Roxy, who is much stronger than he is (Berger 1980: 46), pours out "endearments upon him" and tries to "comfort him" because he will be outcast and friendless if he is disinherited (Berger 1980: 80), he repays her affection and support a page later—after she lets him sell her as a slave so he can pay his gambling debts—by selling her "down the river" to an Arkansas planter (Berger 1980: 81).

However, the main targets of Tom's rancor are the Italian twins and his supposed uncle, Judge York Driscoll. Thanks to their charm, European sophistication, and artistic abilities, the Italians are the only characters in the novel, along with Roxy, who have any charisma—in contrast to Tom who is unpopular and resented for his affectations when he returns from Yale (Berger 1980: 24). When the twins first arrive in town and their landlady, the widow Cooper, and her daughter introduce them to the locals at a party, says Twain, "the twins drifted about from group to group, talking easily and fluently, and winning approval, compelling admiration, and achieving favor from all" (Berger 1980: 29). Moreover, one of the twins, Luigi, is hot-tempered and more courageous than Tom, since he is the one who kicks him into the crowd at the Market Hall, and afterward he is eager to fight the duel with York Driscoll that the Judge initiates to redeem his family honor sullied by Tom's cowardice. Both before and after the kick and the duel,

Tom instinctively dislikes the twins, slanders them when he has the chance, and is delighted when they have difficulties.

The Judge with his F.F.V. devotion to the code duello is far braver than Tom, and he also—within the confines of that code—possesses a sense of what Weisberg might consider a sense of "absolute values." However, the greater source of the covert hatred Tom feels toward the Judge is his role in the narrative as a substitute for Tom's white, biological father, Cecil Burleigh Essex—another F.F.V.—who had died when Tom was an adolescent and before he knew his parentage.[8] After Roxy tells him he has disgraced the white, aristocratic heritage of "yo Essex blood dat's in you," by refusing to fight a duel with Count Luigi, Tom is "stung ... into a fury, and he said to himself that if his father were only alive and in reach of assassination his mother would soon find that he had a very clear notion of the size of his indebtedness to that man and was willing to pay it up in full, even at the risk of his life" (Berger 1980: 70).

Since Essex is not available as a target for Tom's Oedipal rage and revenge, Judge Driscoll becomes the focus of Tom's fear and hatred. After he learns that he is biologically and legally a slave, says Twain, Tom's "hatred of his ostensible 'uncle' [grew steadily] in his heart; for he said to himself, 'He is white; and I am his chattel, his property, his goods, and he can sell me, just as he could his dog'" (Berger 1980: 45, 72). Eventually, due to pressure from Roxy, Tom is forced to graduate from petty pilfering to larger larcenies. In order to escape after he tries to steal York Driscoll's cash box, he stabs the old man with an oriental dagger he had earlier stolen from the Italian twins. Because the twins are, coincidentally, in the neighborhood when this happens, they are immediately arrested. Since Judge Driscoll and the twins were the major targets of Tom's ressentiment envy and rancor, he is delighted and gratified when Count Luigi is accused of the Judge's death: "'One of the twins!' soliloquized Tom; 'how lucky! It is the knife that has done him this grace'" (Berger 1980: 96).

Certain symbolic qualities of the murder scene are especially significant. Early on in the novel, Twain eliminated (or "censored") the melodramatic and psychological potentialities of giving Tom any opportunities to confront his white biological father, Colonel Essex, by specifically excluding Essex from consideration as a significant character with the brusque remark: "Then there was Colonel Cecil Burleigh Essex, another F.F.V. of formidable calibre—*however, with him we have no concern*" (Berger 1980: 4; emphasis added). By eliminating Essex as a character, Twain eliminated the disconcerting possibilities of having a bitter, resentful, legally Black son encounter his white father during the narrative.[9] Nevertheless, the racial implications of Tom murdering his supposed uncle are heavily implied because of the disguise he adopts just before he tries to steal the judge's cash box: "Then he blacked his face with a burnt cork and put the cork in his pocket" (Berger 1980: 93). At the moment he kills Judge Driscoll, the leader of the town's

F.F.V.s, who can be considered a surrogate father, Tom has disguised himself as a Black slave. Therefore, there is an additional, symbolic significance to Twain's description of the murder: "he [Tom] felt the old man's strong grip upon him. ... Without hesitation he drove the knife home—*and was free*" (Berger 1980: 94; emphasis added).

The Judge's standing in the community is high, because of his own aristocratic standards and the respect he receives. "He was fine, and just, and generous. To be a gentleman ... was his only religion, and to it he was always faithful," says Twain. "He was respected, esteemed, and beloved by all" (Berger 1980: 4). For these reasons, and because he is a judge, his murder is a special, symbolic crime: an attack on his entire community's values and its legality as embodied in one of its patriarchs. An additional, Freudian dimension of the murder scene's symbolism is implied by the detail that Tom commits the crime with a knife stolen from another man, Count Luigi, who has been characterized as more "manly" and courageous than he is, and that immediately after he kills the judge he rushes back to his room where he cross-dresses in his "suit of girl's clothes" to escape (Berger 1980: 95).

Tom's behavior and reactions after the crime are also heavily symbolic. Disguised as a veiled woman, he goes to a deserted house, takes off his blood-stained clothing, to "free" himself from "this sort of evidence," as he "cleansed his [bloody] hand on the straw, and cleaned most of the smut from his face. Then he burned his male and female attire to ashes ... and put on a disguise proper for a tramp" (Berger 1980: 95). In effect, Tom thinks he can "free" himself from his past crimes and identities by treating them as "evidence" that can be wiped off like blood or that can be burned like incriminating clothing. As Tom himself believes at the beginning of the twins' trial (in which Wilson is their defense attorney), he is secure because no one will be able to pierce the veil of duplicities and fictions he has created or guess the assumed identities he has supposedly destroyed:

> The Clarksons met an unknown woman in the back lane. ... *that* is his [Wilson's] case! I'll give him a century to find her. ... A woman who doesn't exist any longer, and the clothes that gave her her sex burnt up and the ashes thrown away. ... Lord, it will be pathetically funny to see him grubbing and groping after that woman that don't exist, and the right person sitting under his very nose all the time!
>
> (Berger 1980: 102; emphasis in original)

Unfortunately for Tom and the serenity of Dawson's Landing, the freedom he enjoys after killing Judge Driscoll is brief. What defeats and destroys him is the only existing evidence of his original identity, before Roxy gave him his new social identity as a Driscoll, his fingerprints. Unlike the fictional woman of Tom's disguise, who did not "exist any longer" when he burned the dress he had worn, Tom's fingerprints have remained on his body ever since he was an infant. Therefore, Wilson is able—thanks to Tom giving him the incriminating strip of glass—first to match up his prints with the bloody ones on the dagger and then to demonstrate dramatically to a packed courtroom both Tom's guilt and his original identity as the slave child who was Roxy's son. By the end of the novel, Tom's identities—social, legal, racial, and gender—are so mixed and confused by the fictions he and Roxy have constructed that only this kind of indisputable forensic evidence seems capable of identifying him and achieving justice. For as Wilson tells the judge and jury, fingerprints are "certain physical marks which do not change their character, and by which he can always be identified ... without doubt or question," because they are the individual's "physiological autograph ... [that] cannot be counterfeited, nor can he disguise it or hide it away" (Berger 1980: 108). The narrative's larger, more complicated social, racial, and ethical issues of whether Tom should be considered a Black man or a white one, slave or free, the product of deterministic forces or a responsible agent, are ignored in the novel's climatic courtroom scene that is focused entirely on the questions of Tom's birth identity and who killed Judge Driscoll, and ends with Tom collapsing in a faint when Wilson reveals he is "Valet de Chambre, negro and slave—falsely called Thomas à Becket Driscoll—" and a murderer (Berger 1980: 112).

In an 1893 letter to Fred Hall in which Twain boasts that most of the characters in *Pudd'nhead* were not "important" and that he has eliminated "weather" and "scenery" from the narrative, he implies that the novel was a "success" because "the finger-prints ... is [*sic*] virgin ground—absolutely fresh, and mighty curious and interesting to everybody."[10] Considered from this perspective, the true "hero" of the narrative and the source of its author's enthusiasm is not Tom's human antagonist and the novel's ostensible detective, Pudd'nhead Wilson, but the scientific method Wilson employs in his realist obsession with collecting, labeling, and cataloging facts in the form of fingerprints. One reason Wilson, unlike most fictional detectives, is so "prosaic" and lacking in charisma, the reason Twain had so little interest in him as a character and described him as being "a lever, with a useful function" (Henry Nash Smith cited in Berger 1980: 254), is that his role in the novel is mainly to demonstrate that method. Unlike Doyle's Sherlock Holmes who uses a wide variety of tactics and methods to catch criminals—surveillance, "deduction," research, intuition, and disguises, as well as a bit of science— Wilson's discovery that Tom is a criminal is based entirely on science, the use of fingerprinting to identify criminals that Twain learned by reading Francis Galton's *Finger Prints* in 1892 when he was writing *Pudd'nhead*. As Wilson performs his demonstration of Galton's methods during the trial, he conveys—through this association with science—an assurance that he never possessed earlier in the novel. The awed inhabitants of Dawson's Landing respond with "explosion[s] of applause," as if they are witnessing a magic act or theatrical performance, when he identifies their "natal autographs" to them. Even more significantly, the trial judge exclaims, "'This certainly approaches the miraculous!'" (Berger 1980: 110), implying that forensic science, as represented by fingerprinting, has supplanted supernatural justice as a power that can achieve justice by providing new kinds of divinations and oracles.

Twain was correct when he told the President of Yale that his humor was "the natural enemy of royalties, nobilities, [and] privileges" (cited in Gillman 1989: 12), but this statement did not mean that he was opposed to hierarchy per se. In *Pudd'nhead* it is the "voice" of science—as enunciated by Wilson who becomes its spokesperson and devotee—that achieves discursive dominance and authority. It replaces the supernatural and also the voices of the charismatic humans, who dominate trial scenes in Romantic justice narratives, by becoming *the* force that can reveal "truth" and bring justice to a duplicitous and disorderly society. One of the more significant proofs of the extent to which realist science is more powerful than the merely human characters in *Pudd'nhead* is the way in which Tom responds to Wilson's revelations: "Tom turned his ashen face imploringly toward the speaker, made some impotent movements with his white lips, then slid limp and lifeless to the floor" (Berger 1980: 112–13). Until this moment, Tom had always been able to deceive human antagonists with glib lies and clever rationalizations, with the negative creativity that is possessed by ressentiment characters, but the revelations of science about his identity and guilt are unanswerable, and therefore they render him mute and "impotent."

That Tom is mute and becomes "lifeless" when he is decrowned and his slave identity is revealed can also be interpreted as another difference between how identity is constructed in realist and Romantic justice narratives. In the latter, characters like Vautrin or Stevenson's Dr. Jekyll retain "essential," inner selves beneath their social identities. Even when they are most tested by adversity, most vulnerable to the judgments of others, they are still able to respond with eloquent speeches and/or confessions in which they judge their adversaries or, in Jekyll's case, himself. In contrast, since Tom's whole self is the hollow concoction of lies and fictions that make up his social identity, that entire self dies, becomes "lifeless," and collapses when his fingerprints prove him to be a "negro and slave" (Berger 1980: 112). Moreover, the Romantic novels we have just mentioned all build up to self-narrated revelations of identity that are focused on kinships—Vautrin's leadership of his "ten thousand comrades" who are loyal to their underworld "boss" (Berger 1980: 135), and Jekyll's connection with Hyde, his evil alter ego and other self. In contrast, Tom's silence after his slave name is spoken, discloses his inner emptiness and isolation because—as Roxy said earlier in the novel—"there 'warn't nothing *to* him'" (Berger 1980: 46; emphasis in original).

Yet another reason for Tom's silence is implied by the punishment he receives after he has confessed and been sentenced to life imprisonment in Twain's "Conclusion." Then Percy Driscoll's creditors come forward and point out that originally Tom was Percy's property, not his son; therefore, he belongs to the Driscoll estate and should be sold to pay off a portion of its indebtedness. "If 'Tom' were white and free it would be unquestionably right to punish him— ... but to shut up a valuable slave for life—that was quite another matter," says Twain's narrative persona. Consequently, "when the governor understood the case, he pardoned Tom at once, and the creditors sold him down the river" (Berger 1980: 115). Tom has become, as he was at birth, a chattel slave, mere property. Since property is socially dead and cannot speak, it is appropriate that Tom is mute and dehumanized after his slave identity and name are revealed and that his "confession" is reported but not quoted by Twain in the "Conclusion."

Tom's trial and punishment resolve the disorders initiated by the unjust events of 1830 in bleakly ironic ways that Twain chronicles in a brusque, factual "Conclusion." The injustice of being judged a "pudd'nhead" suffered by Wilson in 1830 is partially remedied by the esteem he receives for revealing Tom's villainies; some of Dawson's Landing's "remorseful" citizens acknowledge that they are the ones who have been the fools for over twenty years—but no one volunteers to compensate Wilson for the years he was considered a "perfect jackass" and unable to practice as a lawyer. The Italian twins are found innocent of Judge Driscoll's murder, but they "were weary of Western adventure, and straightway retired to Europe" (Berger 1980: 114). Roxy is apparently not punished in any legal way for switching Tom and Chambers, but her "heart was broken" and her "spirit ... was quenched," and her only solace afterwards was religion (Berger 1980: 114). Chambers, now recognized as a member of the white gentry in terms of his parentage and "blood," is unable to function as a member of that class because he has become so conditioned to think of himself as being Black and a slave. Even though he is "rich and free," says Twain, he "could neither read nor write, and his speech was the basest dialect of the negro quarter. His gait, his attitudes, his gestures, his laugh—all were vulgar and uncouth. ... Money and fine clothes could not mend these defects or cover them up" (Berger 1980: 114).

However, a rough kind of vengeful justice does prevail when Tom is punished by being sold "down the river," since that act does bring closure to the cycle of injustices and betrayals that were initiated in 1830 when Percy Driscoll threatened to punish his slaves in the same way and continued when Tom sold Roxy to the Arkansas planter. In those instances, being sold to a cruel master was unjust (Percy's slaves did not deserve such a harsh punishment) or grossly unfair (Roxy was sacrificing her freedom for Tom). In Tom's case, however, being sold "down the river" can be considered an appropriate punishment. Unlike the generic "nigger" he describes in his soliloquy in

Chapter 10 after he learns he is one-thirty-second Black ("What crime did the uncreated nigger commit? ... How hard the nigger's fate seems" [Berger 1980: 44]), Tom has committed many crimes. Disguised in the white social and racial identity his mother appropriated for him, he has been a liar, coward, thief, and murderer who would have been delighted if the Italian twins had been wrongfully convicted for his killing of Judge Driscoll. Therefore—unlike Chambers or Roxy and the other Black characters in the novel—it is just for him to suffer the "fate" of being a slave and sold down the river. However, this verdict also restores the racial boundaries and eliminates the racial ambiguity that existed after Roxy switched the babies. Like the Court's ruling in Plessy vs. Ferguson, it implicitly equates justice with segregation and keeping people "with their own kind." Therefore, it defeats Roxy's plan to liberate her son from slavery by giving him their master's son's identity. On the other hand, that son cannot adapt to life as a white person, nor can he remain in his "place" as a slave. He cannot bear to sit in the Driscoll family pew, for example, but he also can no longer take "refuge in the [church's] 'nigger gallery'" (Berger 1980: 114), and therefore Roxy's original revenge against Percy Driscoll remains intact.

Chapter 6

The empire strikes back

Imperialism and justice in E. M. Forster's
A Passage to India

Indians know whether they are liked or not—they cannot be fooled here. Justice
never satisfies them, and that is why the British Empire rests on sand.
(E. M. Forster, *A Passage to India*, Forster 1973: 289)

Even though one of its most important scenes is a dramatic court trial, *A
Passage to India* is only partially a book about justice. It is also about themes
such as friendship, loyalty, visions, and the meeting of the cultures of East
and West, and how this meeting is played out through the lives of its main
characters. Further, as we will argue, it is—as are most books of more than
momentary interest—about the nature of human life and relationships. Yet
all of these things must be seen in relation to the trial of a young Indian
doctor, Aziz, who is accused of assaulting or attempting to rape an Englishwoman in a cave near Chandrapore, the rather seedy and run down Indian
provincial city which is the novel's setting. For what Forster implies about
justice and its limitations and problems in Chandrapore serves to illuminate
and focus the other large issues with which he is dealing. When we view
Passage from that perspective it turns out to have one important similarity
with *Pudd'nhead Wilson*: in both novels the justice process is subverted by
inequality. The institution producing this inequality is different—imperialism rather than slavery—but the effect is roughly similar. Lives are blighted;

the good suffer, and the bad flourish, at least temporarily, because of the assumption that some people are intrinsically better than others and, therefore, have the right and responsibility to rule them.

Equality, as philosophers such as John Rawls and Jürgen Habermas have emphasized, is a crucial component of any genuine justice process. How, Rawls asks, would a just society begin? It would originate in the meeting of its members who would be ignorant of their talents and positions in society and therefore would be willing to accept "equality in the assignment of basic rights and duties" (Rawls 1971: 14). Similarly, in Habermas's formulation of how individuals would communicate in a properly functioning civil society and its public sphere, he emphasizes that, "*All* members must be able to take part in the discourse, even if not necessarily in the same way. Each must have fundamentally equal chances to take a position on all relevant contributions" (Habermas 1996: 182; emphasis in original).

When Rawls and Habermas's principles are applied to an empire or a colonial society, the very term "imperial justice" would seem to be an oxymoron. For empires are built on force and historic conquests, not on equality or hypothetical meetings or communications among equals. This is especially true of the British Empire in India that was based historically on a violent act of resistance, the Mutiny or Rebellion of 1857, which was followed by an even more violent retribution as the British regained control. Moreover, imperialists, including those portrayed by Forster are almost invariably convinced that they are racially, religiously, morally, and/or culturally superior—not equal—to their colonial subjects. Therefore, according to a great deal of twentieth- and twenty-first-century thinking on this subject, a colonial society is by its very nature unjust. Imperialism or "the conquest of the earth," warns Marlow, the narrator of Conrad's *Heart of Darkness*, "which mostly means the taking it away from those who have a different complexion or slightly flatter noses than ourselves, is not a pretty thing when you look into it too closely" (Conrad 2002: 107). The language of a more recent commentator, Edward Said, is more temperate but just as negative: "At some very basic level, imperialism means thinking about, settling on, controlling land you do not possess, that is distant, that is lived on and owned by others. For all kinds of reasons, it attracts some people and often involves untold misery for others" (Said 1994: 7).

Seen through the lens of Forster's novel, many aspects of Indian life are not "pretty," including some which would foster justice and equality in a non-imperial society. Politics, for example, is a major area in which the "disadvantaged" can improve their positions if they have the opportunity to do so. In *Passage*, however, politics is an activity in which the British have most of the power while the Indians mostly have slogans, protests, meetings, and promises.[1] As for Indian nationalism, the idea that Indians have an equal right to govern themselves and have their own laws, Forster's brief comments on that subject are not especially serious or respectful. Thus one of the consequences of Aziz's trial is the formation of a "committee of notables, nationalist in tendency, where Hindus, Moslems, two Sikhs, two Parsis, a Jain, and a Native Christian tried to like one another more than came natural [sic] to them. As long as someone abused the English, all went well, but nothing constructive had been achieved, and if the English were to leave India, the committee would vanish also" (Forster 1952: 114–115).

On the other hand, more vigorous or violent efforts by the Indians to gain power could be disastrous. This possibility was dramatized most memorably by an ugly incident that occurred shortly before Forster began writing his novel, which was published in 1924. This event is not mentioned explicitly in *Passage*—even though it almost undoubtedly influenced the behavior of some of Forster's characters. In April 1919, political rallies in the Punjabi city of Amritsar turned violent. Banks were looted, buildings were burned, dozens of Europeans were attacked, four were killed, and an Englishwoman, named Marcia Sherwood, was beaten by a gang of Indian youths. Punjab's Lieutenant Governor, Sir Michael O'Dwyer, decided that the province was on the verge of becoming the scene of a second 1857 Mutiny and called in the army. When troops commanded by Brigadier General Reginald Dyer arrived, the General banned meetings and ordered punishments, including one forcing Indians to crawl down the lane where Sherwood was attacked. When Indian leaders called a meeting at a walled garden called Jallianwalla Bagh to protest these punishments, Dyer responded by bringing troops to seal the garden's only exit and then ordering them to open fire, even though the crowd of 10,000 was unarmed and peaceful. Nearly 400 were killed, and 1,500 were wounded, but the General was neither court-martialed by the army nor prosecuted in a civil court.[2] Twenty years later Sir Michael O'Dwyer was assassinated by Udham Singh, a Sikh militant who had witnessed the massacre and vowed to avenge it (Lal 2008), but Dyer escaped retribution. Instead, in a strictly political process he was relieved of his command by the Secretary for War, Winston Churchill, and forced to retire from the army (Swaminathan 2002).

Though this leniency outraged Indians, it mollified Dyer's British supporters, a group that included powerful members of parliament and the nation's media establishment, particularly the *Morning Post*, which raised a sum of £26,000 for the General. An additional sign of Dyer's popularity in England was that when Churchill defended the government's decision, he did not condemn the General himself, though he made it clear that he abhorred the massacre. It was, he said, "an episode which appears to me to be without precedent or parallel in the modern history of the British Empire. ... It is an extraordinary event, a monstrous event, an event which stands in singular and sinister isolation." But it was not, he asserted,

> the British way of doing business. ... The British power in India does not stand on such foundations. It stands on much stronger foundations. ...

Our reign in India or anywhere else has never stood on the basis of physical force alone, and it would be fatal to the British Empire if we were to
try to base our-selves only upon it. The British way of doing things ... has
always meant and implied close and effectual co-operation with the people
of the country.

(Churchill, 8 July 1920)

Considered from this perspective, the Anglo-Indian colonial officials in *A
Passage to India* seem to be trying to do things in "the British way."
Chandrapore has the amenities of imperialism. Taxes are collected and spent
on public works; there are laws and courts to enforce them; a hospital, trains
that run on time, schools and colleges to train clerks, teachers, and professional persons who will supposedly become cooperative subalterns in the
imperial system. But observed more closely, as Forster observes it, the
"British way" is based more on paternalism than cooperation, and beneath
the paternalism there is a bedrock of contempt. When things are going
smoothly in Chandrapore, the Collector Turton refers to Indians as "the
Aryan Brother" and invites the westernized ones—barristers, teachers, and
"Government people"—to a "Bridge Party" that is supposed to "bridge the
gulf between East and West" and thus be a kind of imperial public sphere in
which the British and Indians will meet on a social basis (Forster 1973: 27,
28). But the equality that is a prerogative for a valid public sphere cannot
exist because of the arrogance of the Anglo-Indians and the dependency they
impose on their subjects. Thus, Turton, surveying his Indian guests, sneers,
"We know why he's here, I think—over that contract, and he wants to get
the right side of me ... and he's the astrologer who wants to dodge the
municipal building regulations ... " (Forster 1973: 41).

The Anglo-Indian women are worse. When Adela Quested (who is
supposed to marry Heaslop, the colonial magistrate) and Mrs. Moore (who is
Heaslop's mother) arrive from England, they encounter the colonial wives at
the Anglo-Indian club. These women, such as Mrs. McBryde and the other
habitués are eager to initiate them into the right, puck attitudes toward
Indians.

> " ... I was a nurse before my marriage, and came across them a great
> deal, so I know. I really do know the truth about Indians. ... One's only
> hope was to hold sternly aloof."
> "Even from one's patients?"
> "Why the kindest thing one can do to a native is to let him die," said
> Mrs. Callender.
>
> (Forster 1973: 25)

Mrs. Turton, the Collector's wife, is just as direct and even more arrogant at
the "Bridge Party." In response to Mrs. Moore's question about the female

Indian guests, Turton claims, "You're superior to them, anyway. Don't forget that. You're superior to everyone in India except one or two of the Ranis [Hindu queens], and they're on an equality" (Forster 1973: 42).

In a more general way, however, virtually all of the characters in *Passage* judge one another, and a very high percentage of these judgments are derogatory and influenced by prejudice, suspicion, contempt, and/or fear. The novel's English characters (the Schoolmaster Fielding, Quested, Mrs. Moore) criticize the Anglo-Indians (Heaslop and the other "Turtons and Burtons") for being rude and racist. The Anglo-Indians, in turn, more or less openly despise or patronize all Indians (Aziz, Mahmoud Ali, and the Nawab Bahadur), and the Muslim Indians, in *their* turn and among themselves, criticize and ridicule the Anglo-Indians, the English, and the "slack Hindus" (Forster 1973: 72). "The spirit of the Indian earth ... tries to keep men in compartments," remarks Forster's narrative persona midway through the novel (Forster 1973: 140), and all of these communities suspect the others of spying on them, bribing their servants, and conspiring against them. As Forster makes clear in the novel's early scenes, however, it is the Anglo-Indians who do the most to create and maintain this cycle of mutual contempt and suspicion.

This attitude breeds fear and distrust. Indeed, says, Forster's narrative persona, "Fear is everywhere [in India]; the British Raj rests on it" (Forster 1973: 192). Even when events are going smoothly, as they do at the beginning of the novel, before the disastrous journey to the Marabar caves, the Indians like Aziz have to fear the large and small humiliations, the snubs and insults that the Anglo-Indians inflict. On this level and in this context, injustice in *Passage* often takes the form not of crimes but of refusals to give other persons, chiefly the Indians, their just deserts and respect. Most of Forster's Indian characters are middle- or upper-class Muslim professional men and landowners—doctors, barristers, police officials, engineers, and a wealthy landowner, the Nawab Bahadur. Some have degrees from British universities, and they are just as well educated, intelligent, articulate, and "civilized" as their British or Anglo-Indian counterparts—and the Nawab is considerably richer—yet they are denied membership in the colonial "club" and treated with patronizing disdain, or worse, on social occasions. Or, like the obsequious Dr. Panna Lal, they may become *babus*, superficially westernized Indians who try to ingratiate themselves with their colonial masters by mimicking their values and manners, a course of action that earns them the contempt of the Anglo-Indians and the hostility of their fellow Indians.

Since the Indians are confronted with these attitudes, it is inevitable, the novel implies, for them to react with their own defensive prejudices and over-generalizations. So they claim that all Englishmen become bigots after they have been in India for two years, but that Englishwomen are even worse since they are transformed in only six months (Forster 1973: 9). Thus, when two mem-sahibs commandeer Aziz's waiting carriage early on in the novel, he responds with his own contemptuous judgment: "the inevitable snub—his bow ignored, his carriage taken. It might have been worse, for it comforted him somehow that Mesdames Callender and Lesley should be fat and weigh the tonga down behind. Beautiful women would have pained him," and he promptly wishes to "shake the dust of Anglo-India off his feet! To escape from the net and be back among manners and gestures that he knew!" (Forster 1973: 14–15).

Then, when things go badly, as they do after Aziz's arrest, the Indians have good reason to fear the wrath of the Anglo-Indian authorities. Then the Collector Turton no longer speaks of Indians as his "Aryan Brother" when he tells Fielding that, based on his "twenty-five years of experience of this country ... I have never known anything but disaster [to] result when English people and Indians attempt to be intimate socially. Intercourse, yes. Courtesy, by all means. Intimacy—never, never. The whole weight of my authority is against it" (Forster 1973: 182). Or there is the Collector's colleague, Major Callender, who rules the hospital where Aziz is a surgeon and calls Indians "buck niggers," and wants to "call in the troops" (Forster 1973: 207). Or there is Turton's own wife who says Indians "ought to be spat at, they ought to be ground into dust." It is likely that some of this anger is caused by fear, for many of the Anglo-Indians who are listening to Mrs. Turton and the Major at the club shortly after Aziz's arrest seem convinced that Chandrapore is on the verge of another 1857 Mutiny, because its citizens are expressing support for Aziz with protests and strikes. Fortunately for all concerned, the head official, Turton, is capable of responding to more realistic fears, and he resists calling in the army. For even though he wanted "to flog every native that he saw," he also wanted to do nothing that would lead to a riot or to the necessity for military intervention. "The dread of having to call in the troops was vivid to him; soldiers put one thing straight, but leave a dozen others crooked. ... The Collector sighed. There seemed nothing for it but the old weary business of compromise and moderation. He longed for the good old days when an Englishman could satisfy his own honour and no questions asked afterwards" (Forster 1973: 211).

Presumably Turton has Amritsar or a similar incident on his mind, a potential disaster in which a local official (like himself) becomes the scape-goat. Therefore, he urges moderation, and the Anglo-Indians rely on the legal system, their legal system, to avenge Quested and to restore order.

The innocent defendant is one of the most stereotyped characters and motifs in popular culture justice texts, many of which culminate in exciting courtroom scenes in which the real criminal is discovered through a melo-dramatic revelation, usually one that is factual in nature, such as Tom Dris-coll's fingerprints in *Pudd'nhead Wilson*. Though the specifics of this motif vary, the outcome is the same: injustice is defeated when falsehood is destroyed by some kind of solid, empirical fact. The clever criminal with the brilliant alibi proving he was in Boston is trapped by the humble parking ticket proving he was in Manhattan a block from the crime scene on the day of the murder. One reason *A Passage to India* is more of a modernist than a popular culture text is that it contains none of these generic clichés, and the factual "truth" of what happened to Quested in the Marabar cave is never revealed. Fielding, the rational Englishman, looks at the hills and wonders like a realist detective "what miscreant lurked in them, presently to be detected by the activities of the law? Who was the guide, and had he been found yet? What was the 'echo' of which the girl complained? He did not know, but presumably he would know. Great is information, and she shall prevail" (Forster 1973: 191).

Unfortunately for all concerned, the facts available to Fielding are simple but opaque. Aziz, seeking to impress his English friends, arranges an elaborate excursion to the Marabar Caves. Fielding and Professor Godbole miss the train that takes Aziz, Quested and Mrs. Moore to the hills. The first cave they visit, accompanied by a guide and villagers, is crowded and has an unpleasant echo that causes Mrs. Moore to become ill. Aziz, Quested, and the guide go on. She enters a cave by herself; Aziz goes into a different cave, and then steps outside to smoke a cigarette. When he tries to rejoin Quested, Aziz cannot remember which cave she was in—they all look alike—panics, and strikes the guide who flees. He has found Quested's binoculars with a broken strap and puts them in his pocket; then he sees her at the bottom of the hill, near a road talking to another woman. Fielding suddenly arrives; a Miss Derek has driven him there. Quested disappears, and we learn she is being driven back to Chandrapore by Derek. At this point in the novel, readers have seen the entire incident through Aziz's point of view. They know that he did not join Quested in a cave, and therefore he is innocent when he returns on the train and is arrested because Quested has alleged that he molested her.

The event in the cave, as she recounts it later, was brief and confusing.

> I went into this detestable cave. ... and then as I was saying there was this shadow, or sort of shadow, down the entrance tunnel, bottling me up. It seemed like an age, but I suppose the whole thing can't have lasted thirty seconds really. I hit at him with the [field] glasses, he pulled me round the cave by the strap, it broke, I escaped that's all. He never actually touched me once. It all seems such nonsense.
>
> (Forster 1973: 214)

Aziz has no way of proving that he did not follow Quested into the cave to assault her, but on the other hand she cannot prove that the "shadow" that she encountered was Aziz. It could have been the guide, a stray villager, or even a hallucination—though the broken strap on the binoculars suggests that some kind of physical conflict did occur. From a strictly legalistic standpoint it is a stalemate, since neither party can prove beyond a reasonable doubt that her or his narrative is the true one. But while this logic would be relevant in a society in which both persons had roughly equal status and therefore equal degrees of credibility, it would be naïve to imagine that it will be applied in an imperial courtroom. In such a court racist stereotypes will prevail, and one party (Aziz) will be seen as a treacherous liar and the other (Quested) as a pathetic victim who must be avenged by a guilty verdict and a stiff prison sentence.

British legalism may be adequate, the novel implies, for the kind of utilitarian justice Ronnie Heaslop dispenses as Chandrapore City Magistrate.

> Every day he worked hard in the court trying to decide which of two untrue accounts was the less untrue, trying to dispense justice fearlessly, to protect the weak against the less weak, the incoherent against the plausible, surrounded by lies and flattery. That morning he had convicted a railway clerk of overcharging pilgrims for their tickets, and a Pathan of attempted rape. He expected no gratitude, no recognition for this. ... It was his duty.
>
> (Forster 1973: 51–52)

But it lacks the sensitivity needed to deal with a case like Aziz's. Moreover, it is an imported, alien system of justice without deep roots in the cultures or historical experiences of India's three main, most powerful communities—Hindu, Muslim, and Anglo-Indian. Because of the limitations of Heaslop's level of legalism, Forster's characters do not passively or fully accept it. They imagine alternatives to it or they try to manipulate or circumvent it—but these efforts are not very successful. For example, Aziz, before the incident at the Caves, loves to imagine himself living in the golden age of the Mogul emperors who ruled India in the sixteenth and seventeenth centuries. To Aziz, Alamgir and Babur are as important as Napoleon or Elizabeth I are to nostalgic French or Englishmen, and when he imagines himself as possessing power, he fantasizes that he would display it like a Mogul ruler. "Sometimes I shut my eyes and dream I have splendid clothes again and am riding into battle behind Alamgir," he tells Fielding. Later, during his lunch with Fielding, Mrs. Moore, and Quested, Aziz

> peopled [the] room with clerks and officials, all benevolent because they lived long ago. "So we would sit giving [rupees] forever—on a carpet instead of chairs, that is the chief change ... , but I think we would never punish anyone."
>
> The ladies agreed.
>
> "Poor criminal, give him another chance. It only makes a man worse to go to prison and be corrupted." ... "We punish no one, no one," he

repeated, "and in the evening we will give a great banquet ... and all shall be feasting and happiness until the next day, when there shall be justice as before—fifty rupees, a hundred, a thousand—until peace comes."

(Forster 1973: 66, 75)

Unlike Heaslop's justice with its petty crimes and punishments, Aziz's Mogul justice would be generous and humane. But it is also naïve and unrealistic. As Forester's narrative persona tartly comments, Aziz's justice expresses the "tenderness of one incapable of administration, and unable to grasp that if the poor criminal is let off he will again rob the poor widow" (Forster 1973: 75).

A second alternative vision of justice, which is also not very satisfactory, is the Hindu metaphysical or supernatural justice that is the subject of Godbole's comments at the end of Chapter 19. Confronted by Fielding with the plain question of whether Aziz is innocent or guilty, Godbole refuses to give a direct answer; instead he subjects the schoolmaster to a lecture on Hindu philosophy:

"according to our philosophy. ... nothing can be performed in isolation. ... I am informed that an evil action was performed in the Marabar Hills ... My answer to that is this: that action was performed by Dr. Aziz." He stopped. ... "It was performed by the guide." He stopped again. "It was performed by you." Now he had an air of daring and of coyness. "It was performed by me." He looked shyly down the sleeve of his own coat. "And by my students. It was even performed by the lady herself. When evil occurs, it expresses the whole of the universe. Similarly when good occurs."

(Forster 1973: 197)

Godbole's theology mocks the most fundamental bases of western legality and logic, and he knows this—hence his "air of daring and coyness"—but he uses the occasion to illustrate his idea of justice by then telling Fielding the legend of the Tank of the Dagger, involving a Rajah who murdered his nephew and spent years with a dagger clamped to his hand until he came to a spring when "he was thirsty ... but saw a thirsty cow and ordered the water to be offered to her first, which, when done, 'dagger fell from his hand, and to commemorate miracle he built Tank'" (Forster 1973: 198). For Fielding the story is irrelevant, because it has nothing to do with Aziz; for Godbole the story is appropriate since it presumably illustrates a Hindu conception of justice. Rather like Coleridge's *Ancient Mariner*, the Rajah's guilt was signified by supernatural means (the dagger clamped to his hand equals the albatross around the Mariner's neck); his rehabilitation was shown by another miracle, the dagger falling from his hand, so there were no troublesome questions about guilt or innocence like the ones in Aziz's case. The Professor may be a very wise man, but his wisdom has little or no relevance to Aziz's fate or the quality of justice as it is practiced in Chandrapore.

The most important concept of justice in the novel, which is derived from history, is the collective memory of what we would call Mutiny justice that takes control of the Anglo-Indian community before and during Aziz's trial. It is, in effect, a demand for revenge, no matter how unfair, that exists beneath the outward, legalistic forms of British justice that will be displayed at the trial. Like Aziz's nostalgic Mogul court, this kind of justice is based on history, but it is a vindictive, nightmare narrative of India's history, not a generous dream. Moreover, instead of being an obvious and rather harmless individual fantasy, it is a malevolent, collective melodrama that gives unity and coherence to the Anglo-Indian community at moments of crisis. When Fielding tries to argue with Police Super-intendent McBryde about Aziz's guilt or innocence, the Superintendent's main argument is a simple one: "When you think of crime you think of English crime. The psychology here is different. ... Read any of the Mutiny records; which, rather than the Bhagavad Gita, should be your Bible in this country" (Forster 1973: 187). Even though that Mutiny by Indian Army troops (or sepoys) took place in the middle of the previous century, McBryde considers it a convincing explanation of Aziz's guilt. For the Anglo-Indians, as Forster represents them, still consider that Mutiny proof that virtually all Indians are perfidious, lustful barbarians. Aziz, to them, is only following in his ancestors' footsteps, albeit on a small scale, and his arrest triggers both their panicky fears and their panicky desire that the British should retaliate fiercely.

Looking at the families gathered for the meeting in the club on the evening after Aziz's arrest, Forster notes that the building has the "air of the residency at Lucknow" during the siege of 1857. During the meeting Major Callender, the most blatantly racist of the Anglo-Indians, calls for actions similar to General Dyer's. And though Callender's "outbursts were dis-counted," they made people uneasy because they aroused "the unspeakable limit of cynicism untouched since 1857" (Forster 1973: 207). Equally revealing is Mrs. Turton's diatribe as she tries to spur on her husband and the other Anglo-Indian males by impugning their manhood: " ... you men. You're weak, weak, weak. Why, [Indians] ought to crawl from here to the caves on their hands and knees whenever an Englishwoman's in sight, they oughtn't to be spoken to" (Forster 1973: 240).[3] As the discussion continues, the malevolence becomes so intense that Fielding experiences it as a palpable force, an "evil ... propagating in every direction. It seemed to have an existence of its own" (Forster 1973: 207–8).

Later, relatively temperate historians have acknowledged that both sides committed atrocities during the Mutiny or that English troops slaughtered innocent Indians at Delhi as vigorously as the sepoys massacred English women and children at Cawnpore. But to many Victorian and early twentieth-century English historians and novelists, and to many of their readers, the Mutiny was all the evidence they needed to believe that Indians were too dangerous to be trusted if they were not kept under the strict control of the Raj. But even though the Mutiny might be a fearful collective myth for Anglo-Indians, it was also a powerful source of racial and national pride. A popular history of British imperialism, published in the same year as Forster's novel, advised its readers to "dwell with admiration and gratitude on the many heroic deeds" performed by English officers and soldiers during the Mutiny (Gibbs 1924: 221), and another historian has commented that for British troops killed in the Mutiny "death in battle meant a hero's crown; they were the martyrs of the secular religion of the age" (Spear 1972: 272).

Forster also acknowledges that the desire for heroism is one element of his Anglo-Indian characters' response to Aziz's alleged crime, but he emphasizes that this heroism is vindictive and irrational as well as chivalrous. When Turton first tells Fielding about Quested's accusation, his face is "white, fanatical, and rather beautiful ... fused by some white and generous heat" (Forster 1973: 163), but he quickly becomes furious when he realizes that the Englishman, loyal to his friend Aziz, is trying to respond rationally to the situation:

> the Collector looked at [Fielding] sternly, because he was keeping his head. He had not gone mad at the phrase "an English girl fresh from England," he had not rallied to the banner of race. ... All over Chandrapore that day the Europeans were putting aside their normal personalities. ... Pity, wrath, heroism, filled them, but the power of putting two and two together was annihilated.
>
> (Forster 1973: 183)

The Collector Turton's male compatriots become even more irrational as they begin imagining themselves heroic defenders of their families against riots or a new Mutiny. "They had started speaking of 'women and children' — that phrase that exempts the male from sanity when it has been repeated a few times," comments Forster's narrative persona; "Each felt that all he loved best in the world was at stake, demanded revenge, and was filled with a not unpleasing glow. ... 'But it's the women and children,' they repeated, and the Collector knew he ought to stop them intoxicating themselves, but he hadn't the heart" (Forster 1973: 205). In this way, the atrocities of the Mutiny are used as justification for being vindictive and—at the same time—a dream of melodramatic male heroism that justifies (to use Heaslop's words) their determination to "hold this wretched country by force" (Forster 1973: 52).

Despite their rage, the novel's Anglo-Indians cannot reenact the bloody retributions that British troops considered "justice" in 1857 and 1858, nor can they emulate General Dyer's actions at Amritsar—though some of them might like to do so. Instead, they have to be satisfied with a show trial that will dramatize Indian malevolence and contrast it, at least ostensibly, with British fair play and devotion to the rule of law. Among themselves, however, as Forster reveals, the Anglo-Indians are dissatisfied by their own legal system and the form the trial must take. Because they wish they could do more for Heaslop, whom they consider a "martyr ... bearing the sahib's cross," they feel "craven sitting on softness and attending the course of the law" (Forster 1973: 185). When Heaslop must disqualify himself as Magistrate—since Quested is his fiancée—and appoint his Indian assistant Das to take his place, McBryde, the Police Superintendent, "grew bitter over the arrangements, and called them the 'fruits of democracy.' In the old days an Englishwoman would not have had to appear [in court] ... She would have made her deposition, and judgment would have followed. He apologized to her for the condition of the country ... " (Forster 1973: 217).

Nevertheless, the Anglo-Indians are so convinced that Aziz will be convicted by their court system that they speak of it as a process that will function with mechanical efficiency. Even when Quested herself begins to doubt whether Aziz is guilty, Heaslop and Mrs. Moore tell her, "the case has to come before a magistrate; it really must, the machinery has started" (Forster 1973: 229). McBryde will give his speech for the prosecution; Quested will narrate her version of her "terrible adventure in the cave," carefully rehearsed with McBryde beforehand (Forster 1973: 212); other prosecution witnesses will testify to Aziz's allegedly bad character; Fielding and Aziz's Indian friends will offer their testimony in vain; the magistrate will find Aziz guilty; and the "nightmare of history," originally created by the Mutiny and now supplemented by the "machinery" of imperial justice, will continue to destroy lives.

The Anglo-Indians must go through the motions of giving Aziz a fair trial, if only to persuade themselves that they are in India to "do justice" (Forster 1973: 50), but since they are so prejudiced and since they control the system, it would seem to be impossible or at least unrealistic to expect that any Indian could receive what Said describes as "impartial justice" (Said 1994: 75). Nevertheless, their court turns out to be nothing but a "flimsy framework" (Forster 1973: 256) rather than a formidable machine when Quested recants her testimony. Then procedural justice does operate effectively in the novel. Aziz is innocent of the crime with which he was charged, and all the charges against him are withdrawn. If the system is unfair, as we have argued, then where does justice come from? How can it emerge from such biased or inequitable circumstances? In a novel filled with mysteries, is the answer to this question just one more "muddle"?

The best answer to this question is that Quested recants and Aziz is saved by visions: two moments of extraordinary perception that Quested experiences, first, as she enters the courtroom, and a little later as she is giving her testimony. These visions are mysterious in the sense that they do not seem to be related to any specific religious or spiritual tradition. And though Forster described them vividly, he never explained them. They simply enter Quested's mind, change the outcome of the trial, and transform the lives of the novel's main characters.

The first vision conveys a sense of ironic relativism that makes Quested question the significance of what she is doing by testifying in court. She has a sudden sense of detachment from immediate concerns and customary values as she notices the room's punkah wallah who operates the fan. The man's extraordinary physical beauty stuns her; and his "aloofness," his absolute lack of any reaction to the events around him, "impressed the girl from middle-class England, and rebuked the narrowness of her sufferings. In virtue of what had she collected this roomful of people together? Her particular brand of opinions, and the suburban Jehovah who sanctified them— by what right did they claim so much importance in the world?" (Forster 1973: 242). Such a statement strikes at the very heart of the British faith in their imperial mission, their assumption that they are a superior race and civilization that must avenge "insults" like Aziz's with elaborate trials and harsh sentences. By seeing the lowly punkah wallah in this way, Quested has already begun to doubt the value of what she and the Anglo-Indian community consider justice.

Quested's second experience of this sort, which Forster twice specifically refers to as a "vision," occurs in the midst of the trial when McBryde is questioning her about what happened in the Marabar caves. Along with Mrs. Moore, Quested heard an unpleasant echo there. It continued to haunt her, and she associated it with her own uncertainty about what really happened in the cave. "Adela was always trying to 'think the incident out,'" says Forster's narrative persona,

> always reminding herself that no harm had been done. ... For a time her own logic would convince her, then she would hear the echo again, weep, declare she was unworthy of Ronny, and hope her assailant would get the maximum sentence. ... And consequently the echo flourished, raging up and down like a nerve in the faculty of her hearing. ... Only Mrs. Moore could drive it back to its source and seal the broken reservoir.
>
> (Forster 1973: 253)

Since Mrs. Moore does not give her the help she seeks, Quested is still uncertain and haunted by the echo until the trial. Then, as she and McBryde start to recite the narrative they had rehearsed, she has a much more positive vision of her experience at the caves that comes into her consciousness spontaneously as she begins to speak.

> A new and unknown sensation protected her, like magnificent armour. She didn't think what happened or even remember in the ordinary way of memory, but she returned to the Marabar Hills, and spoke from them across a sort of darkness to Mr. McBryde. The fatal day recurred in every detail, but now she was of it and not of it at the same time, and this double relation gave it indescribable splendour.
>
> (Forster 1973: 253)

This vision is the obverse of Mrs. Moore's, for whereas the old woman's echo made everything seem vile and trivial, in Quested's vision her experiences have "splendour." Moreover, in Quested's vision she stands outside herself—a version of her ability to look with some objectivity at her own faults and virtues; but in the vision she does so literally, watching herself in the scene at the caves. When McBryde asks the crucial question—did Aziz follow her into the cave?—she waits for him to appear: "Her vision was of several caves. *She saw herself in one, and she was also outside it, watching its entrance, for Aziz to pass in.* She failed to locate him. It was the doubt that had often visited her, but solid and attractive like the hills" (Forster 1973: 253–54; emphasis added). Relying on the vision, rather than on her rehearsed memories, she recants her earlier deposition and says, "Dr. Aziz never followed me into the cave." In the tumult that follows, bolstered by her "vision," she refuses to return to the narrative she had constructed earlier with McBryde. What is also significant about Quested's vision—as the sentence we have emphasized indicates—is how much it defies realist criteria for truth and certainty. Neither Heaslop's "evidence," nor Fielding's "information," nor Sherlock Holmes' "science of deduction" can encompass a perspective in which a person can be in a cave by herself and at the same time also be outside it watching for Aziz.

Quested's vision enhances her great virtue, which is honesty, and allows her to exercise it in a way that enables her to save Aziz and herself, but she is only able to do this bravely and fully through the vision that replaces her earlier confusion and uncertainty. Once that happens, her echo is cured, for as she tells Fielding afterwards, "My echo is gone—I call the buzzing sound in my ears an echo. You see I have been unwell ever since that expedition to the caves" (Forster 1973: 265). What Quested's vision does disrupt is at least one small part of the British empire. Visions and contingency are antitheses of mechanism, and when Quested recants the trial becomes very much a Bakhtinian carnival in which the Anglo-Indians are humiliated and decrowned as they lose control of the "machinery" of their own judicial system. McBryde tries to keep questioning Quested, and Major Callender, the Anglo-Indian surgeon, tries to stop the trial "on medical grounds," but their imperial voices are overwhelmed by those of the Indian magistrate, Das, and the Nawab Bahadur.

> "You withdraw the charge? Answer me," shrieked [Das] the representative of Justice.
>   Something she did not understand took hold of the girl and pulled her through. Though the vision was over, and she had returned to the insipidity of the world, she remembered what she had learnt. ... It was in hard prosaic terms that she said, "I withdraw everything."
>   "Enough—sit down. Mr. McBryde, do you wish to continue in the face of this?"
>   The Superintendent gazed at his witness *as if she was a broken machine*, and said, "Are you mad?"
>   "Don't question her, sir; you have no longer the right."
>   "Give me time to consider—"
>   "Sahib, you will have to withdraw; this becomes a scandal," boomed the Nawab Bahadur suddenly from the back of the court.
>
> (Forster 1973: 256; emphasis added)

However, as Forster makes very clear, Quested's recantation and Aziz's acquittal is not the kind of conclusive, happy ending that terminates so many popular culture justice narratives. Victory for the Indians and defeat for the Anglo-Indians encounter one another in a polarized, antithetical form that is "complete [only] for one moment," and then "life returned to its complexities" (Forster 1973: 257). In fact, after the "flimsy framework of the trial [breaks] up," it takes Forster ninety-one more pages and fourteen more chapters to deal with the "complexities" and issues that have been created or left unresolved by the trial and its immediate aftermath.

Though Das's verdict is, in effect, "not guilty," because Quested recants, the Indians' anger toward her is not assuaged. Mere formal justice, Forster's narrative persona explains, "never satisfies them" (Forster 1973: 289), because it is too "cold," impersonal, and unemotional. Aziz's friend Hamidullah sums up the Indians' reaction by deciding that if Quested

> had shown emotion in court, broke down, beat her breast, and invoked the name of God, she would have summoned forth his imagination and generosity. ... But while relieving the Oriental mind, she had chilled it, with the result that he could scarcely believe she was sincere. ... For her behaviour rested on cold justice and honesty; she had felt, while she recanted, no passion of love for those whom she had wronged.
>
> (Forster 1973: 272)

Nor is Das's verdict enough to assuage the Indians' anger toward the Anglo-Indians who supported and encouraged Quested. Inflamed by wild rumors that the Nawab Bahadur's grandson Nureidden, injured in a car accident, has been tortured by Major Callender in the hospital, a mob leaves the courtroom determined to rescue and avenge Nureidden and then attack the hospital, the Major, and the Anglo-Indian civil station—an event that might have initiated a real disaster, since it probably would have forced Turton to call in the military. But this is averted by a comic decrowning, the self-abasement of Dr. Panna Lal who had planned to ingratiate himself with Major Callender by testifying against Aziz. Confronted with a mob "desirous of his blood," Lal ridicules himself and his own subservient role as the Anglo-Indians' *babu*:

> "Oh, forgive me," he whined. ... "Oh, Dr. Aziz, forgive the wicked lies I told. ... I was afraid, I was mislaid here, there, and everywhere." ... Agitated but alert, he saw them smile at his indifferent English, and suddenly started playing the buffoon, flung down his umbrella, trod through it, and struck himself upon the nose. ... Of ignoble origin, Dr. Panna Lal possessed nothing that could be disgraced, and he wisely decided to make the other Indians feel like kings.
>
> (Forster 1973: 263)

After this carnivalistic performance, a harmless way of ridiculing imperialism and its collaborators that makes the "Indians feel like kings," order and the rational values of the public sphere are restored by the Nawab Bahadur, who "had great possessions and deprecated anarchy," and gives a speech "about Justice, Courage, Liberty, and Prudence, ranged under heads, which cooled the passions of the crowd" (Forster 1973: 264). In effect, hierarchy and reason have been restored, but, at least on a local level, it is more of an Indian hierarchy since the Nawab is one of the district's richest and most respected landowners.

Politically, the trial's outcome at first seems a great victory for the Indians. Heaslop's assistant, Das, becomes the "representative of Justice," because he "had shown that an Indian can preside" (Forster 1973: 238). Even before the trial began, Chandrapore's Indians had already become more politicized by the case. Students at the Government College went on strike, and by the morning the trial starts the Anglo-Indians were aware that "the temper of Chandrapore was altering. ... The Sweepers had just struck, and half the commodes of Chandrapore remained desolate in consequence—only half ... but why should the grotesque incident occur? ... A new spirit seemed abroad, a rearrangement, which no one in the stern little band of whites could explain." There is, at least temporarily, an entente between Chandrapore's Muslims and Hindus who ignore their mutual suspicions and become friendlier. However, Aziz, deeply embittered by what he has experienced from imperial justice, becomes virulently anti-British and abandons his chances for a successful medical career by becoming the personal physician of a Hindu rajah in Rau, a small, independent state where he will not have to deal with British officials. But the empire's Higher Officials react to these events by displaying that capacity for resilience, compromise, and tactical retreat that would enable them to maintain the Raj for two more decades after Forster published his novel. Overt racism is deemed politically incorrect; some of Chandrapore's officials are presumably sacked or transferred; Fielding, no longer a "renegade," is informed by Sir Gilbert, the Province's Lieutenant-Governor, that his attitude was the only "sensible ... view from the first," and the Anglo-Indians who had ostracized him are ordered to invite him to rejoin their club (Forster 1973: 287). "The Marabar caves had been a terrible strain on the local administration; they altered a good many lives and wrecked several careers, but they did not break up a continent or even dislocate a district," concludes Forster's narrative persona, for even though "Sir Gilbert had been courteous, almost obsequious, the fabric he represented had in no wise bowed its head. British officialdom remained, as all pervading and as unpleasant as the sun" (Forster 1973: 289).

Fielding, the most intelligent of the British, realizes this is no real improvement over the pre-Marabar era. He speculates on, then rejects the idea that perhaps mysticism (or what Forster called "visions") might make the British more just and more sensitive to India.

> "It is no good," he thought as he returned past the mosque, "we all build upon sand; and the more modern the country gets the worse'll be the crash. In the old eighteenth century, when cruelty and injustice raged, an invisible power repaired their ravages. Everything echoes now."
>
> (Forster 1973: 309)

In other words, in the eighteenth century, an "invisible power"—presumably religion—could somehow correct inequities, injustices, and cruelties. But in a modernizing society, such as that of colonial India, the echo and its nihilism cannot be contained or explained away by secular forces. Quested's vision on the witness stand, whatever its source, is her own, contiguous experience, and not a paradigm for comparable visions that can defeat future echoes.

On a personal level the great casualty of Aziz's arrest and trial is his friendship with Fielding. Significantly, one of the chief reasons the two men become estranged is because of their very different ideas about how Aziz should deal justly with Quested. After her recantation the Anglo-Indians' chivalrous concern for her welfare disappears instantly, and by chance and irony as the trial ends she literally bumps into Fielding who rescues her and takes her to his College. This encounter and the unromantic friendship that follows it contributes to the "tragic coolness" (Forster 1973: 302) that develops between the Englishman and Aziz. No longer imagining himself a

Mogul ruler who would dispense rupees, Aziz believes the Englishwoman is an ugly "hag" who has besmirched the honor of his family. "I want revenge," he tells Fielding, and he thinks that demanding heavy damages from her—20,000 rupees—will be an appropriate revenge. Fielding is appalled by what he considers his friend's insensitivity; they argue, and in a "passionate and beautiful outburst" (Forster 1973: 290) Aziz renounces everything but his court costs. However, Fielding's intervention on Quested's behalf continues to disturb him, and their friendship first cools and then flounders in a muddle of bad faith, malicious gossip, and misunderstandings in which both men feel the other has been unjust or unfair. At one point Aziz even believes a silly rumor that Fielding was Quested's lover, returned to England on leave to marry her, and had persuaded Aziz not to ask for damages so he could have a rich wife.

Eventually these "stupid misunderstandings" (Forster 1973: 319) are cleared up at Mau when Fielding arrives for a visit with his wife (Stella, Mrs. Moore's daughter) and his brother-in-law (Ralph, Mrs. Moore's other son). In an intricate scene, Aziz's memories of his friendship with Mrs. Moore are reawakened by his encounter with Ralph who has inherited his mother's mysticism and her instinctive sense of kinship with India and Indians. "Then you are an Oriental," Aziz tells Ralph, the same words he had spoken to Mrs. Moore at the mosque in Chandrapore (Forster 1973: 231, 349), and it seems possible that Fielding's and Aziz's friendship also will be reestablished.

At the beginning of the final chapter, it seems that it has when the two men take a horse-back ride together before parting. Aziz has even composed a gracious letter to Quested thanking her for her bravery at the trial. But though Aziz and Fielding may have put the specific injustices of the arrest and the trial behind them, they cannot escape from the larger injustice of imperialism and the effects it has had on their lives and beliefs. Half-seriously and half-ironically they argue politics. "Each had hardened since Chandrapore," says the narrative persona, "and a good knock about proved enjoyable" (Forster 1973: 359). Aziz rages and shouts nationalistic slogans, "India shall be a nation! No foreigners of any sort! Hindu and Muslem and Sikh and all shall be one! Hurrah for India!" Fielding responds by ridiculing his friend's politics and India's nationalistic aspirations: "Away from us, Indians go to seed at once. ... India a nation! What an apotheosis! Last comer to the drab nineteenth-century sisterhood. ... she shall rank with Guatemala and Belgium perhaps" (Forster 1973: 361). Aziz swears that he, or his sons, will "drive every blasted Englishman into the sea," and then

> he rode against [Fielding] furiously—"and then," he concluded, half kissing him, "you and I shall be friends."
>
> "Why can't we be friends now?" said the other, holding him affectionately. "It's what I want. It's what you want."

But the horses didn't want it—they swerved apart; the earth didn't want it, sending rocks through which riders must past single file; the temples, the tank, the jail, the palace, the birds, the carrion, the Guest House, that came into view as they issued from the gap and saw Mau beneath: they didn't want it, they said in their hundred voices, "No, not yet," and the sky said, "No, not there."

(Forster 1973: 362)

Lacking a vision of intuitive, sympathetic kinship comparable to Mrs. Moore's before the Marabar cave debacle or a vision possessing "splendour" as Quested's did during the trial, they can only wrangle and fall victim to the "poison" of nationality and the "spirit of the Indian earth, which tries to keep men in compartments" (Forster 1973: 140). In a flawed universe and society, friendship and justice will surmount separation and prejudice only with sympathy, vision, and great difficulty. Absent such vision and sympathy, where and when are justice and friendship? Not now; not here.

Chapter 7

Race, sex, fear, revenge in Richard Wright's *Native Son*

"I have never known anything but disaster result when English people and Indians attempt to be intimate socially. ... The whole weight of my authority is against it." Then he drove off to his bungalow and gave rein to his passions again. When he saw the coolies asleep in the ditches or the shopkeepers rising to salute him on their little platforms, he said to himself: "I know what you're like at last; you shall pay for this, you shall squeal."

(E. M. Forster, *A Passage to India*, Forster 1952: 182, 183–84)

I demand this [the death penalty] so that others may be deterred from similar crimes, so that peaceful and industrious people may be safe. Your Honor, millions are waiting for your word! They are waiting for you to tell them that jungle law does not prevail in this city! They want you to tell them that they need not sharpen their knives and load their guns to protect themselves. ... Slay the dragon of doubt that causes a million hearts to pause tonight, a million hands to tremble as they lock their doors!

(Richard Wright, *Native Son*, Wright 1991: 835)

E. M. Forster's India and Richard Wright's Chicago are on opposite sides of the world, but they share at least one fear. The speakers of these two quotes, the Collector Turton in Forster's novel and the State's Attorney Buckley in Wright's, have antithetical personalities and political positions. The former is an imperial bureaucrat, appointed by His Majesty's government. The latter is an ambitious, ruthless politician in a city known for its harsh, corrupt politics. Yet both Turton and Buckley see themselves as protecting their communities against the same evil: the malevolent, interracial rapist. Both see themselves as achieving that protection by giving out the harshest possible sentences to persons they consider guilty of sexual crimes against their race. Turton and his fellow Anglo-Indians wish to see Aziz sent to prison for years merely for touching Quested. Buckley—even though he knows that there are extenuating circumstances that might mitigate Bigger's death sentence—ignores them to demand the death penalty, presumably to let the people of Chicago sleep in peace and not tremble with fear that they are about to be attacked.

What are the origins of these fears? In Forster's novel it is the Mutiny of 1857 and 1858. In *Native Son* the origins are depicted as being more contemporary as Wright reveals the prejudices and racism, the inequities, and the resulting injustices of the white society in which Bigger lives—or, to be precise, outside of which Bigger lives—through many details and contrasts. Perhaps the most significant source of prejudice in the novel, because it so influential, is the press. As depicted by Wright, Chicago's newspapers are perfect negative examples of communication in a public sphere that has been corrupted and inflamed by fear, racism, and opportunism. As Wright also makes clear, the press serves as a stand-in for the populace, both creating the "public mind" of its white audience and reflecting it. Bigger's first encounter with that media, while he is still presumed to have no connection with Mary Dalton's disappearance, gives a fair warning of the attitudes that prevail.

"Good God!" said one of the [reporters]. "What a story! Don't you see it? These Negroes want to be left alone and these Reds are forcing 'em to live with 'em, see? Every wire in the country'll carry it!"
    "This is better than Loeb and Leopold," said one.
    "Say, I'm slanting this [story] to the primitive Negro who doesn't want to be disturbed by white civilization."
    "A swell idea!"
    "Say, is this Erlone really a citizen?"
    "That's an angle."
    "Mention his foreign-sounding name."
    "Is he Jewish?"
(Wright 1991: 645)

Obvious in this exchange are the casual racism, the political xenophobia and red-baiting, plus a strong hint of anti-Semitism, the ratings-driven sensationalism, and the blithe amorality of those entrusted to inform the white public. As portrayed by Wright, the Chicago press has an avid desire to create stereotypes ("the primitive Negro") that will inculcate, not diminish, racism.

The second great source of fear and prejudice in the novel are Chicago's city officials, who keep the press supplied with the lurid details they need for inflammatory headlines. As Bigger's defense attorney, Boris Max, rightfully complains how can he make his voice of "sober reason" prevail when a thousand newspaper and magazine articles have dragged "every conceivable prejudice" into the case, and the "authorities of city and state [have] deliberately inflamed the public mind" (Wright 1991: 805)? The third source is, of course, Bigger himself, since he commits the crimes that provide the raw material for the headlines. However, during much of the early stages of the novel, Wright depicts Bigger as a confused young man who is often himself frightened and insecure as well as angry and bitter. Neither an innocent boy nor yet a criminal, he is especially nervous when he has to interact with white people. The differences between their way of life and his are so immense that it is almost impossible for him to function emotionally.

During the brief time he is employed by the rich and liberal Daltons, for example, he soon learns they live in a world that is the antithesis of his. In the first scene of the novel, readers see Bigger and his family in their squalid one-room ghetto apartment as Bigger kills a ferocious rat by hitting it with a skillet (Wright 1991: 450). A little later when he arrives at the Dalton's mansion, the first room he enters "was lit by dim lights glowing from a hidden source. ... He had not expected anything like this; he had not thought that this world would be so utterly different from his own that it would intimidate him" (Wright 1991: 487). Yet the these two worlds are connected, as Bigger eventually learns, by the economic irony that the Daltons own his family's apartment, and a microscopic portion of their wealth comes from the rent his mother pays.

During the early sections of the novel, instead of having a stable personality, Bigger speaks in or encounters a number of voices and viewpoints that are all inadequate, superficial, or dangerous answers to the question of how a young Black man from Chicago's ghetto can react to the inequities and injustices imposed upon him by the Jim Crow system that dominated American society for much of the twentieth century. Each of these viewpoints—whether created by Bigger or by other characters—also implies a narrative, a potential constructed identity for him with appropriate attitudes and actions. But all of these stories are impossible for him because they cannot appease his hunger for a better life that he has glimpsed in white Chicago or placate the deadly combination of rage, fear, and resentment that he feels toward white people because they have denied him access to that better life.

Bigger rejects Black religion, as represented, first, by the spirituals his mother sings (Wright 1991: 454) and later by the platitudes of the Reverend Hammond in Book Three (Wright 1991: 710). What is essential to that religion, as Wright depicts it, is a narrative implying resignation and acceptance of the injustices and miseries of Black existence, since life in this world is meant to be painful and insignificant compared to "eternal life." "Jesus let men crucify 'Im; but His death wuz a victory," says Hammond: "He showed us tha' t' live in this worl' wuz t' be crucified by it. This worl' ain' our home. ... Be like Jesus. Don't resist" (Wright 1991: 711). As Bigger hears the preacher's words, says Wright's narrative persona, he "knew without listening what they meant; it was the old voice of his mother telling him of suffering, of hope, of love beyond this world. And he loathed it because it made him feel as condemned and guilty as the voice of those who hated him" and clamored for his death (Wright 1991: 709).

The street life and its language that he shares with his gang—Gus, Jack, and G. H.—is far more congenial to Bigger and constitutes what we would call his pool hall persona. A melange of jokes about whites and racism, Hollywood escapist fantasies purveyed by the movies, and small-time crime—robbing ghetto apartments, newsstands, and fruit stalls—this milieu allows Bigger and his friends to pose as tough guys surveying their condition with "cool" cynicism and humor. Indeed, as Robert Butler points out, one of the few moments when Bigger is relaxed and friendly toward another person occurs when he and Gus "play 'white'" by staging their own carnivalistic parody of what they think are the manners of rich and powerful white folks—Army Generals, J. P. Morgan, and the President of the United States—as they order one another into battle or to "dump" twenty-thousand shares of US Steel.[1] From this episode one can imagine a future for Bigger in which he would be a neighborhood wise guy and small-time criminal—working (or, more likely, stealing) enough to keep himself supplied with cigarettes, dope, and whiskey, hanging out with his gang, and shooting pool. But Bigger is only briefly amused by the game of "playing 'white'" before it makes him start brooding about the racism that controls and limits him. Where do white folks live, he asks Gus, and when Gus mentions white neighborhoods, Bigger corrects him.

Bigger doubled his fist and struck his solar plexus.

"Right down here in my stomach," he said. ... Every time I think of 'em, I *feel* 'em. ... . It's like fire."

(Wright 1991: 463; emphasis in original)

Gus's answers to this dilemma are simple: "Don't think about it," and "Get drunk and sleep it off" (Wright 1991: 464). But Bigger cannot stupefy himself so easily. He has an uneasy awareness that resisting the white world that oppresses him, even on this petty level, may be dangerous when he sees the campaign poster of Buckley, the State's Attorney, staring at him— exactly like Big Brother in Orwell's 1948 novel *1984*—and warning him: "IF YOU BREAK THE LAW, YOU CAN'T WIN!"[2] "Sometimes I feel like something awful's going to happen to me," he tells Gus, and it is significant that he says this "with a tinge of bitter pride in his voice" (Wright 1991: 463)—a tone of voice that is very different from when he was joking about J. P. Morgan.

The Daltons, the rich and liberal white philanthropists who hire Bigger as a chauffeur, have, needless to say, a language very different from ghetto street talk and a scenario for Bigger's future that is far more constructive, by their standards, than loafing in a pool hall. Though they have made much of their fortune as ghetto slumlords whose holdings include the Thomas family's tenement, the Daltons are proud that they have done their part to combat the injustices of racism by recycling five million dollars of their profits into contributions to "colored schools." They also make a practice of hiring young Black men like Bigger as servants, and they have a Black Horatio Alger success story for him to emulate. His predecessor, named Green, went to night school and eventually got a government job, and Mrs. Dalton encourages Bigger to follow the same road to lower-middle-class success (Wright 1991: 502). Green "kept things neat and nice," another servant tells Bigger when she shows him the room he has inherited: "There were pictures of Jack Johnson, Joe Louis, Jack Dempsey, and Henry Armstrong [on the walls]; there were others of Ginger Rogers, Jean Harlow, and Janet Gaynor" (Wright 1991: 501). Black male violence (with Dempsey as a token white boxer) and white female sexuality are blandly juxtaposed and sanitized in Green's choice of fighters and movie stars as idols—his way of being psychologically "neat and nice." But Bigger does not want to go to night school; his attitude toward Mary Dalton's sexuality is not at all "nice"; and the distance between him and her parents is revealed when Mrs. Dalton speaks to her husband in front of him, as if he were an animal in an experiment, by using the sociological/scientific jargon they have read in the reports of welfare agencies.

> "Don't you think it would be a wise procedure to inject him into his new environment at once so he could get the feel of things? ... I think it's important emotionally that he feels free to trust his environment," the woman said. "Using the analysis contained in his case record the relief [agency] sent us, I think we should evoke an immediate feeling of confidence ... "

"But that's too abrupt," the man said.

Bigger listened, blinking and bewildered. The long strange words they used made no sense to him; it was another language. ... He felt strangely blind.

(Wright 1991: 927–28)

The blindness, which is one of the dominant tropes in the novel, is mutual. Bigger does not see the Daltons or understand their language, and they are equally "blind"—Mrs. Dalton literally so—to him as they plan to impose their values upon him.

Mary Dalton and her Communist lover, Jan Erlone, are far more radical than Mary's parents, but their naïve, leftist response to Bigger is just as "blind." When he wrote *Native Son*, Wright was a full-fledged member of the Party (he broke with it in the early 1940s), and he took some elements of Communist theory and ideology seriously. However, in the novel he portrayed his Communist characters (with the partial exception of Boris Max) as being painfully insensitive and ignorant about African-American people. For Jan and Mary, Bigger's story is to become a Black poster boy whom they will recruit because, Jan explains, "We can't have a revolution without [Black people]. ... They've got to be organized. They've got spirit. They'll give the party something it needs" (Wright 1991: 517). In their presumptuous efforts to befriend Bigger, they invoke all the stereotypes. They ask him if he likes fried chicken and cajole him to sing spirituals for them as Jan plies him with rum and Communist pamphlets, and Mary flirts with him and assures him, "After all, I'm on your side" (Wright 1991: 505).

With the exception of the one involving his pool hall, "cool" persona, what is notable about all of these implied narratives, whether religious or secular, is that they are implicitly redemption narratives in which Bigger will be "saved" from his condition as a Black person by following the "way" set down for him by religion and Jesus; by Green, Horatio Alger, and the Daltons' patronage; or by Marx, Jan, and the CPUSA (Communist Party United States of America). However, all of these redemptive alternatives become irrelevant to Bigger because of the outcome of his encounter with Mary and Jan. The more they try to make him relax and enjoy the interracial harmony they are trying to establish, says Wright's narrative persona, the more Bigger feels embarrassed, distrustful, and angry (Wright 1991: 512). The contrast between what Mary and Jan believe they are doing—being friendly and egalitarian, and what Bigger perceives, that they are perhaps laughing at him and certainly making him acutely conscious of his black skin—is acute and bitter.

Mixed into this already potent medley of discomfort, shame, and misunderstanding is sexual desire. As we will emphasize below, much of the outrage triggered by Bigger's alleged crime is produced by the belief that he raped Mary before killing her. Even more than interracial murder, interracial sex is the great taboo because of the legendary lust felt by Black men for white women and of the unexpressed but powerful fear that that lust might be returned in kind. For this reason, Wright could have made Bigger a far more sympathetic character for many white readers if he had depicted him as having little or no sexual interest in Mary and suggested that he was in her room by accident when he killed her. Instead, Wright made Bigger's desire no small element in his encounter with Mary. When he is sitting with her and Jan in the front seat of the Dalton's car, Bigger is aroused sensually by touching her, and later when she and Jan become passionate in the back seat while he is driving, Bigger is "filled with a sense of them, his muscles grew gradually taut. He sighed and sat up straight, fighting off the stiffening feeling in his loins" (Wright 1991: 518). In the car after Jan leaves, the drunken Mary puts her head on Bigger's shoulder, and when he carries her to her room and starts to make love to her, she responds eagerly: "He tightened his arms as his lips pressed tightly against her and he felt her body moving strongly. ... He kissed her again and felt the sharp bones of her hips move in a hard and veritable grind. Her mouth was open and her breath came slow and deep" (Wright 1991: 524).

At that moment contingency, in the person of the blind Mrs. Dalton, enters the room, and "a hysterical terror seized [Bigger], as though he were falling from a great height in a dream. ... Frenzy dominated him" (Wright 1991: 524). Terrified at being found alone in a room with a white woman, he smothers Mary with a pillow to keep her quiet. What could have been, at worst, a drunken, interracial sexual encounter is transformed into a disaster for everyone—except the State's Attorney Buckley and the Chicago press who relentlessly and vigorously exploit Bigger's acts for their own political and racist purposes.

The instant Bigger knows Mary is dead he immediately realizes that no one will believe that her death was an accident, and that he has become "a murderer, a Negro murderer, a black murderer. He had killed a white woman" (Wright 1991: 527). Before that happened, Bigger had a dualistic identity combining two stereotypes about African-Americans, both of which are negative. At one extreme, in his mind and his secret actions, he is the "bad nigger" implied by his own name, Bigger: angry, resentful, and dangerous, filled with hostility toward the white world he fears and hates. But the role that Bigger acts in public before whites is implied by his surname, Thomas, as in Uncle Tom—the antithetical stereotype of the bad nigger—who is cowardly, docile, dim-witted, and polite to whites. By continuing to play that role after Mary's disappearance is discovered, he thinks he can trick the Daltons into paying a ransom and blame Jan and the Communists for Mary's disappearance. "They don't think we got enough guts to do it [kidnap Mary]. They think niggers is too scared," he tells his girl fiend, Bessie (Wright 1991: 581). He believes no one will suspect he killed Mary and decapitated her corpse, so he could cram it into the Daltons' furnace, because the private detective, Britten, and the reporters who question him think he is a meek black boy or "just a black clown" (Wright 1991: 638).

Like many internalized extreme dualisms, such as Jekyll and Hyde, for example, Bigger's dualistic identity is unstable. In his conscious mind he considers himself in control of himself and events because he thinks he can "handle this thing" (Wright 1991: 583), first, by planning the kidnapping story and, later, by brutally murdering Bessie whom he had forced to be his accomplice. But Bigger's body and his unconscious mind know better. At times he almost collapses physically from stress (Wright 1991: 617–18). He has repeated hallucinatory visions of Mary's bloody, decapitated head, and he has a dream in which he sees himself as decapitated and "decrowned" as "he stood on a street corner in a red glare of light like that which came from the furnace and he had a big package in his arms so wet and slippery and heavy that he could scarcely hold on to it ... and the paper fell away ... it was his *own* head—his own head lying with black face and half-closed eyes ... and hair wet with blood" (Wright 1991: 599; emphasis in original). And, at the crucial moment when the reporters accidentally begin to discover Mary's bones and an earring in the furnace ashes, Bigger loses his head metaphorically by fleeing in panic so that everyone will immediately suspect that he is guilty. After he does that, he has only one identity, the one that will be his fate, as he becomes the doomed villain.

As soon as that happens, he also becomes the villain of a racist melodrama created by the Chicago press. In the headlines of the first newspaper published after the discovery of the bones, Bigger learns what his life's story will be, at least for the public: a sensational account of a taboo-breaking crime committed by a monstrous criminal.

> HUNT BLACK IN GIRL'S DEATH. ... AUTHORITIES HINT SEX CRIME ... He paused and reread the line, AUTHORITIES HINT SEX CRIME. Those words excluded him utterly from the world. To hint that he had committed a sex crime was to pronounce the death sentence. It meant the wiping out of his life even before he was captured; it meant death before death came, for the white men who read these words would at once kill him in their hearts.
>
> (Wright 1991: 673)

In spite of the fact that at this point the only evidence of Bigger's involvement is his disappearance, and even though the state of Mary's remains precludes the possibility of finding any forensic evidence of rape, the newspaper's tone is provocative and unequivocal. The headline's original "hint" quickly becomes a "belief" or fact; and the highly emotional reaction to the story is rapid: "Indignation rose to white heat last night as the news of the Negro's rape and murder of the missing heiress spread through the city" (Wright 1991: 673). This reaction is not limited to indignation. Before

Bigger is arrested, Chicago's whites exact retribution from the city's Black population so that the alleged crime of one man results in the hysterical persecution of many others. Newspapers report smashed windows in the city's Negro section; several Negro men are beaten in white neighborhoods, and "several hundred Negro employees throughout the city [are] dismissed from jobs" (Wright 1991: 674).

More hysteria and fear are generated by the reaction of the public authorities. Five thousand policemen and three thousand white vigilantes rush to Chicago's Black neighborhoods and begin searching every building. All cars, buses, el trains, and streetcars leaving the South Side are stopped, and the scene in which Bigger is finally hunted down is an apocalyptic one with sirens and whistles screaming while torrents of water are sprayed from fire hoses on the water tower where he tries to take refuge. When he is in jail and in court, mobs of whites gather to shriek curses and insults at him, and in one scene they erect a cross on a nearby building and burn it where he can see it.

After Bigger is captured and appears in public at the inquest, Wright again uses a lengthy quotation from a newspaper to encapsulate the reaction of the white public and media establishment. Relying on actual newspaper accounts of the trial of a young Black man, Robert Nixon, who was convicted and executed for similar crimes in Chicago in 1938–39 (Wright 1991: 875, 935), Wright demonstrates how emotions and prejudice can be inflamed when an individual can be converted into a dehumanized, demonized stereotype. In the newspaper in the novel, headlined, "NEGRO RAPIST FAINTS AT INQUEST," Bigger is described as a "Negro sexslayer." A comment by a "terrified" spectator that Bigger "looks exactly like an ape!" is amplified in later paragraphs that describe how his

> lower jaw protrudes obnoxiously, reminding one of a jungle beast. ... a beast utterly untouched by the softening influences of modern civilization. In speech and manner he lacks the charm of the average, harmless, genial, grinning southern darky. ... He acted like an earlier missing link in the human species.
>
> (Wright 1991: 706)

Amplifying and encouraging the charged rhetoric of the press and the hysteria of the populace is the State's Attorney Buckley who represents the city's power structure and its justice system. For as Buckley warns Bigger in his cell, "You're dealing with the *law* now!" (Wright 1991: 728; emphasis in original). Here the full irony implied by Buckley's re-election poster, which Bigger saw earlier, becomes more apparent: "IF YOU BREAK THE LAW, YOU CAN'T WIN!" Thanks to Bigger breaking the law and losing his case and life, it is Buckley who will win—another election. A shrewd tactician as well as a demagogue, Buckley elicits a confession from Bigger by letting him hear the mob outside the jail ("Those people would like to lynch you."), frightening him with accusations that he committed other crimes, and then pretending to sympathize with him: "I know how you feel, boy. You're colored and you feel you haven't had a square deal, don't you?" (Wright 1991: 728, 733). In court, however, Buckley shows neither sympathy nor mercy as he demands the death penalty with a series of ferocious racist diatribes. Though he sanctimoniously extols the law as "holy" and "sacred," the "foundation of all our cherished values. ... because it makes us human" (Wright 1991: 829), he deliberately arouses white fears and hatred by echoing the dehumanizing vocabulary of the media when he calls Bigger a "maddened ape" (Wright 1991: 832), and he explicitly proclaims himself the agent of the mob howling outside the courtroom when he tells the judge:

> "It is not often ... that a representative of the people finds the masses of the citizens who elected him to office standing literally at his back, waiting for him to enforce the law. ... " The room was quiet as a tomb. Buckley strode to the window and with one motion of his hand hoisted it up. The rumbling mutter of the vast mob swept in. ... .
> "Kill 'im now!"
> "Lynch 'im!"
>
> (Wright 1991: 794)

Bigger has already pleaded guilty to causing the death of Mary and the premeditated killing of his girlfriend, Bessie. His attorney, Boris Max, has already explicitly said he will not claim Bigger was not guilty by reason of insanity. The trial is being held only so that the judge can decide if there are mitigating circumstances that will justify giving Bigger life imprisonment rather than a capital sentence.[3] Nevertheless, Buckley does everything he can to guarantee that that decision will be made on the grounds of emotion and prejudice rather than in the rational manner that is supposed to prevail in a rule-of-law justice system based on the norms of the public sphere. In an absurd exercise of legal overkill, he calls 60 witnesses—police officers, schoolteachers, almost everyone who has seen or known Bigger—to testify that he is guilty and "sane." In his speeches he uses the word "black" with obsessive frequency to suggest the racial overtones of the case. Bigger, he says, is guilty of "black crimes" (Wright 1991: 435), a "half-human black ape," a "black mad dog," who has committed a "black and awful deed"; and that "[e]very decent white man in America ought to swoon with joy for the opportunity to crush with his heel the woolly head of this black lizard" (Wright 1991: 829–35).

Finally, even though most of Mary's corpse was burned to ashes so no evidence of rape can be found, Buckley, like Chicago's newspapers, emphasizes that alleged part of Bigger's crimes that is sexual and therefore most sensational and likely to arouse white fears and a desire for revenge: "He burned the body to get rid of evidences of *rape*! ... He killed her because he *raped* her! Mind you, Your Honor, the central crime here is *rape*!" (Wright 1991: 833; emphasis in original). Bois Max's appeal to reason, as he well knows, is virtually hopeless, and it is scarcely surprising when the judge sentences Bigger to death, after acknowledging that "In view of the unprecedented disturbance of the public mind the duty of this court is clear" (Wright 1991: 837). In other words, his decision is based on his "duty" to appease the mob outside the courtroom that is howling for Bigger's death, since the "public mind" in *Native Son* is racist and intolerant and has created a society in which inequality is rampant, the rights of minorities are ignored, and the rule of law can be trumped by hysteria.

Considered in other contexts, Richard Wright's Bigger Thomas takes on additional significance. Created near the end of the depression Bigger is an example of that era's fascination with what might be called symbolic or celebrity criminals. Both factual and fictional, this was a rogue's galley that included John Dillinger, Bonnie and Clyde, Jimmy Cagney's *Public Enemy* (1931), and Humphrey Bogart's Duke Mantee in Robert Sherwood's *The Petrified Forest* (1936), who were seen as rebels as well as criminals, because they defied society as well as broke its laws.[4] But as an African-American criminal/rebel Bigger occupies a special status. Created near the midpoint of the long journey of African-Americans striving for equality in the United States—after Uncle Tom but before Martin Luther King, Jr., well after Plessey vs. Ferguson, but before Brown vs. Board of Education and Obama vs. McCain—Bigger revealed the anger and the resistance to the second-class citizenship that was instituted by Plessey. Critic Irving Howe summed up the situation very well when he commented in 1961 that Wright's *Native Son* and his other writings had made him "the American Negro novelist who would speak without hesitation, who for the first time would tell the truth not only about the familiar sufferings of his people but about their varied responses, those inner feelings of anger and hatred which no white man could reach." By doing this, Howe said, Wright "told us the one thing even the most liberal and well-disposed whites prefer not to hear: that Negroes were far from patient or forgiving, that they were scarred by fear and hated every moment of their humiliation" (Howe 1961: 62).

Fear and hatred are powerful emotions, and though they govern much of Bigger's behavior in the novel they do not wholly explain or justify it. And Bigger himself is too inarticulate, confused, and poorly educated to perform that task himself in any public way, as he is himself well aware. After he is captured and while he is enduring the ordeals of the Grand Jury inquest and his trial, he is prey to intense feelings of despair and hope, rebellion and acute indifference. But his most persistent and significant thoughts are derived from his efforts to comprehend and communicate his own feelings. "Yet he knew that the moment he tried to put his feelings into words, his tongue would not move" (Wright 1991: 786). Therefore, since he cannot tell his own story, Bigger knows others will tell it for him, and what will be told about his trial and execution will demonstrate the power of white society to crush any Black person who rebels against its laws and taboos, and he deeply resents this. "It was not their hate he felt; it was something deeper than that," Wright's narrative persona explains as Bigger looks at the white crowd watching him before the Grand Jury inquest at the beginning of Book Three.

> He sensed that in their attitude toward him they had gone beyond hate. He heard in the sound of their voices a patient certainty; he saw their eyes gazing at him with calm conviction. Though he could not have put it into words, he felt that not only had they resolved to put him to death, but that they ... regarded him as a figment of that black world which they feared and were anxious to keep under control. ... they were going to use his death as a symbol of fear to wave before the eyes of that black world. And as he felt it, rebellion rose in him.
>
> (Wright 1991: 702–3)

Bigger will not willingly be reduced to a "figment" or a "symbol of fear." This stubborn sense of his individual worth and significance, conjoined with the racial reasons for his dilemma (which he understands very well), spark him into an interior resistance. He is not articulate enough to be a Vautrin, justifying himself and his crimes before a judge or the police. He does not speak at all at the inquest, and his statements at his trial are limited to a few stammered words. "Y-y-yessuh; I understand," he whispers in response to the judge's questions (Wright 1991: 793). So his rebellion must occur in his mind or in his cell when he speaks to characters such as Jan, Max, and the Reverend Hammond; and much of that rebellion lies in his efforts to find the "words" to understand himself in his own mind.

But even though Bigger may lack the words he needs to explain himself to others, other characters in the novel do not have that handicap. Boris Max, his lawyer, and Buckley, the State's Attorney, are especially loquacious as they portray Bigger in the contexts of their respective ideologies.

Speaking for the racist right in the novel are an unnamed Mississippi editor and Buckley who see Bigger strictly as a criminal, and a particularly despicable one, who must be destroyed to keep Chicago safe and civilized for white people. Buckley shrewdly recognizes that what motivates Bigger and determines much of his behavior is the fear inculcated in him by his Mississippi upbringing. After the State's Attorney manipulates Bigger to confess, he sneers, "Just a scared colored boy from Mississippi" (Wright 1991: 734). Why Bigger was so scared is suggested by one of the newspapers he reads containing a statement by a Jackson, Mississippi, editor advising the North that the way to keep Black men like Bigger "in their places" is to "make them know that if they so much as touch a white woman, good or bad, they cannot live." Strict segregation is also necessary with separate facilities for

> all Negroes in parks, playgrounds, cafés, theaters, and streetcars. Residential segregation is imperative. Such measures can to keep them as much as possible of direct contact with white women had lessened their attacks against them. ... Another psychological deterrent can be attained by conditioning Negroes so that they have to pay deference to the white person with whom they come in contact. This is done by regulating their speech and actions. We have found that the injection of an element of constant fear has aided us greatly.
>
> (Wright 1991: 707)

In other words, racism and lynch law "condition" Blacks to fear whites, and especially contacts with white women, in the same way that Pavlov conditioned dogs to salivate when they heard bells.

When behavior modification and segregation fail to deter men like Bigger, then other, sterner means of repression will be employed. In Bigger's case he becomes the target of both Northern and Southern forms of revenge and repression that are considered to be justice. A lynch mob is allowed to surround the courthouse, to burn a cross, and shout threats. Only the presence of two regiments of the Illinois National Guard prevents the crowd from lynching him. At the same time Buckley uses the full resources of a modern state and metropolis to guarantee that Bigger receives the death penalty. His sixty-three witnesses include professional psychologists from the University of Chicago, fifteen journalists, two schoolteachers, five doctors, and sixteen policemen, among others. For good measure Buckley incites the mob with his racist rhetoric to intimidate the judge. "If this man's life is spared," Buckley shouts at the judge, "I shall resign my office and tell those people out there in the streets I can no longer protect their lives and property. I shall tell them that our courts, swamped with mawkish sentimentality, are no longer fit instruments to safeguard the public peace! I shall tell them that we have abandoned the fight for civilization!" (Wright 1991: 795).

This Bigger, the menacing Black rapist and criminal became surprisingly and disturbingly topical during the 1980s and 1990s, and Wright's novel became prophetic. For Bigger Thomas, properly considered, might be a prototype for many young men—mostly Black and Hispanic—who were described for the past several decades in law-and-order political diatribes and the popular media as the inhabitants of a fearsome and predatory underclass. And that Wright's depiction of public attitudes toward members of that underclass is politically relevant can be seen not only from the way in which mainstream media depict the perpetrators of crimes such as rape, car-jackings, drive-by shootings, and "drug-related" homicides, but also from the outcome of the 1988 Presidential election. American voters voted in droves against Governor Michael Dukakis after they were exposed to negative campaign advertisements featuring photographs of rapist and murderer, Willy Horton, whose crimes were blamed on Dukakis's "liberalism" and whose mug shots "could have been supplied by 'central casting'" as being "emblematic of the national crime issue and a dramatic confirmation of what everybody had heard about … urban ghettos."[5] Like Horton, Bigger is a criminal whose transgressions are used to symbolize the pathologies of a society. But whereas the supporters of George H. W. Bush employed Horton as an indictment of Bush's political opponent's alleged failure to protect society from those pathologies, as embodied in Horton, Wright's leftist, anti-racist portrait of Bigger as a rebel is a means of indicting American society for creating those pathologies in the first place, for producing the Biggers and other native sons that it so fears.

Besides American racism and its influence on Bigger, Wright's analysis also considers the influence of what might be called his historical environment and conditioning that is based on class, the politics of the 1930s, and what Wright describes as the "modernity" of Bigger's situation (Wright 1991: 845–66). The 1930s was a decade of escalating civil and international violence in Germany, Ethiopia, Spain, China, and elsewhere that culminated in World War II in 1939. In the novel itself, Bigger may not know what a capitalist or a communist is (Wright 1991: 475, 494), but he can understand the crude kind of power that could give men like himself a sense of solidarity and opportunities to dominate others by violence. "Of late he had liked to hear tell of men who could rule others," says the narrative persona,

> for in actions such as these he felt that there was a way to escape from this tight morass of fear and shame that sapped at the base of his life. He liked to hear of how Japan was conquering China; of how Hitler was running the Jews to the ground; of how Mussolini was invading Spain. … He felt that some day there would be a black man who would whip the black people into a tight band and together they would act and end fear and shame.
>
> (Wright 1991: 551)

And in his 1940 pamphlet describing Native Son's origins, "How 'Bigger' Was Born," Wright emphasized not only how he had been influenced by his encounters with a series of rebellious young Black men but also by the idea that there were certain conditions of modern life that were creating millions of Bigger Thomases, "dispossessed and disinherited" men, "white and black, [who all] felt tense, afraid, nervous, hysterical, and restless." "From far away Nazi Germany and old Russia," Wright says, "had come to me items of knowledge that told me that certain modern experiences were creating types of personalities whose existence ignored racial and national lines of demarcation" (Wright 1991: 865). These were "modern" men and women, Wright argues, who were attracted to revolution or extreme forms of nationalism—such as Nazism and Japanese militarism—because they were

> living in a world whose fundamental assumptions could no longer be taken for granted: a world ridden with national and class strife; a world whose metaphysical meanings had vanished; a world in which God no longer existed. ... a highly geared world whose nature was conflict and action ... Speaking figuratively, they were [like] chronic alcoholics, men who lived by violence, through extreme action and sensation, through drowning daily in a perpetual nervous agitation.
>
> (Wright 1991: 865–66)

Despite these "potentialities," as Wright was quick to acknowledge (Wright 1991: 521), it was unlikely that a Bigger Thomas growing up in the Chicago ghetto would become either a Fascist or a Communist (like Wright himself). On the other hand, it was also unlikely that persons with these pathologies would be devoted to values such as law and order or democracy and stability. Speaking through Bigger's lawyer, Boris Max, he warns that, executing one lone sociopath, or even hundreds of them, will not make white America any more secure. Bigger is only one of America's millions of Black people who live under similar conditions and can scarcely be expected to respect this nation's laws, since "once you see them as a whole, once your eyes leave the individual. ... [you see] they are not simply twelve million people; in reality they constitute a separate nation, stunted, stripped, and held captive within this nation, devoid of political, social, economic, and property rights" (Wright 1991: 463; emphasis in original). Developing and modifying the ideas about right- and left-wing radicalism that Wright would soon state in "How 'Bigger' Was Born," Max also warns that the conditions that make Bigger feel baffled and deprived have afflicted

> millions of others, Negro and white, and that is what makes our future seem a looming image of violence. The feeling of resentment and the balked longing for some kind of fulfilment and exultation ... stalk day by day through this land. The consciousness of Bigger Thomas, and millions of others more or less like him, white and black ... form the quicksands upon which the foundations of our civilization rest. Who knows when some slight shock ... shall send the skyscrapers in our cities toppling? Does that sound fantastic?
>
> (Wright 1991: 823)

In Max's warning, the rage and ressentiment intuited by Twain, which covertly motivated Tom Driscoll's attacks on the security of Dawson's Landing in *Pudd'nhead Wilson,* have become overt and apocalyptic in scale, and they motivate the rage of white as well as Black Americans who feel themselves to be outcast and frustrated. Read with the benefit of hindsight, Max's jeremiad is disturbingly close to prophecy. What Wright, through Max, is saying anticipates underclass and minority race riots and the Kerner reports issued in reaction to them in later decades and thus applies to America's Bigger Thomases and Willy Hortons. It may also apply to High School massacres; skinhead hate crimes; postal workers who kill co-workers; home-grown terrorists who, inspired by conspiracy theories, destroy federal buildings; and foreign ones who literally topple skyscrapers.

Chapter 8

State terrorism and revenge in André Brink's *A Dry White Season*

"I was speechless, because now we were talking about pure terrorism. I asked him [Police Brigadier Willem Schoon] who gave the orders. He told me it came from the highest authority. I asked if this included the President [P. W. Botha], and he said yes ... "

(Eugene de Kock's reaction when ordered to destroy Cosatu House, Johannesburg, the headquarters of a labor union, in 1987. Cited in Meredith 1999: 52–53)

"Because the State has not seen fit to indict anyone for the death of Steve Biko, it becomes necessary to indict the State. ... This means that the South African government and all its supporters bear the responsibility for what happened to Steve Biko. They bear this responsibility in varying degrees. ... precisely who struck the fatal blows is relatively unimportant. ... The real killer was the [apartheid] System—and all its representatives involved in this tragedy. Two members of the South African cabinet are most responsible for the circumstances under which Steve Biko died—Police Minister J. T. Kruger and Premier B.J. Vorster."

(Donald Woods's reaction to the inquest that exonerated the Security Policemen who killed Steve Biko in 1977. Woods 1978: 355–56)

De Kock and Woods represent polar opposites of the white political spectrum in South Africa's apartheid era. De Kock, a Colonel in the Security

Police, was one of the most ruthless and deadly defenders of apartheid. Involved in over seventy killings in South Africa and neighboring countries, he was sentenced to two life sentences, plus 212 years for a wide assortment of crimes in 1996 (Meredith 1999: 54). Woods, a liberal newspaper editor, was a personal friend and admirer of Steve Biko. When he received a banning order after Biko's death in 1977, he fled into exile in England where he became an anti-apartheid activist. Yet de Kock and Woods might agree on one thing: that in order to defend and implement apartheid the South African government's security forces, including its highest officials, had crossed over the line dividing legality from illegality and become a criminal, terrorist organization.

Confronted by Black African resistance to apartheid, which ranged from peaceful demonstrations and work stoppages to terrorist attacks, the South African government, which was dominated by the Afrikaners' National Party (NP), became increasingly violent and repressive, and its enemies in the African National Congress (ANC), the South African Communist Party (SACP), and the Pan-African Congress (PAC) retaliated in kind by resorting to sabotage, terrorism, and other forms of "armed struggle." The Sharpeville massacre in 1960 and the ANC leadership's 1961 founding of its armed wing, Umkhonto weSizwe (MK—Spear of the Nation), the Soweto school riots and the murder of Steve Biko in 1976–77, the ANC attacks on the Vortekkerhoogte military base and the Koeberg nuclear power plant in 1981 and 1982, the bombing of the ANC's London headquarters by South African security forces in 1982, the ANC's car bomb attack on the headquarters of the South African Air Force in Pretoria in 1983, and the government's destruction of Cosatu House in 1987—these are only a short list of the cycles of attacks, uprisings, revenges, and retaliations that the government and its enemies inflicted in their "total onslaughts" upon one another. Eventually the leadership of both sides recognized how deadly this process had become, and when a peace settlement was finally negotiated by the ANC and the NP, they agreed in the country's new constitution that the reconstruction of their "deeply divided society" depended not only on their willingness to eschew violence but their overcoming "a legacy of hatred, fear, guilt and revenge."

During its struggle to sustain apartheid, the South African government, when it was ruled by the NP, made that nation an almost perfect example of what Ernst Fraenkel called a Dual State with two legal systems. Of course, ever since it was created in 1910, South Africa had been a deeply divided nation both politically and racially. The ruling white minority was divided politically by the Afrikaners' bitter memories of how their independent republics had been destroyed in the Anglo-Boer War, when they had been forced to join the British Empire. "These people—my forebears—understood oppression," F. W. De Klerk said in the NP's "Submission to the Truth and Reconciliation Commission" (TRC) in 1993. "During their freedom struggle their homes were burned, their country was devastated and more than

20,000 of their women and children died in concentration camps"; they "understood resistance" as they "withstood British attempts to strip them of their culture," and they understood "poverty and deprivation" when the depression and drought drove them from their farms into cities during the 1930s (De Klerk 1993).

But even though the Afrikaners might have understood oppression and poverty, their politicians were only too willing to cooperate with their British counterparts and impose these conditions on Black South Africans. Between 1910 and 1948 white legislators of both groups passed an assortment of laws discriminating against their country's Black African, Colored (mixed race), and Asian (Indian) populations—such as the 1913 Land Act, the 1923 Urban Areas Act, the Color Bar Act of 1926, the 1936 Representation of Natives Act, and the 1946 Asiatic Land Tenure Act. But when it took power in 1948, the NP's racism was even more virulent and explicit. Its election slogan, for example, was, "*Die kaffer op sy plek; die koelies uit die land*"—"The kaffir [nigger] in his place; the coolies [Indians] out of the country" (Mandela 1996). In 1948, therefore, South Africa's patch work of de jure and de facto discriminations began to become completely and rapidly de jure (Mandela 1996). Though it had been elected that year with only a small parliamentary majority, the NP passed a plethora of laws implementing and expanding apartheid. In 1950 it also began to adopt a long sequence of national security laws designed to criminalize and crush resistance to apartheid. It was at this point that South Africa began to become a Dual State legally as well as a divided society racially.[1]

Persons who accepted and obeyed the apartheid system with its white dominance and racial inequities were ruled by a conventional, normative justice system based on the rule of law; those who actively resisted or criticized apartheid, including whites, might be treated by security forces with "unlimited arbitrariness and violence" (Fraenkel 1941: xiii), including harassment, murder and torture. Or they also might be prosecuted for crimes such as treason in elaborate and lengthy show trials in which they were sometimes, somewhat to their own surprise, found innocent instead of joining Nelson Mandela and his colleagues on Robben Island for lengthy prison terms.

By the 1970s and 1980s this divided justice system, as described by Adam Hochschild, had become a capricious and

> contradictory amalgam. The government routinely tortures thousands of prisoners ... and, in times of crisis, keeps thousands of them in preventive detention for months at a time. Yet at the same time the British legal tradition and the Afrikaners' Germanic love of order mean there is an elaborate network of magistrates in white cravats and lawyers in black robes, of hearings, writs, stays, and appeals. ... It is entirely up to the government's whim whether it decides to lock someone up in preventive

> detention [and usually torture them], or charge the same person with
> something and have a full-dress trial.
>
> (Hochschild 1990: 179)

Besides the fears and uncertainties generated by its capricious justice system,
the apartheid government (or "elements" within it) was also willing to resort
to a variety of criminal acts to silence, intimidate, or "eliminate" its enemies.
Compared to these "elements," Forster's Anglo-Indians are mere bigots and
Buckley in *Native Son* is only a demagogue, whereas many of apartheid's
defenders were full-fledged felons and murderers. Thus, there were burglaries, fire bombings, and gunshots at the homes and offices of political
activists, the officials of unions and student groups, Black newspaper editors
and reporters, and church officials. In addition, there were mysterious
explosions, like the one at Cosatu House carried out by de Kock and his
team, and mysterious accidents, like the one that kills Ben Du Toit in *A Dry
White Season*. And all of these criminal or extralegal acts then had to be
covered up or at least partially concealed so that their perpetrators, and the
higher officials who gave them orders, could not be identified or face legal
action.

For one of the significant features of state terrorism—whether practiced by
the Nazis in the 1930s, by the Chilean military in the 1970s, or by the
South African police and military during the apartheid era—is its semi-
clandestine quality. Anti-state terrorists, such as Timothy McVeigh, the Red
Brigades, or the men who destroyed the World Trade Center, attack the rule
of law by operating outside and against a nation's criminal law system. They
destabilize the public sphere and seek maximum publicity by sending messages to the media or by choosing symbolic targets or victims such as the
World Trade Center, the Murrah Building, or the politicians and executives
kidnapped in Europe in the 1970s and 1980s. State terrorists, in contrast,
subvert the rule of law by operating *within* their nation's legal system in a
covert manner with the implicit support of their superiors. Crimes such as
murder and torture are committed, usually by military or police units, but
they are concealed by cover-ups, propaganda, and censorship that vitiate the
public sphere. Nevertheless, rumors and censored media reports produce an
environment of fear, terror, and intimidation that helps the government
maintain power without identifying perpetrators in ways that would make
them accountable for their criminal acts. This process then, in turn, creates
an additional web of complicity entangling lawyers, doctors, government
officials, journalists, and ordinary citizens who know or suspect what is
really happening in police stations and detention centers but are afraid or
unwilling to publicize it.

To protect itself from its own normative legal system, the South African
government also created what one churchman described, in a related context, as a "suffocating fog of silence and lies."[2] The "fog" surrounding

preventive detention (a.k.a. detention without trial, detention for purposes of interrogation) was especially pernicious. Grafted onto the South African legal system in 1963 by the General Law Amendment Act and later Acts in that decade, preventive detention eliminated habeas corpus. It allowed the police to detain persons they believed involved with activities such as terrorism, sabotage, and subversion for as long as the police wished to interrogate them. Courts were specifically forbidden to order their release, and though magistrates could see them under strictly prescribed and limited conditions, they had no access to lawyers or anyone else beside the police.

Persons detained under these laws, therefore, were totally under the control of the police. When some of them began dying under suspicious circumstances so it appeared they had been choked or beaten to death, these events harshly contradicted efforts by the government to portray South Africa as a bastion of civilization protecting itself against hordes of Black barbarians, terrorists, and communists. So the police resorted to crude and unconvincing explanations. They claimed prisoners died after falling and hitting their heads on desks or walls; they fell down steps, or they committed suicide by hanging themselves or jumping out of windows. Or it was alleged that prisoners had escaped when actually the police had killed them and destroyed their corpses with fire or explosives.[3] Moreover, as D. P. de Villiers, an eminent South African jurist explained in 1983, a key characteristic of virtually all actions taken under the security laws "was the veil of official secrecy drawn over the reasons for specific bannings and detentions, as well as about what exactly happened during detentions, particularly those for interrogations." Until the mid-1970s, says de Villiers, the South African government was able to keep this veil intact without undue difficulty. "Queries, criticisms, or objections ... were rejected by government spokesmen as politically unloyal ... and based on an ignorance of the critical facts known only to an inner circle of informed officials. ... Ordinary legal processes were said to be inadequate because of intimidation of witnesses, the need to protect informers, secret methods of investigation, and the need to act [against] potential saboteurs *before* they struck."[4] This situation changed dramatically after the 1976–77 school riots that began in Soweto and immediately spread throughout South Africa. According to official and unofficial estimates, between 618 and over 1,000 persons were killed in pitched battles with the police, and over 5,000 were injured. Four hundred and thirty schools, 184 government beer halls, and 124 administration buildings were destroyed or burned down, and more than 21,000 people were arrested for offenses such as arson and unlawful or riotous assembly (Price 1991: 48). The number of persons dying in police custody rose rapidly in 1977—by September when Steve Biko was killed the toll for that year was already 45—and Biko's death itself created a storm of outrage in South Africa and other nations.[5]

Because of Biko's intelligence and charismatic leadership abilities, his murder was a special, symbolic crime that deeply angered millions of South Africans, including whites as well as Blacks and those who disapproved of his politics as well as those who were his followers. The government's response to that anger only worsened the situation. Instead of either punishing Biko's killers or offering more plausible reasons why he and so many other prisoners had died while being interrogated, the government reacted—five weeks after Biko's death—with Draconian efforts to regain control of the public sphere by slamming it shut. In mid-October the Vorster government

> sent shock waves around the world by taking massive security measures, which included the closure of two Black newspapers ... and of *Pro Veritate*, the publication of the Christian Institute, the detention of the editor of the two Black newspapers ... the banning of another newspaper editor, Mr. Donald Woods ... and of an eminent dissenting Afrikaans religious leader, Dr. Beyers Naude, the director of the Christian Institute, the prescription of 18 different organizations, and the detention and banning of a long list of other people.
>
> (de Villiers 1983: 404)

This response precipitated a new crisis. In South Africa itself, says de Villiers, even the NP's own followers' "boundless trust" in their government's rectitude was shaken, and it was clear in retrospect that that government had "seriously underestimated the enduring concerns its actions would create over a broad spectrum of intellectual circles ... cut[ting] right across party-political allegiances" (de Villiers 1983: 405). Abroad, in the international public sphere, the violent repression of the school riots and the Biko case further damaged South Africa's reputation and was a major step toward it becoming a pariah state—"the skunk of the world" as Nelson Mandela and others called it. By the early 1980s, two South African academics commented dryly, their nation had become "one of the most unusual states in the modern world: the international community hesitates to accept its identity, refuses to accept the legitimacy of its government, and ... implicitly denies its sovereignty."[6] In addition, the circumstances of Biko's death and the government's suppression of the school riots and protests exacerbated the cycles of actions and reactions, of resistance and repression that had plagued South Africa since the 1950s (de Villiers 1983: 397). The government continued to adopt more and more repressive laws, to proclaim more states of emergency and attacks on its enemies, and to arrest, detain, and torture thousands more of its citizens. The ANC and its allies (e.g., the Communist Party, the United Democratic Front) worked harder to organize more protests and work stoppages and to recruit militants whom it trained in camps in nearby countries to become guerilias, saboteurs, and terrorists.

It was in this political climate that André Brink wrote and published *A Dry White Season*, his novel about police violence, preventive detention, and state terrorism. Begun shortly before Biko's death in 1977 and completed in 1979 (Brink 1996: 17), it can be seen as an attempt to present in fictional form the truths about preventive detention (and the political crisis it had fomented) that the government had prevented from appearing in factual form with its October 1977 bannings, detentions, and newspaper closures. It is Brink's attempt to pierce the "veil of secrecy" and cover-ups the South African government was using to try to conceal the crimes of its own security forces and the culpability of high officials, including its President.

Considered as a justice story, *A Dry White Season* can be classified as a kind of Romantic thriller, albeit a pessimistic one. Its main character, Ben Du Toit, is an Afrikaner history teacher who becomes radicalized when a Black janitor at his school, Gordon Ngubene, dies while in police custody, a supposed suicide. Outraged by the results of the inquest that—like Steve Biko's—exonerates the police, Du Toit pits himself against the apartheid state and its security forces in an increasingly isolated quest for the truth about Ngubene's death. As this quest becomes more dangerous and frustrating, he also becomes motivated by a desire for revenge, by the hope that, as he tells one of his daughters, some day, "we'll have all of Gordon's murderers lined up against a wall" (Brink 1984: 202). More of a Don Quixote than a Lancelot in his wife's opinion (Brink 1984: 70), he interviews witnesses and doctors, collects affidavits and other documents, and eventually has his suspicions publicized in an English-language newspaper. All of these acts bring Ben to the increasingly hostile attention of the Special Branch police who harass, terrorize, blackmail, and eventually—the novel hints heavily—kill him in a faked hit-and-run car accident.

Before he dies, however, Ben sends a packet of notes, documents, photos, and diaries to the novel's frame narrator, an old college friend, because he happens to be a professional writer and editor—of "popular novels," mainly romances for women whom he describes chauvinistically as his "few thousand housewives and typists" (Brink 1984: 11). Brink portrays his anonymous frame narrator—a genial, apolitical man—as confused and concerned by the changes in his friend's personality. In their brief meeting, before the documents were sent, Ben was rude, nervous, and suspicious, almost paranoid. In the early pages of the novel's "Foreword" the narrator muddles along trying to make connections between the disturbing Ben who's just died and the Ben he'd known in college and afterwards. What had transformed him from a "nice chap" who had seemed "an ordinary, good-natured, harmless, unremarkable man" (Brink 1984: 9) into an angry, obsessed loner who dies under suspicious circumstances?

Then the frame narrator encounters an event that (though he does not fully recognize it) dramatically reveals the larger significance of Ben's lonely search for justice. On the day of Ben's funeral he is in downtown

Johannesburg near the Supreme Court. Suddenly he realizes the normal urban noise has stopped, as has the flow of traffic, and everywhere people are standing still until they see that:

> Down from the [train] station a slow wall of people were approaching in the street pushing the silence ahead of them: a dull, irresistible phalanx of blacks. There was no shouting, no noise at all. But the front lines were marching with raised clenched fists. ... We whites ... began to edge toward the reassurance of walls and pillars. No-one spoke or made a sudden gesture. All action was delayed. ... It was only later I realised that judgment had been set for that day in one of the numerous terrorism trials of these recent months; and this crowd was on its way from Soweto in order to be present at the verdict.
>
> They never arrived, though. While we were still standing there police sirens started wailing and from all directions vans and armoured vehicles converged.
>
> (Brink 1984: 19)

The city square or forum—that is supposed to be a major part of the public sphere, a place where rational negotiations and decisions are made at financial institutions, businesses, and government agencies—has become mute and paralyzed in a defacto racial civil war. Its inhabitants, Black and white, are trapped in a cycle of resistance and repression: the ANC Black Power clenched fists vs. the police sirens and vans. The Blacks are angry and militant, the whites are fearful and huddle together, the two groups separated by a silent abyss of antagonism until it is shattered by the police sirens that have replaced rational discourse. Ben Du Toit tries to bridge that abyss by showing that a white man, even a Boer or *lanie*, could care about justice for a Black man. "I just want justice. Is that too much to ask?" he exclaims midway through the novel (Brink 1984: 145). In South Africa in the 1970s, the answer is "yes," and because Du Toit dares to question a Special Branch cover-up, he is murdered.

But though Ben is the main character in the novel, he does not completely dominate it. *A Dry White Season* is a family drama as well as a thriller, and it is much concerned with the fates of two families: the Du Toits (white, Afrikaner, middle-class) and the Ngubenes (Black and working-class). The years since apartheid was institutionalized were good ones for the Du Toits. Ben's father-in-law, a rich farmer, is an NP MP; Ben's wife Susan has a good job with South African Broadcasting; his daughter Suzette is on the staff of a glossy interior design magazine; and her husband is an up-and-coming young architect who has begun to get contracts from the provincial government. Even the unambitious Ben has benefited from the government's largesse: he was able to attend a university because he received a scholarship. For the Ngubenes the times have been harder. Forced to leave school to support his family after his father was killed in a mining accident, Gordon worked at a variety of menial jobs in the city. Then he tried to live in the country in his family's village and hated it—planting maize, "scouring the veld with a lean dog in search of hares for meat, sitting in the sun in front of the hut" (Brink 1984: 38). Returning to the city and Soweto he marries, has children, and becomes a janitor at Ben's school.

Before their troubles with police began, the relationship between the two families was traditional and paternalistic. Ben loans Ngubene small sums of money, acts as his protector and advisor when he has troubles, and helps him send his son, Jonathan, to school. In return Gordon and Jonathan do chores for Ben like wash his car and help him garden. Then Jonathan is arrested during one of the Soweto school riots, dies afterward, and the Ngubenes receive wildly contradictory accounts of his death—that he had been in a hospital badly injured, that he died of natural causes, and finally that he allegedly had been killed on the day of the riot and had never been in police custody at all, though the medical report ascertaining this is "not available" (Brink 1984: 47). Du Toit responds by discouraging Ngubene's efforts to find out the truth about his son's death, advising him not to do anything reckless (Brink 1984: 48). Then, when Gordon insists on trying to discover the truth about his son's death and is detained, Ben promptly goes to the police to assure them that his friend is a "decent, honest man" who'd never do anything unlawful: the white *Baas* dutifully vouching for a good servant or employee.

In an earlier South Africa Ben's journey to John Vorster Square might have helped secure Gordon's release. But by the 1970s the Special Branch no longer follows the old paternalistic rules. Gordon is tortured and dies under suspicious circumstances, and both families—the Du Toits as well as the Ngubenes—are destroyed after Ben becomes obsessed by Gordon's case and begins collecting documents and interviewing witnesses. Seen from this perspective, *A Dry White Season* is the antithesis of a more conservative and politically conventional thriller, Alfred Hitchcock's *The Man Who Knew Too Much* (1934, 1955). In both versions of that film, the nation state and a middle-class family are menaced by foreign spies who kidnap a child so the child's father will not reveal their conspiratorial plans. Since the nation's security forces are not very effective, the family must act themselves to rescue the child and thwart the spies' plans. Family values and patriotic values are fused as the family both save themselves and become, in effect, the nation's surrogate protectors. In Brink's novel, on the other hand, the Ngubene and Du Toit families are harmed by insiders, their nation's own police, not by evil outsiders or foreign spies. However, since South Africa was a divided society racially as well as legally, the destructive process is different for the two families.

For the Black Ngubenes, it is crude, overt, and harsh. Captain Stolz and his team from the Special Branch arrest Gordon in the middle of the night.

"They knocked so loud we were stiff with fright," Gordon's wife Emily tells Ben.

> "Before Gordon could open for them they kicked down the door ... They turn over the whole house, Baas. ... they roll up the carpet, they tear open the mattress, they throw out the drawers of the cupboard. ... And then they start to beat Gordon and to push him around ... they say: 'You come with us, Kaffir!' ... one man he say to me: 'Ja, better say good-bye to him. You not going to see him again.'"
>
> (Brink 1984: 53)

Even though Ben is probably more troublesome to the Special Branch than Gordon was, the destructive process for the white Du Toits is more complex and sophisticated, almost polite. Ben is not arrested, tortured, and strangled with a wet towel as Gordon was, presumably by Captain Stolz. Instead, Colonel Viljoen gives him discrete warnings and Stolz gives him sterner ones. Then, when Stolz and his men search Ben's house, they arrive in the afternoon, knock on the door with a warrant, wait for Ben to admit them, and the Captain introduces his men formally: "They looked like a group of rugby players waiting for a bus," Ben decides, "all washed and shaven ... all of them beaming with good health, exemplary young men, probably the fathers of small children; one could imagine them accompanying their wives to shop in supermarkets." When Ben's wife Susan enters the room, the Captain apologizes for needing to search their house for incriminating documents: "Sorry about the inconvenience," he tells her (Brink 1984: 152, 153).

Stolz's manners are polite, but he does not shirk what he considers his responsibilities. "If we have reason to suspect that you're hiding anything from us, we'll be back," he warns. "We can turn this whole house upside down if we want to" (Brink 1984: 157). Ben's phone is tapped, he is kept under surveillance, and his mail is read. When these "petty intimidations" (Brink 1984: 223) fail, and Ben persists in his efforts to discover the truth, the police resort to blackmail and other forms of harassment that soon become a covert kind of terrorism. And—in the end—the process is as relentless and lethal as that which killed Gordon Ngubene. Ben's colleagues and pupils are incited against him, and eventually he is fired from his teaching job. Someone cuts up the tires of his car, fires shots into his house, makes anonymous phone calls at three o'clock in the morning, and sends him a letter bomb. Ben's wife's contract with SABC is not renewed, and her mental health and their marriage, both already shaky, collapse. His lover Melanie's passport is revoked, and she is forced into exile. He becomes estranged from his daughters, and one of them tries to help the police find his hidden evidence and documents. His good friend and ally, Stanley Makhaya, a Zulu cab driver, flees to Swaziland. Only Ben's young son, Johan, continues to stand by him until Ben dies in the hit-and-run accident, reported on page four of the evening newspaper, so that presumably only the frame narrator knows the significance of his death.

The fates of the two families are also influenced by two intermediary figures both of whom—in very different ways—can be considered carnivalistic characters: Stolz and Stanley Makhaya, a Zulu cab driver who helps Ben in his search for evidence about Gordon Ngubene's death. Stolz acts as the intermediary between the apartheid state and the two families. As we mentioned earlier, inversion is a carnivalistic motif, and Stolz turns the Du Toits' and the Ngubenes' homes and lives "upside down," both literally and metaphorically (Brink 1984: 53, 157). He is the enforcer who arrests and tortures Gordon and who searches Ben's house, tries to blackmail him, and gives him his final warning before he is killed. A dualistic character, Stolz is polite, almost gracious in his dealings with the Du Toits, and Ben refers to his behavior and manners with words such as "civilized," "congenial," "friendly," and "casual" (Brink 1984: 156, 206–7). But this is only Stolz's public mask. In testimony at Gordon's inquest a young woman, who had recently been detained, describes how Stolz had beaten her with a sjambok, kicked her, made her lick up her own blood from the floor, and choked her with a towel repeatedly until she was unconscious, saying once, "Come on ... speak up. Or do you want to die like Gordon Ngubene?" (Brink 1984: 113).

Stanley Makhaya is a more traditional and flamboyant type of carnivalistic figure. After Gordon's arrest and death he acts as the intermediary between the two families, bringing news from Soweto and Gordon's wife Emily into Ben's white neighborhood and ferrying Ben to the Black township where Ben could not travel himself. With his bellowing, explosive laughter, his irreverent attitudes, and his township *tsotsis* (hoodlum) slang, Stanley is a chthonic character who could have stepped out of the pages of Bakhtin's *Rabelais and His World* (1984), or out of one of Rabelais's own works. A shady but not a sinister figure, Stanley operates his gypsy cab on both sides of the law, and he specializes in giving people what they need to survive in the townships.

> You get a bloke *pasa'd* by the tsotsis, so you pick him up and take him home. ... you get one passed out from *atshitshi:* same thing. ... Others looking for *phata-phata* ... so you find them a *skarapafet.* A whore. ... You pick them up, you listen to their sob stories, you're their bank when they need some *magageba.* ... you're the first to know when the *gattes* are coming on a raid, so you can warn your pals.
>
> (Brink 1984: 84)

A dualistic antithesis to Stolz—who is thin, polite, and brings death to the two families—Stanley is obese, rude, and tries to bring rebirth. When Ben becomes depressed and frustrated, Stanley offers to revive him by taking him to a "solid *stokvel*" that will last from Friday to Sunday, a party "where you dance non-stop until you pass out. Then we bring you round with *popla* [booze] and we push some meat down your throat and there you go again. ... by the time you get to Sunday night ... we just hang you out with the washing for a week, and then you're a new man. Born again" (Brink 1984: 252).

As a defender of apartheid, Stolz can be considered a kind of successor to the nineteenth-century Afrikaner *voortrekkers* who believed it was their religious and historical destiny to rule South Africa by subjugating its native inhabitants. Stanley, however, is specifically referred to by Ben as looking like Dingane, the Zulu king who was the *voortrekkers'* most formidable enemy (Brink 1984: 53), and he lives for the day when apartheid will end. Then, he tells Ben, "I won't have to dodge your neighbours' fucking dogs at night no more. We'll walk out here in broad daylight together, man. ... Arm-in-arm, I tell you. Right through the world, lanie. ... And no bastard to stop us saying: 'Hey, where's that domboek [passbook]?'"[7] Stanley and Stolz can also be seen as related in a dualistic way because Ben feels a sort of kinship with both of them, including Stolz. His kinship with Stanley is easily explained. Both are country boys who have shared memories of growing up in rural South Africa and learned to survive in Johannesburg. Both are outraged by Gordon's death and the inquest cover-up and are determined to discover the truth. Both are opposed to apartheid and try to subvert it: Ben because of its injustices and his desire to punish Gordon's killers, Stanley because he wants his children to have a better life than his own. ("I'm only as free as the white bosses allow me to be. ... But what about my children?" [Brink 1984: 98]). As for Stolz, even though he and Ben are enemies, near the end of the novel and at their last meeting, Ben has an epiphany after he refuses to shake the Captain's hand. Then he is amazed by "the discovery that there was no anger against the man left in him. He almost, momentarily, felt sorry for him. *You're a prisoner just like me. The only difference is that you don't know it*" (Brink 1984: 282; emphasis in original).

What is imprisoning both men is the apartheid system, the NP's policy of segregation and white/Afrikaner supremacy that Nelson Mandela described as being "diabolical in its detail, inescapable in its reach, and overwhelming in its power" (Mandela 1996). Under this system justice meant that, starting in 1948 with the NP's electoral victory when, as Ben's father-in-law tells him, "we have at long last come to power in our own land," South Africa must be dominated by the Afrikaners (Brink 1984: 212). Inspired by their *voortrekker* ancestors' strength and courage, their motto was, "*eie volk, eie taal, eie land*," which may be translated into political terms as "Our own people, our own language, must rule our own nation" (Mandela 1996). Like his factual counterparts, such as Eugene de Kock, Stolz is imprisoned by his willingness to commit any crime, tell any lie, that will help sustain that system for "*Volk en Vaderland*."[8] Ben is imprisoned by his inability to change that system, but in certain important respects Brink portrays him as having partially escaped from the apartheid prison.

Externally, of course, Ben is still a prisoner in the sense that he cannot escape the apartheid state's power to keep him under surveillance, tap his phone, ruin his life, and eventually kill him. Subjectively, however, his quest for justice frees him from a crucial component of the Afrikaners' communal identity that helped them justify apartheid to themselves: their *laager* mentality that made them value loyalty to "*Volk en Vaderland*" more than truth or justice (Meredith 1999: 48). Inherited from the great trek and its historical memory, this mentality elevated "*eie volk*" to the status of a Chosen People who had to assert themselves against others and respond to every crisis by circling their wagons—literally in the nineteenth century and metaphorically in the twentieth—and believing that group solidarity with the *Volk*—"their own people"—was the only way for Afrikaners to survive. When they feel "threatened and beleaguered on all sides," Brink wrote in a political essay, Afrikaners believe "the only safety [is] to be found inside the *laager* of [their] own people" (Brink 1983: 136). Elevated into an ideology and institutionalized as apartheid after 1948, the *laager* mentality repressed the positive side of the Afrikaners' communal mentality and expressed only its negative, Brink charged in one of his political essays, so that they had become driven "by [their] fear, by suspicion, by uncertainty, hence by arrogance, meanness, narrowmindedness, pigheadedness."[9]

The clearest sign of Ben's liberation from the *laager* mentality occurs midway through the novel after he has attended Gordon Ngubene's funeral and after his house has just been searched for the first time by Stolz. Ben's epiphany takes the form of a long, brooding meditation on the patriotic, sanitized version of the history of Afrikaans he has been teaching his students. In this vision of South Africa, which is essentially the same as de Klerk's "Submission" to the TRC, the great trek and the Anglo-Boer War are interpreted not merely as resistance to British imperialism but as a "persistent search for freedom" that makes the Afrikaners "the first freedom fighters of Africa," rather than oppressors (Brink 1984: 160). Ben recites the Afrikaners' paternalistic rationalizations for their racism, that it was proper and part of God's plan for Blacks to live in mud huts while whites lived in houses, that it was right for Blacks to take "our discarded clothes" as "they laid our table, brought up our children, emptied our chamber pots. ... We looked after them and valued their services and taught them the Gospel. ... But it remained a matter of 'us' and 'them'. It was a good and comfortable division ... " (Brink 1984: 162). But now he decides the traditional narrative/ myth is "not good enough. ... suddenly it's no longer adequate" (Brink 1984: 160, 163). He has begun to question the "us," the Afrikaner side of the comfortable old division. All his life he had taken it for granted that "my own people," his *Volk,* were those "speaking my language, taking the name of my God ..., sharing my history" (Brink 1984: 162), but all that has changed. Ben still considers himself an Afrikaner. Later in the novel when a Black lawyer condescendingly calls him a white liberal, he responds "fiercely," "I'm not a bloody Liberal. ... I'm an Afrikaner" (Brink 1984: 181). But after mourning Gordon Ngubene's death, attending his funeral, and trying to console his widow—and then realizing that "that mourning ... had been caused by 'my people'"—Ben must ask again, "who are 'my people' today? To whom do I owe my loyalty? There must be someone, something" (Brink 1984: 163).

There are two answers to Ben's question. The first can be gleaned from Brink's historical and political essays attacking apartheid and criticizing the NP's policies. What Afrikaners who possess their group's traditional, *laager* mentality do not realize, he suggests in those essays, is that their own history has a lively counter tradition of dissidence by a "ruggedly independent race of individuals" (Brink 1983: 15). Indeed, Hendrik Bibault, who was the first person to call himself an Afrikaner, early in the eighteenth century, could be considered an early example. An unruly young man, Bibault defied a command from the colony's governor by proclaiming, "I shall not go. I am an Afrikaner and even if the landdrost [magistrate] kills me or puts me in jail I refuse to hold my tongue."[10] In Brink's reading of South Africa's past, this counter tradition was carried on by a variety of colorful Afrikaner rebels in the early nineteenth century. There was Frederik Bezuidenhout, who defied the British colonial authorities, and his contemporary,

> the almost legendary Coenraad de Buys, outlaw and fugitive, who lived across the borders of the Colony with his black wife and deliberately and extravagantly broke all the colonial laws that came in his way. ... The very first of the Trekkers, Louis Trichardt, was himself a rather off-beat individual who allegedly smuggled guns to the Xhosas for years before he loaded his wagon.
>
> (Brink 1983: 21)

Not surprisingly, in the twentieth century Brink's "heroes' gallery of Afrikaner dissidence" is explicitly political and opposed to apartheid. It includes the Rev. Beyers Naude of The Christian Institute, who was banned after the killing of Steve Biko, and the brilliant barrister, Bram Fischer, who was sentenced to life imprisonment for his political activism. Speaking of the latter, Brink wrote, even though "'his own people' accused him of aligning himself with the enemy [Fischer] was really demonstrating that sense of justice and liberty ... which had been running in the riverbed of true Afrikanerdom for centuries."[11]

Like Bibault and Brink himself with his vigorous opposition to apartheid and censorship, these were individuals who resisted the landdrosts of their respective times. And, through his efforts to find and tell the truth about the Special Branch's crimes, Ben Du Toit also made himself part of that dissident tradition. That Du Toit should be punished for his resistance was not an anomaly. Because of his defiance, Bibault was banished from the colony. Bezuidenhout was killed by British troops sent to arrest him, and by the late twentieth century Louis Trichardt's option, to start on a trek with wagon and oxen, was not very practical—instead, one might need to crawl in the dark through a field filled with landmines to reach the Botswana border. Bram Fischer was isolated and ostracized as well as imprisoned, and the Afrikaner establishment tried to isolate the Rev. Naude in the same way but was less successful (Brink 1983: 22). As for Brink's own situation, in an angry open letter to President P. W. Botha during a State of Emergency in the mid-1980s, he acknowledged that "the very act of committing to paper this open letter to you is a crime. I can be arrested for this. And, if it happens, you may do your best that people in South Africa will not even know that I am among those ... who disappear every day. But I also know that I cannot submit to being silenced forcibly as long as I have a conscience to live with."[12] For the Afrikaner dissident, whether he defies the authorities in the eighteenth century or the twentieth, silence is not an honorable option.

The second answer to Ben's question is implied by the pattern in the second half of the novel of his quest for evidence that will reveal how Gordon Ngubene died. As a white, middle-class Afrikaner with a university degree, Ben is a member of the civil society that existed during the apartheid era. Thanks to his wife's family and its connections, he also has an entrée into the Afrikaner establishment. A logical man, whose favorite game is chess, Ben tries to exploit these connections for support and assistance in a systematic, rational way. But whenever he approaches Afrikaners, he encounters the *laager* mentality and is frustrated. The pastor of his *kerk*, his father-in-law, the NP MP, his brother-in-law who is an executive with a large corporation, the editor of an Afrikaans-language newspaper, a powerful government minister—all disappoint him. Some, like the government minister and his father-in-law, are hostile ("Are you absolutely sure you're not being manipulated by people with dubious intentions, Mr Du Toit?" "Ben, how can you side with the enemies of your people. Those who find in everything that happens ammunition to attack a freely elected government?" [Brink 1984: 253, 211]). Others, such as the editor, are apologetic ("You must realize it's fatal to plunge in right now. ... We cannot afford to put any more ammunition into the hands of our enemies" [Brink 1984: 233]). But the *laager* mindset, and even the metaphors, are the same. We are encircled by enemies; therefore, we must close ranks and not give any "ammunition" to enemies. If truth and justice can be used as "ammunition," then they must be sacrificed.

Yet at the same time, the novel also shows how other South Africans of different races and ethnic backgrounds try to resist repression and cooperate with Du Toit and his quest for justice, often at great risk to themselves. Stanley Makhaya is a Zulu; Ben's lover, Melanie, is half-Jewish, and both become exiles because of their involvement with Ben. During the Ngubene inquest, Black detainees, who had been tortured and forced to sign affidavits exonerating the police, recant their testimony in court even though they will almost certainly be tortured again for doing so. A Black policeman, Johnson Seroke, surreptitiously gives Du Toit information and is "shot dead by unknown persons" a few weeks later. An Asian (i.e., Indian) doctor, who participated in Ngubene's autopsy, noticed certain highly suspicious facts and tells Du Toit about them. The doctor promptly receives a "banning order," exiling him to a remote town in Northern Transvaal for five years. The white editor of an English-language newspaper publishes Du Toit's findings without mentioning his name and under a reporter's by-line. The Department of Justice immediately sues the paper for libel, and the "senior reporter," Richard Harrison, is sentenced to a year in prison when he will not reveal his source (Brink 1984: 119, 205–6, 234, 236, 266).

Like a tumor that metastasizes, state terrorism spreads and harms these people as it attacks and destroys the Ben Du Toits and the Gordon Ngubenes. But the damage is not confined to them. For one of the disquieting insights embedded in *A Dry White Season* is that apartheid and the state terrorism that supports it do not limit their destructiveness to victims who are real or imagined enemies of the government. They also disrupt the larger society of affluent, middle-class whites who made up South Africa's civil society in the apartheid era. This idea is embedded in two major, carnivalistic "feasts," or "scandal scenes," one near the beginning and the other near the end of the novel.

Such scenes, as we said earlier, are festive or formal gatherings that are interrupted by disruptive, irreverent, and/or obscene behavior, language, or laughter that reveals hidden tensions and injustices. Such scenes, Bakhtin claimed, are "linked to moments of crisis, of breaking points in the cycle of nature or in the life of society and man," and they may also be "moments of death and revival, of change and renewal" (Bakhtin 1984: 9). In *A Dry White Season* the first of these scenes is a dinner party that occurs when Gordon Ngubene has been detained but is still alive. Ben and his wife's guests are several of her friends from SABC, a few colleagues from Ben's school, including the Principal, and the pastor of their church. The wine and conversation are flowing smoothly when Stanley Makhaya and Emily Ngubene arrive on Ben's porch with a pair of Gordon's pants the police gave her to wash. The pants are bloodstained and there are three broken teeth in one pocket. Ben makes frantic phone calls to a lawyer who reluctantly agrees to try to get an interdict. The dinner continues; Ben returns, apologizes, and relays the bad news about the pants and teeth. However, these ugly facts only cause a temporary disruption. The government's detention policies are debated in a civil way, and by the time dessert arrives a cautious consensus emerges approving Ben's concern. "Too much secrecy doesn't do anyone any good," the minister opines, and one of Ben's colleagues toasts him:

"Unless we start doing something on our own we're in for an unholy explosion ... Here's to you, Oom Ben ... Give them hell."

And suddenly they were all raising their glasses, beaming with benevolence and amusement, in a show of unity unpredictable barely a minute ago.

(Brink 1984: 72, 73)

This "moment of crisis," as Bakhtin might call it, is a mild one that leads to renewal. As the guests' toasts and the affectionate "Oom" (uncle) suggest, the *laager* is again intact, and Ben is still part of it. In contrast, the second "feast" or Saturnalia is a tragic debacle that signals the destruction of both the Ngubene and Du Toit families. By then Gordon has been dead for months, and his second son, Robert, has disappeared. Ben is being ostracized and threatened after the publication of his suspicions in the English-language newspaper. He has received the letter bomb (which he did not open) and his Principal has given him his "final warning" ("The school cannot afford to keep political agitators on its staff" [Brink 1984: 235]). In the midst of these events, Christmas arrives, and Ben has to preside over a family holiday dinner. Four generations, crowded together in the house, Susan's parents, daughters with husbands and children, immense quantities of rich food, an "interminable prayer" from Ben's father-in-law, plus a variety of family tensions and jealousies all set the stage for Stanley Makhaya's arrival just as the traditional family pudding is being served.

This time Stanley does not wait patiently on the porch but instead charges into the house "like a great black bull." Very drunk, he roars with laughter, shocks everyone with a grotesque parody of holiday bonhomie, and trades sarcastic insults with the father-in-law who demands, "Who is this kaffir?" In the pandemonium that follows, Ben's relatives—led by Susan's parents—depart en masse, and Ben discovers the reason for Stanley's bizarre behavior as the man's laughter is transformed into sobs of grief. The Ngubene's son Robert had been in Mozambique and had trained to become a guerilla. Returning across the border with weapons, he and his companions had encountered an army patrol and been killed. When his mother Emily learned this news, she committed suicide by throwing herself in front of a train at the Soweto station on Christmas morning.

This chain of events destroys the Ngubene family physically, and Stanley's disruption of the Christmas dinner accelerates the emotional destruction of the Du Toit family. Ben becomes estranged from his daughters, and his marriage enters its final throes, leading to the divorce that is in process when he is killed in the hit-and-run "accident" that was presumably arranged by Captain Stolz and the Special Branch. This outcome may be considered another example of inversion. Early on in the novel, when Ben first went to the Special Branch to vouch for Gordon, Colonel Viljoen dismissed his fears by telling him, "I assure you we know what we're doing, Mr Du Toit—and it's for your own good too. To make sure you and your family can sleep peacefully at night" (Brink 1984: 62). Torturing and murdering political prisoners may have been intended to protect the homes and hearths of good Afrikaners like the Du Toits, but—colliding with Ben Du Toit's stubborn and courageous insistence on learning the truth and achieving justice—the results had been very different.

Where had South Africa begun to go wrong? According to Phil Bruwer, the father of Ben's lover and the wisest of the characters in the novel, it was—once again—the *laager* mentality: the acceptance of complicity with criminality as long as it is "our people" who are the criminals. "Perhaps it's something ... we neglected when there was still time to stop the rot," he tells Ben during their final conversation, "When we turned a blind eye just because it was 'our people' who committed the crimes" (Brink 1984: 291). Considered from this perspective, Ben Du Toit's quest and defeat have a redeeming element. At great cost to himself and the people who help him, he has made it more difficult for white South Africans, including his fellow Afrikaners, to remain blind to their government's crimes. Moreover, in the novel's final epiphany, in its "Epilogue," the frame narrator implies that he may carry on Ben's quest by telling the story he has reconstructed from the dead man's notes and diaries. Though he suspects that the police may know Ben sent these materials to him and may put him under surveillance, he now, like Ben, has a conscience that will not let him rest. And a story that demands to be told. Therefore, he intends "to write it down. To report what I know. So that it will not be possible for any man ever to say again: *I knew nothing about it*" (Brink 1984: 316; emphasis in original). On the other hand, justice in the form of retribution seems impossible. Ben's bold assertion that someday, "we'll have all of Gordon's murderers lined up against a wall" (Brink 1984: 202), seems extremely unlikely by the end of the novel.

What Brink and *A Dry White Season* offer in place of retribution is revelation, an attempt to revitalize the public sphere by telling fictional truths instead of the propaganda and lies used to explain the deaths of Steve Biko and other persons detained by South Africa's security forces. For by the end of the novel at least Ben Du Toit, the frame narrator, and—by implication—Brink and his readers—are no longer imprisoned by the web of complicity, the "fog of silence and lies," that engulfed South Africa during the apartheid era. Brink's novel is prescient in its implication that discovering truths about the apartheid era would be more likely than achieving revenge or retribution.

As part of the political negotiations that allowed elections and a less violent transition to a more democratic government to occur in the early 1990s, the NP and the ANC had to reject two of the more obvious options for dealing with past, apartheid-era crimes. One was a blanket amnesty that would have, in effect, tacitly allowed the lawlessness of the apartheid era to go unpunished and maintained the "veil of secrecy" that de Villers described; this option was anathema to the ANC. The other, legalistic option of holding Nuremberg-style trials for some of the main perpetrators of apartheid, was anathema to the South African military leaders who threatened to revolt if such trials were initiated (Boraine 2000: 143). Confronted by these choices between reconciliation and revenge and between peace and all-out civil war, the negotiators discovered a third way. Its key principles were articulated by Albie Sachs, an ANC leader whose right arm and sight in one eye had been destroyed by a car bomb set by government agents. "If there is a general amnesty and it brings peace and democracy to our country, I would be thrilled," Sachs told Anthony Lewis. "... What is important is to expose the crimes, that is very healing, whereas endless trials might simply keep the wounds open" (Lewis 1990). The TRC, the Commission created by this compromise, allowed selective amnesty under certain conditions. Thus, for example, an ANC terrorist could receive amnesty if he could persuade the Commission that his terrorist acts were motivated by political convictions, and policemen who had committed crimes could receive amnesty if it was evident that they had acted out of a sense of duty. In addition, applicants for amnesty had to make full disclosures of what they had done, and this provision was a strong incentive for killers, torturers, and terrorists to testify and reveal their own crimes and the complicity of others.[13]

The granting of amnesty to many of the perpetrators who confessed was bitterly resented by some victims (or the families of victims) who believed that criminals must be punished so retribution can occur. On the other hand, as our quote earlier from the 1996 South African constitution implies, the politicians who created the TRC felt that in the past their nation had had a surfeit of revenges accompanied by "hatred, fear, [and] guilt," and what it needed for the future was understanding, reparation, reconciliation, and *ubuntu*—a Bantu word meaning humanness and a sense of collective unity.[14] According to Patti Waldmeir, "scores of [the] black South Africans" she interviewed during the transition to democracy agreed with this idea. When she asked Sipho Maduna, a young ANC militant who had been tortured by the police, about revenge, he replied "that God had exacted revenge on his behalf." When she asked if this meant that "his tormentors were dead already? He laughed. The 'revenge' ... was the ANC's victory in the [1994] elections. 'We were fighting for Madiba [Nelson Mandela], and today Madiba is free, we are all free.' And that for Sipho was the sweetest revenge of all. It was a matter of *ubuntu*, he said" (Waldmeir 1997: 277).

As for Madiba, aka Mandela, he of course was his nation's prime example of an individual embodying reconciliation and *ubuntu* rather than revenge and divisiveness. He achieved this, first, by showing an amazing lack of bitterness for his long years spent as a political prisoner. And, second, even though he hated apartheid and did much to destroy it, he clearly demonstrated that he did not bear any grudges against the Afrikaners, either as individuals or as a group. In 1995, for example, in one of his most eloquent gestures of reconciliation, he attended the World Cup final rugby game between New Zealand and South Africa's Springboks in Johannesburg—which was significant in itself since rugby had been a whites-only sport dominated by Afrikaners. He also visited the team at its training camp and came on the pitch at the beginning of the game to wish them luck—wearing a green Springboks cap and jersey. The symbolism was shrewd and dramatic; it was what South Africans called "Madiba Magic" at its most effective. "The best thing was to see him wear a Springbok jersey," recalled one of the players, Joost van der Westhulzen. " ... Then we realised that the whole country is behind us, and for this man to wear a Springbok jersey was a sign, not just for us, but for the whole of South Africa, that we have to unite"—and the crowd of 72,000 mostly white South Africans responded by cheering and chanting Mandela's name (Bond 2007). When the Springboks won 15–12, in a double overtime, Mandela came out to present the Cup to the Springboks' team captain, Francois Pienaar; he was still wearing the Springboks cap and jersey, and the two men embraced while a television audience estimated at two billion watched and the stadium crowd cheered this "spontaneous gesture of racial reconciliation."[15]

Besides such acts of reconciliation with Afrikaners who may have supported apartheid, Mandela also demonstrated his kinship with ones like Brink who had opposed it and contributed to the long struggle against it. Here his purpose was not reconciliation, which was unnecessary, but appreciation. In Brink's case, Mandela did this handsomely in the form of a 1996 Preface to that writer's collection of essays, *Reinventing a Continent*. After praising South African writers and intellectuals in general for "countering and breaking the tyranny of silence" apartheid had imposed "to keep untold the suffering it inflicted," Mandela singled out Afrikaner intellectuals who

> added their voices to those denouncing injustice. ... That long road we have walked ... carries indelibly the tracks and the footmarks of these courageous men and women who dared to challenge the powerful structures of their own ethnic group to proclaim their allegiance to the ideal of a greater South Africa. ... The quality of our freedom in the future will depend on the creative and critical input of our writers.
> (Mandela, Preface to *Reinventing a Continent vii-viii*, Brink 1996)

Mandela's comments are even more significant because some of the later, post-apartheid essays in *Reinventing* are strongly critical of a number of the ANC's policies and several of Mandela's own political decisions. Brink's critical instincts did not die with apartheid, even though compared to his earlier furious attacks on the NP's policies and its leaders, especially P. W. Botha, his strictures on the ANC seem almost mild. Yet they are sharp criticisms, and the relationship between the writer and the politician, implied by both Brink's criticisms and Mandela's Preface, is a hopeful omen for the future of a "greater South Africa." It is, after all, a nation that both men worked to create, a nation in which telling critical truth will be treated with respect and *ubuntu*, not anger and retaliations.

Chapter 9

Rogue cops and beltway vigilantes

Torture, redemptive violence, and "American ideals"

We meet here during a crucial period in the history of our nation, and of
the civilized world. Part of that history was written by others; the rest
will be written by us. (Applause.) On a September morning, threats that
had gathered for years, in secret and far away, led to murder in our
country on a massive scale. As a result, we must look at security in a
new way, because our country is a battlefield in the first war of the 21st
century. ... . The first to benefit from a free Iraq would be the Iraqi
people, themselves. Today they live in scarcity and fear, under a dictator
who has brought them nothing but war, and misery, and torture. Their
lives and their freedom matter little to Saddam Hussein—but Iraqi lives
and freedom matter greatly to us. (Applause.)

(Guardian.co.uk., 2003, "Full text: George Bush's Speech to the
American Enterprise Institute")

Human beings can be awful cruel to one another.

(Huck Finn in *The Adventures of Huckleberry Finn*,
Mark Twain 1999: 239)

In December 2006 when Augusto Pinochet died, and while his nation's
citizens were either mourning the dictator's demise or celebrating it by
drinking champagne on the streets of Santiago, the American government

did not offer the usual condolences. Instead, a White House spokesman, Tony Fratto, said tersely: "Augusto Pinochet's dictatorship in Chile represented one of most difficult periods in that nation's history. Our thoughts today are with the victims of his reign and their families" (Bonnefoy 2006). Persons with keen memories noted that in 1999 former President George H. W. Bush had been one of the people, along with Henry Kissinger, who had urged the British government to allow Pinochet to return to Chile instead of being extradited to Spain, as Judge Balthazar Garzon had demanded. And a few of the harsher critics of the second Bush Presidency made unpleasant comparisons between American tactics in the War on Terror and Chile's policies under Pinochet. Were Americans doing anything disturbingly similar to the "Caravans of Death" in Chile that had seized leftists so they could be tortured and killed? In fact, in April 2009 a group of American Human Rights lawyers announced that Judge Garzon, the same Spanish jurist who had been Pinochet's nemesis, was becoming involved with efforts to begin criminal proceedings against six Bush administration lawyers, who had written opinions justifying torture, and that these efforts might lead to investigations of Donald Rumsfeld and Dick Cheney (Center for Constitutional Rights 2009).

> During the last days of the second Bush regime such accusations, particularly regarding torture, grew increasingly vigorous, and many Americans had to confront the grim possibility that between 2002 and 2009 their government had behaved in ways, although not to their own citizens, that were not too different from certain practices in Chile and South Africa during the 1970s and the 1980s. Confronted and challenged by terrorists, enemies, and insurgents, determined to avenge past attacks and/or prevent future ones, the George W. Bush administration, the Chilean military and the National Party's apartheid regime had all used what were called "extreme" or "alternative" interrogation procedures.
>
> (Danner 2009: 20)

The euphuisms for these methods varied, but certain outcomes were similar: first, they were cruel, caused severe bodily pain and psychological damage to their victims, and were violations of national, international, and military law; second, they were concealed with widely varying amounts of skill by the torturers themselves and by their governments; third, the cover-ups failed, and the governments of all three nations' reputations were badly sullied. In the cases of the United States and South Africa some of the criticisms were all the harsher because these were elected governments that had condoned or encouraged human rights abuses of prisoners at the same time that they were trying to maintain a veneer of legality and claiming a moral high ground.

There were differences of course. One was that because the United States is such a rich, powerful country it could provide its torturers with conceal-ments and amenities that Brink's Captain Stolz and his Chilean counterparts could only dream of, such as "torture taxis," executive jets to ferry prisoners to secret torture centers elsewhere in the world. A second difference is that in South Africa and Chile there were relatively clear chains of causation. In the case of South Africa, described in the previous chapter, there was the fear of communism, plus the *laager* mentality that can be related to the Afrikaners' history. In Chile there was an even more virulent anticommunism, plus his-torical class antagonisms. America was attacked by Islamic radicals, but that didn't set up an equally direct set of historical American motivations for how some prisoners came to be treated. Some Americans, who presumably knew their nation's history well, were genuinely bewildered as well as shocked by Abu Ghraib and what it told them about their nation's twenty-first-century mentality. For Rory Kennedy, Robert Kennedy's daughter, who made a documentary film about that prison, for example, the tortures seemed a betrayal of 200 years of American history. When George Washington was told that the British were horrendously mistreating American prisoners and asked how the Americans should treat British prisoners, Kennedy said, the General replied, "Treat them with dignity and respect," and she claimed that such attitudes had been America's "moral compass" for two hundred years, and losing them had created "a country that is completely unfamiliar to me" (Longworth 2007). *The New York Times* reached a similar verdict at the end of 2007 when it denounced the Bush administration in an exceptionally bitter editorial. Commenting on efforts by CIA operatives to destroy evi-dence of how they had tortured prisoners, the writer said such acts made it impossible to

> "recognize our country," because "it was impossible to see the founding principles of the greatest democracy in the contempt these men and their bosses showed for the constitution, the rule of law and human decency. ... This sort of lawless behavior has become standard practice since Sept. 11, 2001 ... [but] there is no safety for Americans or their country when those ideals are sacrificed."
>
> (The New York Times 2007: A20)

Besides this seeming lack of historical contextuality, there was also a kind of geographical and institutional discontinuity. Until recently Americans have learned about this torture in two ways and in two main venues, because much of it was occurring on two separate operational levels at opposite ends of the chain of command. At the bottom of the chain, at Abu Ghraib itself, there were relatively simple exposés of "abuses" by Privates, Corporals, and officers from Military Intelligence (MI) and Military Police (MP) units assigned, respectively, to interrogate and guard prisoners. As we mentioned earlier, one section of Abu Ghraib was called Camp Ganci to remember and, by implication, to avenge a firefighter who died in 9/11. Yet another section of the prison was named Camp Vigilant, and during the fall and winter of 2003–4 some of the MP guards began dispensing their own brand of vigilante justice and punishments, including beatings, sexual humiliations, dog attacks, and threats of electrocution. They also began recording these activities on digital cameras. The resulting images of what Philip Gourevitch calls "primal dungeon scenes" were crude technically, but the crudity was appropriate because it echoed "the bleakness and misery of the medieval tableaux" being enacted by the guards and prisoners (Gourevitch 2008: 262).

While this was happening, the Insurgency became stronger, and under pressure from Washington, the commander of ground forces in Iraq, Lieutenant General Ricardo Sanchez, ordered more aggressive interrogations and the use of dogs to control prisoners (Gourevitch 2008: 32). Several of the MP guards who had photographed prisoners being abused began showing the photographs to friends; the photos began circulating though the prison, and Specialist Joe Darby showed them to an agent of the CID (Criminal Investigation Command). Sanchez then, in January 2004, ordered investigations to deal with instances of "detainee abuse, escapes from confinement facilities, and accountability lapses, which indicated systemic problems within the [MP] brigade and suggested a lack of clear standards, proficiency, and leadership" (Taguba Report 2004). One of these investigations—by General Antonio Taguba—confirmed the abuses in his report, but the story became a global scandal in the late spring of 2004 when the images were shown on CBS News's *Sixty Minutes* program. Only seven of the Americans at Abu Ghraib were punished with well-publicized court martials, prison sentences, and dishonorable discharges providing just closures in accordance with a narrow application of the rules of military justice. The guard considered the ringleader, Corporal Charles Graner, received a ten-year sentence. No one above the rank of sergeant served jail time; however, a number of officers were reprimanded or fined, and one, General Janis Karpinski, who had been in command of the American prisons in Iraq, was demoted. Two dog handlers were punished, but the officer, who authorized the dogs, and more forceful interrogation techniques, General Sanchez, was not reprimanded (Gourevitch 2008: 268–69).

But there was another side to Abu Ghraib and also Guantanamo: the other Americans there whose moral compasses continued to function even in contaminated environments. Some were capable professionals who managed to do difficult jobs under chaotic conditions and were saved by their professionalism. Tim Dugan, a civilian interrogator, said he never abused detainees, because that violated the basic purpose of interrogation. "One of the things an interrogator does every time is evaluate the truthfulness and reliability of the information given," he said. " ... So, if I get information through torture, I have no way to verify anything, because I would just assume that you're going to tell me whatever the hell you want so the pain stops" (Gourevitch 2008: 204). In other cases the resistance or protest was ethical. FBI agents stationed at Guantanamo in 2002 and 2003 objected so strongly to the interrogation tactics being used by the military that they began documenting them in a file labeled, "War Crimes." The file became a 437-page report detailing the agents' vehement objections to "practices like intimidating inmates with snarling dogs, parading them in the nude before female soldiers, or 'short-shackling' them to the floor for many hours in extreme heat or cold." The agents and some of their superior officers believed these practices were unlawful, and took their concerns to the National Security Council and the Departments of Justice and Defense, but nothing happened (Lichtblau, Shane, 2008)—which might not have been the outcome if the agents had had photographs that they could have leaked to the media.

At the other end of the chain of command, Washington, D.C., additional evidence regarding torture began to seep and then pour into the media. Much of it was connected to "senior officials," such as the now former President, Vice President, and Secretary of Defense, who have become prime suspects in a global detective story whose code words are phrases like "rendition" and Guantanamo and whose events were influenced by legal opinions by lawyers like John Yoo and David Addington. In this story secret crimes (if they are crimes) happened not only in Tier 1B in Abu Ghraib but also in airports and torture centers on several continents. What occurred in those places was due to once secret (but now public) memorandums by "senior officials" in Washington that often seem to have been meant to destroy the protections provided by the Geneva Conventions and to blur the difference between legal and illegal ("aggressive") techniques by authorizing the latter and then "redefin[ing] the law to create the appearance of their legality" (Truthdig 2008).

Closure in the form of just or even unjust verdicts may not come easily or quickly to end this story. There are no images of naked Iraqis or menacing dogs to inspire horror and disgust. Instead there are images like the one by Trevor Paglen that appears in the January 11, 2007 *New York Review of Books*: a collection of seemingly innocent airplanes at a regional airport in North Carolina. Yet according to the plane spotters and air traffic controllers who track them these may be the more notorious "torture taxis" and "ghost planes" used to transform the "war on terror" into an attack on "American values." But this connection, as we said, was tenuous, a detective story until recently when it began to seem more factual. When President Obama decided to declassify previously secret memos authorizing torture and signed by Donald Rumsfeld, he created an immediate political firestorm and a longer-term possibility that the truth may eventually emerge regarding how much legal linkage there is between, say, Camp Ganci and the Oval Office.

But that will occur well after this book is finished and after the judges, lawyers, investigations, commissions, and politicians have finished their work.

In the meantime it is important to remember that just as there were individuals like Tim Dugan at Abu Ghraib who maintained their commitment to what was lawful and in accord with the Geneva Conventions in a climate of lawlessness, there were individuals and agencies in the Pentagon and within the Beltway who did the same. The Naval Criminal Investigative Service (NCIS), for example, realized that the "dark side" of the torture scandal had begun to manifest itself as early as the fall and winter of 2002 when NCIS agents assigned to interrogation activities at Guantanamo reported to their superior officer, David Brant, that detainees were being abused. He agreed and reported that "the abuse was serious, that it most probably violated American law and certainly violated American values" to Alberto Mora, the Navy's Consul General or chief civilian lawyer. At first Mora believed that this "policy of cruelty" was the work of "rogue elements," but he soon learned otherwise. "I was horrified. I was dumbfounded. I was concerned. I was stupefied. I was astonished that this could have taken place," he recalled, "that Secretary [of Defense] Rumsfeld himself would have been asked, much less gotten involved in these kinds of matters. And as I reviewed the documents ... I saw that the legal memorandum that originated in Guantanamo was wholly inadequate and, as I felt instantaneously, an incompetent piece of legal work ... And I felt that all of it was some horrific mistake" (Touring Democracy 2007). Despite the vigorous opposition of individuals like Mora, the "policy of cruelty" prevailed and expanded to Iraq.

That individuals such as Brant, Mora, and the Guantanamo FBI agents should have opposed bad policies based on bad legal thinking speaks well for their integrity, but it also testifies to how firmly legalism is embedded in American life both as an ideal and as an actuality. Before Guantanamo and Abu Ghraib, the history of legalism in America was largely a success story, and some of the successes were impressive. Even before the United States became a nation, its leaders had demonstrated their respect for the rule of law and due process, for "civilized" codes of conduct, and for safeguards to prevent abuses by despotic governments. The colonists responsible for the 1776 Virginia Bill of Rights, for example, included four safeguards to protect defendants, including number 9, that prohibited "cruel and unusual punishments," and number 8 that said:

> That in all capital or criminal prosecutions a man hath a right to demand the cause and nature of his accusation, to be confronted with the accusers and witnesses, to call for evidence in his favour, and to a speedy trial by an impartial jury of his vicinage, without whose unanimous consent he cannot be found guilty, nor can he be compelled to

give evidence against himself; that no man be deprived of his liberty except by the law of the land, or the judgment of his peers.

(Virginia Bill of Rights 1776)

The writers of the Declaration of Independence included, along with other complaints about the King of England, charges that he had deprived "us, in many cases, of the benefits of trial by jury" and transported "us beyond [the] seas to be tried for pretended offenses." And when they wrote the constitution for their own government a few years later, they promptly added a Bill of Rights to protect themselves and their descendents from dictatorial behavior by that government.

Nineteenth-century Americans were also a legalistic lot. As Alexis de Tocqueville commented, lawyers were a dominant class in American society, and their professional mentality had a strong influence on their nation's policies and culture. "In America there are no nobles or literary men [public intellectuals], and the people are apt to mistrust the wealthy; lawyers consequently form the highest political class and the most cultivated portion of society," he wrote in Chapter 16 of *Democracy in America*.

> . ... If I were asked where I place the American aristocracy, I should reply without hesitation that it is not among the rich, who are united by no common tie, but that it occupies the judicial bench and the bar. ... [Therefore] the lawyers, as a body, form the most powerful, if not the only, counterpoise to the democratic element. In that country we easily perceive how the legal profession is qualified by its attributes, and even by its faults, to neutralize the vices inherent in popular government. When the American people are intoxicated by passion ... they are checked and stopped by the almost invisible influence of their legal counselors.
>
> (Tocqueville, Book 1, Chapter 16, 1835)

Though they did certain things—such as create laws to justify the taking of Native American land and to treat those peoples as sub-human, as well as oppress African-Americans first as slaves and then by Jim Crow laws and Klan terrorism—that many twentieth-century Americans would condemn as evil and unlawful, nineteenth-century ones did these practices with the approval of their lawyers—all the way to the Supreme Court that, for example, justified slavery and Jim Crow with rulings such as Dred Scott vs. Sandford and Plessy vs. Ferguson. To be sure, there was also the American frontier, a region whose inhabitants often seemed susceptible to intoxication by strong drink combined with passions that resulted in vigilante hangings, whippings, and brandings by nightriders and vigilante committees. However, most American vigilante movements were in existence for too brief a time to be considered significant parts of their nation's or their communities' legal cultures. The great majority appeared only sporadically on the frontier as it moved west and south into regions like Appalachia, the lower Midwest, the Ozarks, California, the western Plains states, Texas and the deep South. According to Richard Brown, the longevity of these vigilante movements varied considerably, but ones "that lasted as long as a year were long lived. More commonly, they finished their business in a period of months or weeks" (Brown 1975: 97). The major exception to this pattern was of course the deep South where the Klu Klux Klan used vigilante and terrorist tactics to maintain white supremacy. In other regions, most vigilante movements came into existence to destroy or drive out a specific gang of bandits or horse thieves preying on a frontier community, and—after that goal was achieved—the communities relied on conventional legalistic justice methods with trained judges, formal trials, prison sentences, and legal executions.

By legalistic standards this is a change for the better, since it takes justice, punishment, and revenge out of the hands of lynch mobs, vigilantes, and/or victims (or victims' relatives). Instead, says Paul Gewirtz, "an abstraction of the 'state' calls the wrongdoer to account ... because the wrong is seen as one against the community as much as any particular victim ... substituting the state for the victim ... is a great achievement. It keeps at bay the unmediated passions of an injured victim, especially unmediated revenge. It transforms a private vendetta into a public concern" (Gewirtz, "Victims and Voyeurs" 1996: 157). It was also a process of cultural and historical transformation. Law and lawyers followed the line of white settlement West to record deeds, regulate commerce, and achieve statehood. The frontier barbarian, the wild Indian, the lawless bandit, and the unruly vigilante mob had little to contribute to this process, and they were driven west or destroyed, as America became a prosperous, civilized nation.

During the early part of the twentieth century, when the line of settlement reached the coast and the United States was becoming a regional power, its leaders brought their legalistic outlook with them when they intervened in the affairs of their nation's poorer, smaller neighbors. That is, they saw themselves as judges and America as a policeman correcting the lawless or barbaric behavior of those countries. They did this in accordance with the guidelines of an appendage to the Monroe Doctrine—established by Theodore Roosevelt and called the Roosevelt Corollary—that was based on claims that the United States had the right to intervene as "an international police power" whenever the behavior of its Southern neighbors exhibited "chronic wrongdoing, or an impotence which results in a general loosening of the ties of civilized society [that] may in America, as elsewhere, ultimately require intervention by some civilized nation" (Roosevelt Corollary 1904). Less obtrusive than the traditional or formal de jure imperialism of European powers, the Corollary fostered a more discrete, de facto hegemony or "lite" imperialism that could be expanded when necessary. Franklin Roosevelt, who was involved with a Haitian intervention when he was Wilson's Undersecretary of the Navy in 1915, described the process in 1928. Haiti was in "chronic trouble," Presidents were murdered, and governments were overthrown, he recalled, but the United States intervened and landed its

> marines and sailors only when the unfortunate Chief Magistrate of the moment [Guillaume Sam] was dragged out of the French Legation, cut into six pieces and thrown to the mob. Here again we cleaned house, restored order, built public works and put governmental operation on a sound and honest basis. We are still there. It is true, however, that in Santo Domingo and especially in Haiti we seem to have paid too little attention to making the citizens of these states more capable of reassuming the control of their own governments. But we have done a fine piece of material work, and the world ought to thank us.
>
> (Roosevelt 1928: 573–86).

During the Hoover administration and Roosevelt's own first term, the United States gradually phased out its hemispheric military occupations and interventions and replaced them with the Good Neighbor policy. This policy relied on diplomacy instead of force, and for the next twenty years, until the onset of the Cold War, it allowed America's Caribbean and Latin American neighbors to police themselves either democratically or dictatorially, depending on the proclivities of their ruling elites. The United States was still the dominant, hegemonic state in its hemisphere, but restrained by this policy it would exercise that power in a more strictly legalistic and respectful way.

Justice goes to the movies

During this time period, from the 1920s through the 1950s and the 1960s, legalism remained a strong force in American life and culture. Concern for topics such as due process, rigged trials, biased verdicts, and coerced confessions can be found in discourses such as jurisprudence, legislation, and popular culture. Dramatizations of these subjects were ubiquitous in popular media ranging from radio serials and television shows like *Perry Mason* (1957–1966), pulp fiction books, magazines and B-level movies to serious novels like *Native Son* and Theodore Dreiser's *An American Tragedy* (1925).

In the field of jurisprudence, courts, including the Supreme Court, began taking a closer look at America's courtrooms and police stations when suspects were arrested, interrogated, and put on trial. What they found was often at odds with the Constitution, especially as it applied to African-Americans relative to the Fourteenth Amendment, which forbids any "State [to] deprive any person of life, liberty, or property, without due process of law; nor deny to any person within its jurisdiction the equal protection of the law." In Brown vs. Mississippi in 1936, to give an important example, the Supreme Court unanimously (9–0) reversed a Mississippi verdict that had convicted three Black men of homicide on the basis of a rigged trial and confessions that had been coerced by torture. Chief Justice Hughes did not bother to conceal the Court's contempt as he referred to the "so-called trial" and its "pretended convictions," but he was even more scathing in his explanations of why such confessions violated the Fifth Amendment (which says that no person shall be "compelled to be a witness against himself"). "Further details of the brutal treatment to which these helpless prisoners were subjected need not be pursued," Hughes wrote,

> It is sufficient to say that in pertinent respects the transcript reads more like pages torn from some medieval account than a record made within the confines of a modern civilization which aspires to an enlightened constitutional government. ... The rack and torture chamber may not be substituted for the witness stand. ... And a trial equally is a mere pretense where the state authorities have contrived a conviction resting solely upon confessions obtained by violence.
>
> (Brown v. Mississippi 1936)

Combined with Gideon vs. Wainwright (1963), which enforces the Sixth Amendment's right to counsel, Brown would evolve into Miranda vs. Arizona (1966). That controversial decision, which forces police to tell suspects their rights, would foment police discontent and make rogue cops and vigilantes, like Popeye Doyle and Dirty Harry, even more popular because they ignored Miranda.

Legislative efforts to ban extralegal executions by lynch mobs by making lynching a federal crime were less successful than the Court's efforts to ban coerced confessions. More than 200 anti-lynching bills were introduced in Congress, many of them by the National Association for the Advancement of Colored People, in the first half of the twentieth century; the House passed three, but they were then defeated in the Senate by filibusters by Southern Senators. In 2005, however, the Senate did pass a non-binding resolution apologizing for this failure in which it "expresses the deepest sympathies and most solemn regrets of the Senate to the descendants of victims of lynching, the ancestors of whom were deprived of life, human dignity and the constitutional protections accorded all citizens of the United States" (Democracy NOW 2005).

If one surveys the popular media for approximately forty years, starting in the 1920s, there is considerable evidence to justify the assumption that many Americans, who were not lawyers or judges, nevertheless shared the concerns expressed by the Supreme Court in Brown vs. Mississippi. Though the examples chosen might differ in details, one can discern a consensus regarding concepts associated with justice such as fairness, accountability, evidence, and the need to achieve retribution by lawful means. These concepts were dramatized in both the factual and fictional media in a variety of genres. Accountability was a particular concern that these texts applied to the entire justice process and not just to criminals and defendants. That is, a text might be critical of a trial and blame a judge or prosecutor for an unfair verdict, which is what *Native Son* does. Or in the case of *To Kill a Mockingbird* it is Bob Ewell and the jury that are implicitly blamed for an unjust verdict. Or in the factual media of what is now called true crime, there were controversial cases and trials such as those of Sacco and Vanzetti, the Lindberg Kidnapper, Bruno Hauptman, and the Scottsboro Boys. Each of these causes célèbres involved issues of fairness and concerns that politics, nationality, or race could taint judicial processes and decisions.

Concern about such issues could also have a political significance in the 1930s and afterwards. America's enemies and adversaries in World War II and the Cold War had justice systems, but they were not ones that would havebeen approved by Justice Hughes. During the 1930s the Soviets had their show trials in which defendants were coerced to make abject confessions, indictments were treated as statements of fact, and guilty verdicts for all defendants were foregone conclusions and used for propaganda purposes. As for the Italian Fascists and the German Nazis, their conceptions of justice were criminal by American standards. Thus, in his important speech of January 3, 1925, Mussolini insisted he had not ordered Fascist *squadristi* thugs to kill Socialist Deputy Giacomo Matteotti, in retaliation for Matteotti's virulent verbal attacks, but he nevertheless asserted that he assumed "the political, moral, and historical responsibility for all that has happened," including Matteotti's murder, and he then used the ensuing political crisis to consolidate his political power (Ridley 1998: 162). Perhaps deliberately imitating Mussolini, Hermann Goring assured his "Fellow Germans, my measures will not be crippled by any legalistic hesitation," when Hitler appointed him Prussian Minister of the Interior in 1933 after the Reichstag fire: "Each bullet which leaves the barrel of a police pistol now is my bullet. If one calls this murder, then I have murdered. I ordered all this. I back it up. I assume the responsibility" (Conot 1993: 121). Such statements and events such> as the massacre of Ernst Roehm and other Strum Abteilung (SA) leaders in 1934, the 1938 Kristallnacht attacking Jews, synagogues, and Jewish business throughout Germany, the two regimes' use of secret police, the Gestapo and the Italian OVRA (Organization for Vigilance and Repression of Anti-Fascism) founded in 1927, to torture and/ or kill enemies at home and abroad—each was a clear signal that these regimes were willing to commit (or take responsibility for) criminal acts, and the perpetuators would not be punished as members of the Gestapo, OVRA, or mobs of the party faithful as they avenged injuries, punished enemies and otherwise acted as semi-official vigilante lynch mobs and death squads. Due process and the rule of law were destroyed and replaced by what the

Germans called the *Führerprinzip*, the principal that a leader's commands were equivalent to law or even superceded law. The individual's only option was to obey "superior orders," and therefore it was impossible (and dangerous) to question the legality or morality of a command by the Führer or, in Italy, by *Il Duce*.

Having faith in democracy, supporting America's justice system, even if it was not perfect, could have patriotic overtones and be a way of asserting that one had "American values." Interestingly, focusing primarily on films because they were the dominant entertainment media of the period from the 1920s to approximately 1970, one can find examples of movies scrutinizing virtually every stage of the criminal justice process from initial arrests to final verdicts, incarcerations, and executions.

Wrongful Arrest occurs in the *Wrong Man* (1956 directed by Alfred Hitchcock), for example, when a hardworking musician (played by Henry Fonda), a good family man, and a devout Catholic is mistakenly identified as a robber. He survives the ordeal and is exonerated, but his wife has a nervous breakdown and has to spend two years in a mental hospital.

A Questionable Confession is the major problem in Elia Kazan's *Boomerang* (1947): a drifter in Ohio (Arthur Kennedy) is arrested carrying a gun used in a Bridgeport, Connecticut murder, and the Bridgeport police chief (Lee J. Cobb), under heavy pressure from venal politicians and the local newspaper, coerces a confession from the suspect. Fortunately, an idealistic prosecutor, Henry Harvey (Dana Andrews), courageously proves that the suspect is innocent despite the tainted confession, a false witness, and political pressure.

Perjured Testimony by Bob Ewell and his daughter's perjury cause an innocent Black man to die in *To Kill a Mockingbird* (1962), and not even Atticus Finch's (Gregory Peck) brilliant cross-examination can produce a just verdict.

The Reliability of Circumstantial Evidence is questioned and found wanting in Sidney Lumet's 1957 film version of *12 Angry Men*—but only because Juror Number 8 (Henry Fonda) has a "reasonable doubt," refuses to give in to the majority, and eventually persuades them to accept his viewpoint.

Cruel and Unusual Punishments in Mervyn LeRoy's *I Am Fugitive from a Chain Gang* (1932) are suffered by James Allen (Paul Muni) after he is wrongfully convicted and falls into the clutches of a Southern (i.e., Georgia) prison system. Allen escapes, but his life is nevertheless ruined; however, he still manages publicly to indict the chain gang system for its iniquities and cruelty.

Wrongful Arrest and Conviction, Overzealous Prosecutors, Suspect Testimony, and much more make the justice process in Errol Morris's *Thin Blue Line* (1988) seem dangerously unfair. Though produced in a different time frame than the other films in this section, *Thin Blue Line* is too important to leave out. A documentary reconstruction of a Dallas, Texas, homicide allegedly committed by Randall Adams, the film features all the major figures in the case, such as Adams, telling their own stories. The results, including an on-screen implicit confession by the actual murderer, were controversial but so persuasive that Adams was freed.

Considered as a group, these films can be considered cautionary tales. All show flaws and shortcomings in America's legalistic justice system. But they also implicitly apply the concept of personal accountability in a positive way by showing how individuals can still function honorably and sometimes effectively within that system. In fact, one could create a kind of judicial "dream team" with characters from these films. The best defense lawyer, Peck's Atticus Finch; the perfect prosecutor, Andrews's Henry Harvey; the ideal juror, Fonda's Juror Number 8; and the best media interpreter of a crime, Errol Morris when he made *Thin Blue Line*. Even Muni's James Allen could be considered an exemplary victim of injustice, because of the courage and resilience he displays in resisting the system and exposing its evils.

Support for legalism could also be conveyed by criticizing its antithesis, either in the form of mob rule or vigilante violence. The former type of extralegal justice was the target of the first part of Fritz Lang's *Fury* (1936) in which he depicts the mob as gullible cowards and liars who—when they cannot lynch an innocent stranger, Joe Wilson (Spencer Tracy)—try to burn him alive by torching the town jail. The majority of the lynch mob in William Wellman's 1943 *Ox-Bow Incident*, set in 1880s Nevada, are depicted as foolish and vindictive as they avenge the death of a popular rancher, Larry Kincaid, by lynching three strangers. Twenty years before the Milgram experiments would demonstrate the same idea scientifically, Clark's novel and Wellman's film imply how in moments of stress, the first thing many persons lose control over is their minds, and they will obey someone in authority, even if his or her commands may have lethal consequences. In *Ox-Bow* a former Confederate officer, Major Tetley, takes control of the mob, and a large majority of its participants (twenty-one out of twenty-eight) simply obey his orders. They make no effort to find out if the doomed men's stories were true or not or even if Kincaid is really dead. They overrule the pleas of the minority, including Henry Fonda, for fairness and reason only to learn that Kincaid is actually alive and the sheriff has already captured the rustlers who attacked him.

As this detail of *Ox-Bow* illustrates, one notable feature of these films is that the quality of the justice process they depict is dependent upon the quality of the information available as evidence, testimony, and/or confessions and how it is communicated and received. One of the major reasons for Randall Adams's wrongful conviction, for example, was the Dallas court's willingness to accept suspect prosecution testimony from "surprise" witnesses, whereas in *Boomerang*, it is the prosecutor's unwillingness to accept a coerced confession that saves an innocent defendant from conviction and possibly execution. But punishment and accountability can be applied to mobs and their leaders as well as to other individuals in these films. In *Fury*, Wilson, who miraculously escaped the fire, has *his* revenge by letting everyone in the town think he is dead, so that the mob will be convicted of homicide. Only at the last moment, however, does he reveal that he is alive as he gives an eloquent but sober speech condemning revenge as a motive for seeking justice. In the *Ox-Bow* film the enraged Sheriff vows that he will learn who was in the mob, and that he will not show them any mercy. Then, Major Tetley, the man most responsible for the "incident," is condemned by his own son, who calls him a

> murderous beast. There are only two things that have ever meant any-thing to you, power and cruelty. You can't feel pity. You can't even feel guilt. In your heart, you knew those men were innocent, yet you were cold—crazy to see them hanged. ... I could have stopped you with a gun just as any other animal can be stopped from killing, but I couldn't do it 'cause I'm a coward.
>
> (*Ox-Bow* filmscript, 1943)

Apparently the Major can feel some guilt since he walks into the next room, closes the door, and kills himself.[1] Though they can be placed in a variety of genres, including westerns, social realism, and film noir, and followed the conventions of those genres, these films shared certain other characteristics besides having justice as a theme. By late twentieth-century standards, they were not politically representative, since the dominant characters were almost invariably white men portrayed by actors such as Fonda, Tracy, and Peck that audiences would consider serious, credible male authority figures. Even when these characters and the actors who were playing them were victims of society and injustice, they might be depicted as the films' moral centers (for example, Muni in *I Am a Fugitive from a Chain Gang* (1932) and Tracey in *Fury*). Moreover, these films, with the exceptions of *Mockingbird* and *The Ox-Bow Incident* which are based on Lee's and Walter Clark's novels, are all derived from factually true stories and can be considered docudramas, a feature that adds to their earnestness and credibility.

However, pulp fiction authors and Hollywood script writers of the period, from the 1930s through the 1960s, were adept at producing narratives that exploited the appeal of vigilante violence, its romanticism and individuality, but they were careful to do this without coming into overt conflict with legality per se. They did this by setting the narratives in generic times and spaces that were implicitly or explicitly outside the boundaries of effective legality, environments where legality is so weak or non-existent that a good gunfight (or fistfight) is the only credible way to resolve differences or achieve justice. In westerns, which valorized marksmanship and male valor and were set in deserts or small towns in the "old," "wild" west, just closures were likely to be achieved by actors like John Wayne armed with revolvers or rifles. Or in thrillers and film noirs, which lamented lost loves and doomed relationships and were set in modern cities with corrupt or incompetent police, such closures were most likely to come from hard men with automatic pistols, like Sam Spade (Humphrey Bogart) in John Huston's

1941 *The Maltese Falcon* and Rick Blaine (Bogart again) in Michael Curtis's 1942 *Casablanca.*

The advent of Dirty Harry and Popeye Doyle

> This is a movie about a couple of killers. Harry Callahan and a homicidal maniac. The one with the badge is Harry.
>
> (Dirty Harry trailer 1971)

> Doyle fights dirty and plays rough. Doyle is bad news, but he's a good cop.
>
> (The French Connection trailer 1971)

In 1971 Hollywood released two films, both thrillers, whose main characters are rogue cops. These characters' violent behavior is very different from Wayne's and Bogart's chivalry, and their vision of justice and legality is virtually antithetical to that of the films discussed earlier in this chapter, such as *The Wrong Man, Fury, Boomerang*, and *12 Angry Men*. Instead of courtroom drama, Don Siegel's *Dirty Harry* featured Inspector Harry Callahan (Clint Eastwood) and his version of street justice enforced by Harry's massive phallic 357 Magnum handgun, the film's unsubtle way of equating justice with firepower and male sexual prowess. Instead of concern for the rights of the accused, the two films' attitude toward those rights, and similar legalistic niceties, is epitomized by a scene in William Friedkin's *The French Connection*: when its tough cop/antihero, Popeye Doyle (Gene Hackman), shouts, "Hold It!" then promptly shoots a fleeing suspect, Frog 2 (Marcel Bozzuffi), in the back and kills him. Or, earlier in the film, Doyle—wearing a Santa Claus suit that was his disguise in a stakeout—and his partner Russo (Roy Scheider) chase a drug dealer who resists arrest and slashes Russo with a knife. They pursue the man through an urban wasteland and catch him in a huge vacant lot strewn with rubble. Russo kicks the dealer; Doyle pistol whips him, then bewilders him with a parody of a police interrogation, shouting threats ("I wanta bust him!") and crazy questions about Poughkeepsie and foot picking until the terrified man confesses that he had been in Poughkeepsie and picked his toes there. Those scenes and Harry's taunting ("You've got to ask yourself one question: do I feel lucky? Well, do ya punk!") were examples of what critic Roger Greenspun called a "new kind of movie" (Greenspun 1971), whose protagonists were harbingers of new or different attitudes about legality, evil, revenge, and justice in America. Alpha males with good aim and bad attitudes, to paraphrase one of Eastwood's interviewers (Boucher 2008), Dirty Harry and Popeye Doyle are both plain-clothes detectives who represent fusions of an external legalistic identity with an internal vigilante mentality. Officially each wears or carries the badge that allows his use of force to protect the state and his fellow citizens from harm, that authorizes him—like Special Agent 007, James Bond—to share in that monopoly on the legitimate use of violence that the state enjoys. But whereas Bond is supposedly officially authorized by Her Majesty's Government to use violence, including homicide, in order to "save civilization" from barbarous enemies all while wearing expensive clothes and using state-of-the-art weapons, Doyle and Harry are not upper class and they are getting rid of bad guys, not saving civilization.

Doyle and Harry and the films in which they appear (including the sequels to *Dirty Harry*) are also important examples of the kind of redemptive violence, mentioned earlier in this study and described by theologian Walter Wink (1999).[2] Seen in narrative form as myth, says Wink, redemptive violence, "is the story of the victory of order over chaos by means of violence"; it is an "ideology of conquest" in which the gods "favor those who conquer," and the world "is a theater of perpetual conflict in which the prize goes to the strong." Variations upon these mythic themes, Wink argues, are ubiquitous in contemporary American culture, but especially in television where they are dramatized in "the structure of children's cartoon shows" as well as in "comics, video and computer games, and movies." For adults, dramatizations of redemptive violence, and the mentality that underlies it, can be encountered in "the media, in sports, in nationalism, in militarism, in foreign policy. ... in the Rambo movies ... and by the general pursuit of machismo" (Wink 1999: 48, 49).

Considered in the context of justice narratives, as we said earlier, redemptive violence can be seen as synonymous with or a substitute for the justice process. Whether they appear in comic books, TV cartoons or in R-rated thrillers at mall theatres, narratives based on this kind of violence follow certain familiar patterns. Violent revenges and retributions become replacements for due process and conventional police procedures; certitude regarding guilt and innocence is taken for granted; constitutional safeguards are ignored or ridiculed, and punishment becomes the sole goal and only criteria for just actions. The psychodynamics of such narratives, writes Wink, encourage viewers to identify with the films' heroes while projecting "their own repressed anger, violence, rebelliousness, or lust" onto the villain. Then as the film ends they can reassert control over their own violent impulses, repress them, and identify with the avenging hero as he punishes the villain in a cathartic, "guilt-free orgy of aggression" (Wink 1999: 49). These punishments, which are usually lethal, are also often highly melodramatic and conclusive; time itself seems terminated until the credits begin scrolling down the screen after Harry kills Scorpio, the pathological serial killer (Andy Robinson) in *Dirty Harry*, or after the firefight between the police and the drug smugglers in *The French Connection*. As the trailers for these two films suggest, the heroes who purvey these violent closures are notable chiefly for their toughness, their willingness to "play dirty," and their use of sheer physical force to resolve conflicts. For the admirers, first, of Eastwood and later of Charles Bronson (in *Death Wish* in 1974) and Sylvester Stallone (in three *Rambo* films between 1982 and 1988), the characters portrayed by these actors were not mere action figures; they were heroic avengers ridding the world of punks, thugs, rapists, homicidal maniacs, and other evildoers. It was dangerous, gory work, so no one should be squeamish if their heroes' tactics sometimes seemed ruthless and lawless. For their detractors and critics, these characters' heroism is actually rather circumscribed. As Allen Redmon noted, they come into action when order is threatened by evil forces until a "stronger hero" emerges "who is able, through surpassing violent force to annihilate the powerful evil that threatens human existence ... life is reduced to combat, and personal and communal concord is sustained," says Redmon, if and when "the physically powerful can purge the world of evil through righteous violence" (Redmon 2004: 316). What is notable about Redmon's insight is not only its emphasis on physical power, but also what it omits about the myth's avenging heroes. They have no need, it seems, for sensitivity; raw force is their answer for every problem. As for morals or scruples about the way this violence is used, Wink points out that it often degenerates into a "sadistic enjoyment of evil pure and simple" in which redemptive violence "is no longer the means to a higher good, namely order," but "an end in itself ... an aphrodisiac, sheer titillation" (Wink 1999: 56). And if that is true, it does not matter very much if the power comes from the barrels of the sniper rifles fired from rooftops, the weapons of choice for the villains in both *Dirty Harry* and *The French Connection*, or from Harry's .357 Magnum and Doyle's .38 Police Special.

Thus like many other American films of the 1970s, the 1980s, and later—*Straw Dogs, Bonnie and Clyde*, Charles Bronson's *Death Wish* films, and so on—these are violent films in which the physical consequences of the violence are shown in bloody detail. Characters like Major Tetley no longer went into an adjoining room and closed the door behind them before killing themselves. Now audiences expected suicides and homicides on screen in full color. However, as Pauline Kael argues these films are often emotionally "bloodless" in the sense that even though the mayhem "is totally realistic—hideously, graphically so—yet it's without emotion, it has no impact on us. We feel nothing toward the victims ... and no memory of them afterward. As soon as one person gets it, we're ready for the next" (Kael 1976: 251–52). The screaming victims of vampire and chain saw massacre spatter flicks, the punks, muggers, and other riff-raff gunned down in the *Death Wish* and *Dirty Harry* films and their sequels, plus the small-time pushers brutalized by Doyle and Russo, all can be put in this category. Or, at the other extreme, the major villains in Eastwood's *Dirty Harry* series are depicted as being so "disgustingly cruel and inhuman," loathsome and despicable that, as Kael says, "Harry can spend the rest of the movie killing them with a perfect conscience" (Kael 1980: 254), and audiences will cheer him on. As for the killers and avengers who perform these violent acts, they are often portrayed as being like William Munny, before his wife reformed him, as being as "cold as snow." Or as Kael said of Eastwood's *Dirty Harry* films, their "lack of reaction makes the whole show of killing seem ... unreal. ... daydream-nightmares of indiscriminate mayhem and slaughter" (Kael 1976: 251–52). Killing people, these films suggest, can be a cool, nonchalant, casual activity. This is illustrated very well in the bank robbery scene early on in *Dirty Harry* when Harry is having his "usual" lunch—a "foot-long hot dog," of course. When he is interrupted by the robbery, he blasts the robbers' speeding car to a halt, and mows down the fleeing thieves—all the while calmly chewing on his hot dog. The same attitude is exhibited in a different setting in *The French Connection.* In that film's opening scene, made in Marseilles, a sharp-faced man, presumably an undercover policeman, is keeping a large American car under surveillance. When his shift is done, he starts home, stopping to buy a baguette on the way; as he enters the hallway to his flat, a man—later identified as Frog 2—shoots him in the face. Stepping over his victim to leave, the killer breaks off the end of the baguette and takes it with him. The value of human life in both scenes is not high, a hot dog in America, a baguette in France. That difference is negligible. But Frog 2 is an enforcer for a drug cartel and a cop killer, not the sort of man an audience would identify with, whereas Harry Callahan is a killer cop who is presented as an admirable hero. That difference is significant, and there are other differences as well that make *Harry* both a more complete and ominous example of redemptive violence (an 8 or a 9 on a scale of 10) than *The French Connection* (a 6 or 7) and also a more political film. As we suggest elsewhere in this study, from the Virginia Bill of Rights to the present, American culture and history has often been an elite concern, a systematic effort to protect citizens from both despotic rulers and hysterical lynch mobs by insisting on due process, rules of evidence, and rights for the accused. Both *Harry* and *Connection* have a populist and anti-elitist ethos, and their protagonists' reliance on distinctly unorthodox procedures also puts them in conflict with establishment figures such as city officials and their police superiors.

In Doyle's case this anti-elitism is more a matter of lifestyle than of ideology or politics. With his pork-pie hat, cheap, rumpled suits, askew ties, and casual racism ("Never trust a nigger"), Gene Hackman's Doyle is very much a blue-collar barbarian and proud of it. But his elite antagonist, Frog 1, played with impeccable suaveness by Fernando Rey, is a symbol of decadent European elitism, and therefore there is little or no political resonance to his conflict with Doyle, only a contrast between a very affluent criminal who drinks wine and eats snails in a warm luxury hotel, while Doyle and/or Russo huddle in a doorway eating cold pizza and trying to keep him under surveillance on a cold New York winter night. In addition, with his Santa suit and his tendency to trust his gut instincts, his taste for booze (preferably in big noisy night clubs) and casual sex (preferably with women wearing boots), Doyle is a carnivalistic figure, one who has more in common with, say, Vautrin than he does with a more normal policeman. Moreover, despite the Trailer's claim that he is a "good cop," his superior officers, who are also portrayed as tough cops, don't trust him because some of his past hunches have been wrong. But Doyle's chief critic is Mulderig, a FBI agent he is forced to work with even though the two men hate each other. Mulderig (Bill Hickman) is another tough cop, just as hard-nosed and abrasive as Doyle. Midway in the film when Doyle argues that he is "dead certain" about a drug deal, Mulderig volunteers the information that the last time Doyle was dead certain, the result was "a dead cop," and the two men charge each other until other policemen pull them apart. This blemish on Doyle's record is never explained, but that is not necessary. As the film's justly famous chase scene reveals, as Doyle in a car pursues an elevated subway train, the man is fearless but he is also reckless, dangerously impulsive and probably a little insane. This verdict is justified in *Connection*'s final scenes. Filmed on Ward's Island—whose garbage, abandoned hospitals, insane asylums and potters fields have made it one of New York's most desolate wastelands—the film ends with Doyle and Russo stalking Frog 1 in one of the empty buildings, a dank nether world of madness, filth, and shadows. Doyle sees a motion, opens fire without identifying his target, and kills Mulderig. Still obsessively fixated on Frog 1, he pauses only long enough to reload his gun, growls, "The sonofabitch is here. I'm gonna' get him," and rushes into the shadows. The screen goes black; one more shot is heard, and the film ends. This bleak, enigmatic ending and Hackman's brilliant portrayal of Doyle as a tough cop with irredeemable flaws, make *The French Connection*—despite its violence—a relatively limited example of the redemptive violence myth. In addition, the film does not neatly conform to the idolizing/demonizing process described earlier in this study (see, for example, The Introduction and chapter 7 of Wright's *Native Son*). Not only is Doyle too flawed to be idolized; the film's villains are seen too rationally to be demonized. Both are amoral criminals, and Frog 2 is a very dangerous one, but their crimes lack the gratuitous, wanton sadism that is displayed by Harry Callahan's criminal antagonists. In *Dirty Harry* the idolize/demonize process functions at full strength. As played by Eastwood, Harry is a kind of plaster saint—a characterization well suited to Eastwood's good looks and monotone voice. His Inspector Callahan's only apparent interests are battling criminals and protecting San Francisco's citizens. His demonized criminal opponent is Scorpio, a sniggering psychopath who gloats as he targets his victims and has a penchant for preying on innocent, vulnerable persons, children and adolescents. However, Harry's enemies in this film and its sequels are not limited to homicidal sadists. He also has to contend with his elite, non-criminal antagonists, a variety of liberal twits and wusses, city and police officials, who refuse to applaud his zeal and instead castigate him for not following proper legal and police procedures. Because of these characters' legalistic qualms and caveats, Harry's predatory instincts are often frustrated, and it is more difficult for him to protect San Francisco from assaults by homicidal maniacs, such as Scorpio, whose political liberalism is signaled by his long hair (= hippie) and belt buckle shaped like a peace sign (= anti-war protestor). Indeed, Harry and the sequels are so anti-liberal that, as Kael argues, they align themselves with the conservative, right-wing, law-and-order politics of the early 1970s that were being promoted by Richard Nixon and Spiro Agnew (Kael 1976: 206). In the case of *Harry* itself the film goes a step farther and displays what Kael and Roger Ebert call a "fascist" mentality, a judgment it partly deserves (Harris 2008). Generally speaking, conservatives are as much or even more legalistic and respectful of the rule of law as their liberal counterparts are. When they raise law and order as a political issue, this usually means they either want more conservative laws or judges that will interpret existing laws in a harsher, more conservative manner. Either way, they generally do not condone it when agents of a state ignore or break that state's own laws. Fascists, on the other hand, often more or less openly despise legalism, erase the boundary between legal and extra-legal violence, and ignore existing laws—or replace them with decrees—because they are seen as limiting the power of a Duce or Fuehrer. Thus Mussolini, whom we quoted earlier, speaking as head of state, took "responsibility" for the murder of Socialist Deputy Giacomo Matteotti, and Hermann Goring declared, "Each bullet which leaves the barrel of a police pistol now is my bullet" (Ridley 1998: 162; Conot 1993: 121). A logical implementation of this attitude was that, along with the other repressive features we describe in our chapter on Brink, fascist regimes almost always have death squads or some kind of Gestapo or secret police who specialize in killing, torturing, and kidnapping groups or individuals perceived as hostile to the ruling party or its interests—even though laws forbidding such acts supposedly remain in force and are used to prosecute non-governmental criminals.

In *Dirty Harry* that film's antipathy to legalism surfaces most clearly in two confrontation scenes. The first, with a liberal District Attorney (D.A.) midway through the film, occurs after Harry has just tried valiantly but unsuccessfully to thwart a particularly noxious crime: Scorpio had kidnapped, raped, and buried a girl alive, promised to release her for a ransom and then reneged so that she died. During his desperate efforts to save the girl, Harry collects evidence, including Scorpio's rifle, without a search warrant, chases the killer, wounds him, and then tortures him so he will confess and reveal the girl's location. Instead of giving Harry a medal and putting his staff to work to find a legalistic loophole to remedy Harry's blunders and keep Scorpio locked up, the D.A. claims all the evidence Harry collected is too tainted to be used in court, lets the criminal "walk," and berates Harry for ignoring the killer's "rights." To back himself up, the D.A. has an Appellate Court judge handy, a mousy little man who also teaches constitutional law at Berkeley, a sure sign of his elitist, liberal bias. Neither the D.A. nor the judge expresses any appreciation to Harry for his efforts nor do they express any concern or sympathy for the dead girl. All that matters to them is Scorpio and his "rights," and Harry responds by telling them, "The law is crazy!"

In his wrong-headed way Harry is right. Even in a city as liberal as San Francisco, only a D.A. who was insane, or wished to commit political suicide, would sound so much like a Defense lawyer and be openly pro-defendant and so solicitous of a homicidal killer's rights and so little concerned about his victims' fates. Despite its lack of realism, however, this scene sets up the audience for the film's final confrontation. By insinuating that the state has abdicated its responsibility to act as avenger by becoming a protector of the accused, it justifies Harry's vigilante justice at the film's conclusion. After thwarting Scorpio's last crime, an attempt to hijack a school bus and hold the children for ransom, Harry and the killer confront each other by the bank of a river that is deserted except for a boy fishing. Cowardly as ever, Scorpio grabs the boy to use him as a shield, but Harry, with a brilliant trick shot worthy of John Wayne, wounds him. Scorpio is down, completely at Harry's mercy, but his gun is within easy reach. Instead of reading the killer's Miranda rights to him and arresting him, Harry—with his face distorted by righteous rage—taunts Scorpio by daring him to reach for his gun in the "lucky" hope that Harry's Magnum is empty. It isn't, and Harry blasts Scorpio backward into the river where he drifts downstream, presumably on his way to Hell.

It's a beautiful sunny day in an almost pristine California landscape—no enigmatic shots in the dark on Ward's Island obscure *Dirty Harry*'s sense of closure. Mythically speaking, the land has been purged of evil, and order has been produced by redemptive violence. What is less certain is the status of the killing itself. Is it homicidal police brutality, as the film's D.A. might claim? Is it vigilante justice that the *Ox-Bow* mob would have voted for, or a fascist bullet for which Goring would have taken responsibility? Whatever it is, it is not legalism. The film forecloses that remote possibility symbolically in its penultimate scene. As Scorpio's corpse floats out of sight, Harry takes out his Inspector's badge and throws it into the river. It is a simple, stark, and eloquent closure.

Dirty Harry, Death Wish, and the politics of torture

If Eastwood had ended Harry's saga with this scene, he would have resolved the conflict between conventional, liberal legality and Harry's right-wing vigilante ethos with a kind of stark dignity. But Hollywood is an industry, and box office receipts and surveys of potential audiences are more important than dignity. Consequently, Harry's brand of vigilante justice proved to be so popular and commercially successful that four sequels to the original 1971 Harry were made between 1973 and 1988 that followed the formula of portraying Harry as a combination judge, jury, and executioner. But the original film's ideological focus becomes inconsistent. This is especially true of the second film in the series, the 1973 *Magnum Force*; in that film, directed by Ted Post, the villains are a death squad of vigilante motorcycle cops who look like Storm Troopers (Kael 1976: 254), wear glittering aviator-style sunglasses, and kill criminals who have escaped from the justice system through luck or chicanery. Instead of joining them or applauding their efforts, Harry does unto the Troopers as they have done unto others. For even though Harry is not an admirer of the Bill of Rights, he did, as even Kael admits, develop a minimal tolerance for organized justice. "I hate the goddam system," he tells the vigilantes' leader, Lieutenant Briggs (Hal Holbrook), "but until someone comes along with some changes that make sense, I'll stick with it" (Magnum Force Script 1973; Kael 1976: 254). Briggs defends his "team" by connecting it with San Francisco's pioneer past—"A hundred years ago in this city people did the same thing. ... Anyone who threatens the security of the people will be executed." Harry is skeptical; eventually Briggs's cops will be executing people for jaywalking, he says. And, elsewhere in the film there is an allusion to the death squads that were operating in Brazil in the 1960s and 1970s. Often composed of off-duty policemen, they not only killed criminals but also harmless, though troublesome, street people such as beggars, eccentrics, and abandoned or runaway children. Presumably this was a connection too dirty for even Harry's taste, and Eastwood maintained Harry's persona as a romantic loner who reacts to situations spontaneously as an individual rather than as a member of a team.

What developed next in the field of vigilante justice, Charles Bronson's *Death Wish* (1974) and its four sequels (1981 through 1994) were not something better than Eastwood's Harry; in fact, judged by Pauline Kael's criteria, it was worse. Nevertheless, *Death Wish* had four sequels—further proof of the genre's durability and popularity—even though the sequels all had pretty much the same plot line. Bronson's vigilante hero, Paul Kersey, is a mild-mannered architect, who spent the Korean War working in a medical unit because he was a conscientious objector. But when a gang of thugs kills his wife and attacks his daughter, leaving her catatonic, he is transformed into a one-man death squad. The differences between his version of vigilante justice and Eastwood's are moderately significant. Both commodify violence and death, but Harry does this on a piecework basis, whereas Kersey's specialty is high-volume, low-overhead, wholesale mayhem, Wal-Mart-style vigilante justice. Given the chance to join a death squad in São Paulo or Rio de Janeiro, Kersey might not have had any of Harry's scruples.

Considered as a setting, Harry's San Francisco is depicted as a relatively pleasant city even though it is governed by liberals and menaced by Scorpio. Because of its diversity, wealth, and cosmopolitan culture it is—like New York and Los Angeles—one of America's great imperial cities. But in Bronson's and his Director Michael Winner's films the latter two cities are imperial in the sense that they resemble the last days of Rome with the Goths arriving. As manufacturing jobs were moved to foreign countries and many thousands of their middle-class citizens moved to the suburbs, cities like New York discovered they had an underclass: poorly educated people who were qualified for unskilled jobs that no longer existed and who often succumbed to plentiful opportunities for arson, crime, alcohol, and drug abuse. Some Americans and some of the media confronted this aspect of their society's "urban crisis" by criticizing "the system," the network of institutions that are supposed to make urban life smooth and productive. Here, for example, is a New York police chief speaking to Bill Moyers on public television about life in the Bronx in the 1970s and the 1980s. "We are creating a permanent underclass of unemployed and desperate people. ... they drop out of—they stop looking for jobs—they drop out of everything but the welfare rolls," the chief said.

> America, take a look around! Look what you're doing in your ghettos! You're creating a permanent underclass of disaffected and poor, drugged on alcohol, on welfare, living in bombed-out situations, an educational system that doesn't educate, a bureaucracy that doesn't respond, the sanitation doesn't clean, the police don't police. ... . I suppose some of us are working reasonably hard, but the fact of the matter is we're all failing.
>
> (Rosenthal 2000: 85)

Other Americans and the media, including Bronson and the *Death Wish* films, responded by demonizing the underclass and portraying them as violent, predatory criminals lurking in every dark alley: what Wink would call a "a paranoid view of reality, where violence is the only defense against those plotting our doom" (Wink 1999: 55).

In the first *Death Wish*, New York's diversity has become mongrel and polarized into class war zones in which "we," middle-class "decent people" (Death Wish Script 1974) have to struggle with "them," barbaric underclass criminals. Unfortunately these barbarians are not only within the gates and their own neighborhoods; they also are learning our names and addresses, so they can kill or rape our women (*Death Wish I* 1974), kidnap our daughters and murder our housekeepers (*Death Wish II* 1981), kill our friends (*Death Wish III* 1985), sell drugs that kill our friends' children, and invade our fiancé's business (*Death Wish IV* 1987 and *V* 1994). The police, of course, are too inept or overwhelmed to be helpful, and so Kersey avenges these crimes by going into underclass nocturnal strongholds like parks, subways, and "bad" neighborhoods. Using himself as bait, he invites attacks and then kills the attackers. Especially in *Death Wish I* he acts as if New York's entire underclass is collectively guilty. And, behaving more like an exterminator than an executioner, he trolls for thieves, muggers, and "punks" and kills them as if they were noxious pests.

Unlike Harry's antagonists, such as Scorpio and the vigilante cops, who are intelligent enough to be formidable, many of Kersey's enemies are like targets in a shooting gallery in which the vigilante never misses. Moreover, Bronson is so stolid a screen presence that the *Death Wish* films are prime examples of the "bloodlessness" Kael deplored, in which audiences have neither empathy for nor memories of the victims of the violence they see in films (Kael 1976: 252). Like Buckley's portrayal of Bigger Thomas, and even more than Dirty Harry's generic "punks," Bronson's evil "others" have a collective, demonized identity. They gloat, swagger, and brandish weapons to terrify their intended victims, and BANG! much to their surprise (but not the audiences') they are dead.

As for culture and politics, even though Harry disapproves of death squads and is willing to defend the "system" he hates, he remains a devout anti-liberal who relies on force rather than reason to resolve crises. *Death Wish* goes a step farther; it is not only anti-liberal, it is also anti-civilization as well. Civilized people, the film says, are cowards when they face danger. "What are we? What do you call people who are faced with a condition of fear and do nothing about [it], just run and hide?" Kersey asks rhetorically, and his son-in-law tamely replies, "Civilized." From this opinion it is a short step to the vigilante, "pioneer" code of, "What about the good old custom of self-defense? If the police don't defend us maybe we ought to do it ourselves" (Death Wish Script 1974). The film's logic is crude but plausible. In an environment inhabited by violent, predatory criminals whom the police cannot control or punish, self-defense is the only way to survive, and a con-cealed handgun is a mandatory deterrent. Guns become a simple panacea for urban crime and blight. As a citizen of Tucson tells Kersey, who is from New York, his Arizona city has less crime because everyone carries weapons, and therefore, "Unlike your city, we can walk through our parks and streets at night and feel safe. Muggers out here just plain get their Asses blown off" (Death Wish Script 1974).

Bigger guns cure bigger problems. In *Death Wish III* when Kersey has to clean up a New York neighborhood infested by street gangs, he uses a huge Wildey .475 handgun and a 30 caliber Browning machine gun to massacre dozens of enemies. In that film, the borderline between lawful and vigilante behavior has been erased as a police official, named Shriker (Ed Lauter), conscripts Kersey and orders him to use vigilante tactics rather than legal ones. "It'll be just like before, Mr. Vigilante," he tells Kersey, "with one important difference, you're going to be working for me" (Death Wish 3 trailer 1985). As the carnage commences and Bronson starts firing the machine gun, however, the borderline between reality and fantasy also disappears. Then, in the final scene, the gangs' leader, Manny Frakker (Gavan O'Herlihy) tries to defeat Kersey by wearing a bullet-proof vest, but the vigilante has a bazooka, an anti-tank rocket or grenade launcher, within reach, loaded and ready to fire, and the film becomes self-parody. Both Bronson and his victims are so lacking in human qualities that, as one reviewer pointed out, "there is a great deal of entertainment to be had watching ... Bronson running about and shooting bad guys like some demented video game character" (Green 1985).

But this "entertainment" takes on another significance particularly after one learns that some of the guards at Abu Ghraib were devotees of a video game, called Max Pain, that has the same plot line as *Death Wish I* and the same general plot line as that film's sequels. Its hero is a former policeman who is seeking to avenge the murder of his son and wife. "He goes on his own, takes everything into his own hands, trying to find out the [bad] guys," one of the guards told Errol Morris. "He succeeds at the end. He kills them all ... That was a way to entertain yourself" (Gourevitch 2008: 174). In the meantime, other guards, either led by Corporal Graner or on their own initiative, entertained themselves by beating, torturing, and humiliating prisoners, or by terrifying them with dogs. The latter activity was so popular they had a name for it, the "doggy dance," and the two dog handlers who participated in it, "had an ongoing contest to see which of them could make the most prisoners piss in fear" (Gourevitch 2008: 238).

These details and Inspector Shriker's assertion that now Kersey is working for him cause several paths we mentioned in our Preface to converge as the parallels that link them to one another and to Abu Ghraib and the American government become more evident. First, whether they are factual or fictional and whether or not they have personal reasons for revenge, these vigilantes are always "tough" in the sense that they rely almost entirely on force, and they are willing and able to inflict pain, injury, and/or death on anyone they consider "bad guys." This violence conforms to the redemptive myth Wink describes in that the "bad guys" are demonic villains who are so powerful that they cannot be defeated by democratic means or a criminal justice system; instead they must be destroyed by an invincible "avenger, a man on a white horse" (Wink 1999: 51) who is treated as if he is above the law or democratic restraints.

Their styles and the extent of the violence may vary. Hackman's Doyle relies mainly on physical brutality and intimidation. He and his partner Russo do not hesitate to charge into a Brooklyn bar filled with African-American men whom they shove, punch, and shout at when they want to make a "bust." Eastwood's Harry is cool and laconic; even when outnumbered by three or four to one he is always ready, Magnum in hand, for a good gun battle accompanied by a witty remark such as "Make my day" (*Sudden Impact*: 1983), "Are you feeling lucky?" (*Dirty Harry*), or "You forgot your fortune cookie" (*The Dead Pool*: 1988). Bronson's Kersey, though the least demonstrative of the three, does permit himself an occasional smug smirk when he kills someone in a clever way. Despite these minor differences, they have the same response to resistance or hostility—to dominate it completely by brutality in Doyle's case or by the lethal but conclusive violence that occurs at the end of *Dirty Harry* and *Death Wish III*. They also have the same attitude toward authority, a sense of defiant superiority. In Doyle's case, however, this attitude is dramatically questioned by his killing of the FBI agent, Mulderig, and the film's enigmatic ending, which implies that the rogue cop's or vigilante's brand of justice is just as flawed as the legalism it is meant to supplant.

In contrast, Harry's and Kersey's acts of violence are doubly conclusive in that they both destroy evil and justify extralegal or lawless responses to evil. *Dirty Harry* and *Death Wish III* further resemble one another in that there are not any bad consequences from the violence they depict. Their heroes often play dirty, shoot first, and—thanks to their superior weapons—defeat evil. But they never suffer any serious wounds; no one ever hunts them down to avenge the persons they kill, and, unlike William Munny in *Unforgiven*, they never seem to suffer from guilt or remorse. For them, violence and aggression lead to redemption without suffering—an attractive proposition.

These details—especially the reliance on force and violence, the fear of demonized enemies, the justifications for lawlessness, and the certitude that dominance over others is necessary—all parallel the attitudes certain American leaders expressed toward their nation's military forces and its enemies both before and after 9/11 in what was called the Bush Doctrine. These attitudes were not closely guarded state secrets. They and their rationales were clearly expressed in public speeches and policy statements whose implications are not difficult to decipher.

The American reliance almost exclusively on powerful military forces to protect itself and its interests can be traced back to the 1950s and Eisenhower's Doctrine of "Peace through Strength," the national security equivalent of Dirty Harry's .357 Magnum. However, a more ambitious and militaristic version of this idea was produced at century's end by a neo-conservative group, the Project for a New American Century (PNAC), whose membership in 1997 included Dick Cheney, Donald Rumsfeld, Paul Wolfowitz, and the future President's brother, Jeb. Composed mainly of Reagan era officials, the PNAC had no interest in how Eisenhower and his successors, including Reagan, had supplemented military strength with diplomacy and relied on allies to help them achieve their objectives. Instead they projected the vision of a unilateral global policeman that "stands as the world's preeminent power." But cuts on defense spending by the Clinton administration were:

making it increasingly difficult to sustain American influence around the world. ... America has a vital role in maintaining peace and security in Europe, Asia, and the Middle East. If we shirk our responsibilities, we invite challenges to our fundamental interests. The history of the 20th century should have taught us that it is important to shape circumstances before crises emerge, and to meet threats before they become dire.

(Abrams 1997)

The last sentence may sound innocuous, but it isn't. Stated in more general terms in the PNAC's September 2000 policy statement and stated even more explicitly in speeches by both Bush and Cheney after 9/11, it evolved into a nightmare scenario in which an evil dictator builds atomic bombs and gives them to terrorists. Thus it became one of Bush's rationales for "pre-emptive" wars like the one in Iraq. If any nation was hostile or tried to challenge America's status and dominance, then the United States would strike first to maintain that dominance.

Tough-minded and militaristic, this Doctrine might have been used by the Japanese to justify their attack on Pearl Harbor, but of course Cheney and Bush saw it more positively as a protection against a new 9/11—Bush in his June 1, 2002 West Point speech and Cheney in his September 22, 2003 Hartford speech when he said, in comments that obviously applied to Iran and North Korea, as well as Iraq, "It's been suggested that it's wrong for the United States to strike before an enemy strikes us. ... . the President is acting to protect us against further attacks, ... even when it means moving aggressively against would-be attackers" (Phil Taylor website 2003). So, like the vigilante films, the Bush Doctrine justifies shooting first in self-defense, which surely would have been justified in August 2001 if we had known what was planned to happen on September 11. But in their application of the Bush Doctrine to Iraq, Bush and Cheney relied on "intelligence" claiming the existence of weapons of mass destruction that no one so far has been able to discover: a development that badly damaged their credibility—whereas even in *Death Wish I*, for example, we see the mugger brandishing a switch blade leap out to attack Bronson who *then* wheels and fires.

Besides the Bush Doctrine, there was the question of the Bush style. His cowboy bravado was the Texas equivalent of Dirty Harry's taunts, except that in 2003 he was the American tough guy challenging the world. When asked about the insurgency in July of that year, he replied, "There are some who feel like ... they can attack us there. My answer is, bring 'em on! We've got the force necessary to deal with the security situation." The tough American military response to the insurgency was, like Bush's rhetoric, counterproductive. As Colonel Janis Karpinski commented later, rounding up thousands of "security detainees," most of them innocent, and holding them without any reason or evidence did not win hearts or minds. Instead it fueled desires for revenge that caused Iraqis to join the insurgency (Gourevitch 2008: 44). In the case of the guards at Abu Ghraib, this valorization of toughness and aggression was displayed by the MP guards who beat, humiliated, and tortured naked prisoners, or posed for photographs with them as if they were sexual trophies. Unfortunately for America and its interests, especially in Muslim nations, first, reports of abuses and then the resulting images from Iraq became potent motivations for enemies seeking revenge. According to Alberto Mora in testimony before the Senate Armed Services Committee in 2008, "there are serving U.S. flag-rank officers who maintain that the first and second identifiable causes of U.S. combat deaths in Iraq—as judged by their effectiveness in recruiting insurgent fighters into combat—are, respectively the symbols of Abu Ghraib and Guantanamo" (Mora 2007: 5). Mohammed Haez reaches a similar conclusion in his study of suicide bombers in Iraq. Many jihadi websites, he writes, "stress the importance of taking revenge for the transgressions in Abu Ghraib prison," as well as for insults, humiliations, and false arrests by coalition troops during anti-insurgency operations (Haez 2008: 44). During those operations troops seized thousands of Iraqis, many of whom were innocent, and jailed them, and as a result Abu Ghraib soon became one of the factors that made Iraq the perfect setting for the kind of cyclical patterns of revenges and retaliations that became so mutually destructive.

Another resemblance between the Bush government and the redemptive vigilante mentality was their tendency to demonize their antagonists, to see them not merely as enemies but as evil incarnate: Scorpio in *Dirty Harry*, Manny Frakker in *Death Wish III*, and Saddam Hussein both before and after 9/11. Bush displayed this attitude not only in his famous 2002 State of the Union reference to the "Axis of Evil"—North Korea, Iraq, and Iran—but in many other speeches which are litanies of Saddam's evils that, like the films mentioned, invoke the myth of redemptive violence. They do this by arousing the audience's fear and anger so that it will applaud the villain's destruction even if the hero uses "dirty" or unfair tactics. Similarly, in his speeches, Bush almost invariably included Saddam's cruelty and use of torture as signs of the dictator's depravity, and it is significant that he did this at the same time that he, Cheney, and Rumsfeld were demanding that Americans involved in the War on Terror resort to what most people consider cruelty and torture to get "actionable intelligence." For good measure much of this cruel and/or illegal activity occurred in a prison built by Saddam. Yet, while it was happening, Bush also was claiming that the war would be an idealistic effort to bring prosperity and democracy to Iraq. This contradiction reveals more than hypocrisy, projection, or insensitivity. It also reveals a dualism that exists in many characters in this study (and outside it) who manipulate the boundaries between legality and lawlessness or vigilante behavior and end up in a limbo that possesses bad features of both kinds of justice.

Because of their positions, Bush, Cheney, and Rumsfeld had access to what Joan Didion called an "alternative infrastructure" in her noir thriller about the Iran–Contra scandals, *The Last Thing He Wanted* (Didion 1996). (This type of infrastructure is a governmental agency, such as the CIA, that has access to governmental resources but is allowed to operate without some of the constraints and transparency that usually apply to government operations.) With the assistance of their lawyer "team" and this kind of infrastructure, the administration tried to create an alternative justice system that ran by its own rules rather than by existing laws and the Geneva Conventions. They authorized a wide variety of painful procedures to be used by the CIA and the US Army and backed them up with long memos and legal opinions that would seem in line with high standards of military legalism—if one is not a lawyer or does not know these documents were produced by a small cadre of lawyers who excluded any dissenting lawyers or persons with military experience—including Bush's Secretary of State, General Colin Powell. On a much smaller scale Shriker and Lieutenant Briggs from *Death Wish III* and *Magnum Force* also belong in this group as each provides his vigilantes with an alternative chain of command, an alternative source of authority, one that links the governmental with the vigilante or criminal—and thus give that linkage a spurious legitimacy.

General Corman (G. D. Spradlin), the MI commander in *Apocalypse Now*, who made a cameo appearance earlier in this study, is another dualistic individual with access to an alternate infrastructure. His dualism is embedded in his name: Roger Corman was famous (or infamous) as a director of Grade-B horror movies, and thus the perfect person to deal with the horrors that will terminate the film version of Conrad's *Heart of Darkness*. Courtly and civilized, the General does not need to go into Cambodia himself to hunt for Colonel Kurtz. Instead he sends Captain Willard (Martin Sheen), an experienced (six definite kills) assassin, who is presumably on loan from the CIA to "terminate" Kurtz. As he briefs Willard the General presents himself as a thoughtful man with a serious answer for why Kurtz is running amuck. It is, he says,

> Because there's a conflict in every human heart between the rational and the irrational, between good and evil. And good does not always triumph. Sometimes the Dark Side overcomes what Lincoln called "the better angels of our nature." Everything has got a breaking point. You and I have. Walter Kurtz has reached his. And very obviously, he has gone insane.
>
> (Cited in Dirks 2001)

It's an intelligent comment, but it does not go far enough. As the rest of Coppola's film illustrates, the conflict Corman describes can occur in institutions as well as in individual hearts. Armies, security forces, prison guards, and even Presidencies can have their dark sides (to use the General's and Vice President Cheney's language). Strategically placed groups and individuals within such institutions can control budgets and launder money, abuse prisoners, manipulate information and give commands that are obeyed but not recorded. "You understand, Captain, that this mission does not exist," Willard is told at the end of the briefing in *Apocalypse Now*, "nor will it ever exist." Similarly at Abu Ghraib Tim Dugan recalled that when the new guidelines to "break the back of the insurgency" came from Secretary Rumsfeld via General Sanchez, only interrogators who volunteered to use them could stay in the room, and if they stayed they could not "talk about this to anybody" (Gourevitch 2008: 211). Not only were the interrogation techniques at the prison secret, so were the existences of many of its prisoners. "Ghost detainees," for example, were put in custody for the CIA, but not registered, so the Red Cross would not know about them (Gourevitch 2008: 96).

As if to demonstrate that it was not limited to turning live Iraqis into ghosts, the American government sometimes turned nothing at all into ghosts that nevertheless legally existed. How else can one explain the existence of Leonard Bayard who appears in Paglen's and John Crewdson's torture scandal investigations? Bayard has "no residence address, no telephone number, no Social Security number, no credit history, no automobile or property ownership records." Yet as of 2005 he was the registered owner of a Gulfstream V executive jet widely believed to have been used by the CIA to fly detainees to torture sites in Europe, Egypt, and Syria. His application to register the plane, reproduced in Paglen's book, has very similar wording and handwriting as a similar request sent to the Federal Aviation Authority (FAA) nine days later. This request is from a Tyler Howard Tate to register a Boeing 737 widely reputed to be used for the same purpose. Both applications have letterheads with business names and addresses, but apparently neither Tate nor Baryard has been seen alive and well at either of these addresses (Crewdson 2005; Paglen and Thompson 2006: 161–64).

Combining contradictory realities in dualistic, clandestine systems that are rife with duplicities is not a recipe for either institutional or personal stability. Language becomes evasive, designed to conceal rather than communicate. "Torture" meant whatever the speaker wished. "Terminate" means murder in *Apocalypse Now*. "Security detainee" was a term used to "sidestep" the Geneva Conventions in Iraq; it meant prisoners captured by American troops who could not be freed because the evidence was too "thin" either way to decide whether to release them or not from Abu Ghraib. Acronyms, military jargon, euphemisms, and clichés ("take off the gloves," "dark side") proliferated. But the situation at Abu Ghraib was especially toxic, too dirty to be contained by euphemisms. Located in a Sunni district filled with insurgents, subject to frequent mortar attacks and attacks on its convoys hauling prisoners to and from Baghdad, overcrowded and understaffed, it was not an environment that could be ruled by Lincoln's "better angels" but rather by men like Corporal Graner who confided to Specialist Darby that the Christian in him knew what he was doing was wrong, but the "corrections officer in me can't help but love to make a grown man piss himself"—a statement that led Darby to conclude that Graner had a "very, very dark side" (Gourevitch 2008: 234).

As more of Graner's and other Americans' dark sides surfaced, behavior became more bizarre—cruel and capricious for the guards, unspeakably humiliating for the prisoners. You opened a door, recalled a Sergeant, and you saw, "Guys naked. ... Guys in women's panties. Guys handcuffed in stress positions, in isolation cells, no lights, no windows. Open the door, turn the light on—Oh my God, Allah. Click, turn the light off, close the door. It's like, whoa, what is that? What the hell is up with all this stuff? Something's not right here" (Gourevitch 2008: 88). Images of dogs dominating men cowering in fear or, in one of the most notorious images, one sees a woman soldier posed by a corpse. She is smiling or grinning broadly, and her hand is in a thumbs-up position. It is a party or carnival smile and gesture, the way Americans look when they signal that they believe they are really having fun.[3] The Sergeant was right; some things were very wrong at Abu Ghraib and Guantanamo and probably in Afghanistan as well. But perhaps Tim Dugan said it best when he was approached by a Sergeant from Military Intelligence who suggested that he use the MPs to "help soften up your detainees." Dugan said, "I told him I thought he was out of control. I thought the MPs were out of control" (Gourevitch 2008: 205).

"Out of control." How did that begin to happen? In the context of this study it started when many Americans, including the nation's leaders, reacted like vigilantes to the shock, grief, and fear generated by 9/11. Such a response, a mixture of righteous rage and fear disguised as rage, was inevitable in the aftermath of the attack. But prolonged and made the basis for major policy decisions, it was bound to come into conflict with the legality that constrains any nation that wishes, in Justice Hughes' words in Brown vs. Mississippi, to be considered modern and civilized and ruled by an "enlightened constitutional government" that does not replace the witness stand with torture.

Legality is deeply concerned, as we said earlier, with order, including the orderly supervision of revenge and punishment. Its procedures are designed to control the emotions aroused by crime and violence so that a court is reasonably certain the right person receives the right punishment. Its iconic movie heroes are Peck's Atticus Finch and Fonda's Juror number 8: rational men who want to prevent injustice. The vigilante mentality is less scrupulous in such matters. Its iconic figures, Eastwood's Harry and Bronson's Paul Kersey, are tough guys, predators who shoot first, think later, and see their mission as ridding the world of bad guys. Their mentality also wants certainty, but of a different kind: the certainty of punishment.

A great deal of that part of the justice process did occur between 2001 and 2008, but only at a fearful cost to America's reputation as well as immense material costs and horrendous human costs: the guilty and the innocent, Muslims and Christians, Sunnis and Shiites, Americans, Afghans, Iraqis, and many others. Some suffered far more than others, but no group was spared. Moreover, much of this punitive justice took place under conditions, such as military actions and crises, that encouraged violent emotional reactions and covert responses rather than public, rational considerations of relevant legal and ethical principles and how they applied to twenty-first-century events and situations. Under those conditions many Americans did not want to listen patiently to any equivalents to Atticus Finch or Juror Number 8. They wanted "dark side" heroes who could respond to violence and chaos by committing equal or greater redemptive violence that punishes evildoers (Saddam Hussein, Osama bin Laden) and re-establishes order in the form of a Pax Americana for the Middle East and Central Asia. Instead there was the Insurgency and civil war in Iraq, plus a resurgence of the Taliban in Afghanistan that forced Americans to recognize the limitations on and some of the negative consequences of their use of military power. For as an official of an older empire, Turton in *A Passage to India* might have warned them, resorting to military force is always risky, because "soldiers put one thing straight, but leave a dozen others crooked" (Forster 1973: 202).

At the same time that the United States began to retreat from its Bush Doctrine militarism by planning to remove its troops from Iraq, it also began to retreat from its Bush-era policies. By a 5–4 vote on June 18, 2008 the Supreme Court ruled that one of the most important principles of legalism, habeas corpus, could not be denied to the prisoners in Guantanamo. By the fall of 2008 a federal judge had used habeas corpus and applied legal common sense to one of the Guantanamo cases. Reviewing the evidence that had been the basis for imprisoning five Algerians for seven years without any charges filed against them, Judge Richard Leon discovered that the men—who had been living in Bosnia and were accused of planning to go to Afghanistan to become terrorists—were imprisoned by the United States on the basis of a single unsubstantiated "intelligence" source (Trenton Times 2008: B1).

Moreover, in January 2009 the United States inaugurated a new President, who was a graduate of Harvard Law and clearly intended to apply the rule of law and due process to governmental operations during his regime. Inaugurated on January 20 he began the process of restoring legality on January 22 when he announced an Executive Order pledging to close Guantanamo prison within a year, honoring habeas corpus at that prison, applying the Geneva Conventions, and forbidding torture. Actually closing Guantanamo and achieving these goals may be difficult, and the process may not be swift.

In the event that President Obama and his administration need an inspiration for their legalism they might consider one of the great success stories of American legalism, the Nuremberg trials. As early as May 1942 the Roosevelt administration made punishing war criminals a major war aim in a speech by Undersecretary of State Sumner Welles. The time and place of his speech were significant: Memorial Day, Arlington National Cemetery. Here, Welles was telling his countrymen, was what Americans were going to work and die for in World War II. His list of war aims included a pledge that after "utterly and finally crush[ing] the evil men, and the iniquitous systems which they have devised, that are today menacing our existence," then justice would "be done, inexorably and swiftly to those individuals, groups, or peoples, as the case may be, that can truly be held accountable for the stupendous catastrophe into which they have plunged the human race" (Welles 1942). But what sort of punishment would be appropriate for men as evil as Hitler, Himmler, and Goring and how should it be performed? Even before the details of the Holocaust were known, the Nazis' wanton cruelty, lawlessness, and destructiveness had made them perhaps the most hated nation in the history of the world. Stalin simply wanted to kill 50,000 to 100,000 Nazis en masse as revenge for what they had done to the Soviet Union. The Nazi leaders' crimes, said Winston Churchill, "surpass anything that has been known since the darkest and most brutal ages. ... Retribution for these crimes must henceforward take its place among the major purposes of the war" (Bass 2000: 147, 184). "The guilt of such individuals is so black" said Churchill's Foreign Secretary, Anthony Eden, that "they fall outside and go beyond the scope of any judicial process" (Bass 2000: 185), and therefore the British wanted summary executions for the top Nazis and trials for the mid-level ones. Roosevelt's own Secretary of the Treasury, Henry Morgenthau, considered trials and investigations unnecessary for the Nazi leaders. He believed they were so obviously "arch criminals" that they should be punished by summary executions. Mid-level Nazis would be given trials, and as for the remaining Germans who survived the war, they were to be treated as collectively guilty and would become the subjects of a peace so punitive it made the Treaty of Versailles look generous. Vast tracts of their nation would be given to Poland, France, and Denmark; its industrial infrastructure of mines, steel mills, and factories in the Ruhr would be destroyed, and Germany would become a "pastoral" country (Bass 2000, 152–54).

Despite these strongly held, emotional opinions, and despite Morgenthau's fierce opposition, the Roosevelt administration decided in January 1945 to try the leading Nazi war criminals in full dress trials that would follow "the judicial method"—that is, American legal procedures as much as possible— because summary executions might transform criminals into martyrs (Bontecou Papers 1945). The jurist selected in May 1945 to implement this plan, Supreme Court Justice Robert Jackson, did not come from an elite or an especially sophisticated legal background. He was a successful "country lawyer" from upstate New York, who had attended an Albany law school for one year, then dropped out to "read" for the law by clerking for a Jamestown lawyer, and then passed the bar exam. A liberal Democrat in a conservative stronghold, he had defended suspected radicals and communists in the 1920s, even though this had harmed his law practice. While serving on a New York State Commission on the Administration of Justice, he became acquainted with Franklin Roosevelt who was then Governor of the state. Recruited by Roosevelt as a general counsel for the Internal Revenue Service in 1934, he had risen swiftly in the ranks to become Solicitor General in 1938, Attorney General in 1940, and then a Supreme Court justice in 1941. Determined to make the trials a success, Jackson recruited a staff of 640 people, including 150 lawyers. To accommodate journalists and the public during the trials, the Americans completely refurbished the immense Palace of Justice in Nuremberg, entirely rebuilt the courtroom, and added such amenities as a travel bureau, post exchange, barbershop, and even a pub in the basement (Bontecou Papers 1945).

The obstacles the Americans faced in 1945 were formidable. The trials would have to be conducted in four languages, and they would have to follow legal principles that could be aligned with those of five nations— American, British, French, Soviet, and German. Moreover, there were no successful precedents for an international trial of this sort, only failures such as the ones attempted after World War I by the British. Yet they would have to be performed skillfully enough to mollify critics who opposed them either on principle, because they considered them "victor's justice," or because they favored summary executions. For as the British lead prosecutor at the trials, Hartley Shawcross, acknowledged, "There are those who would perhaps say that these wretched men should have been dealt with summarily without trial by 'executive action', that their personal power for evil broken, they should be swept aside onto oblivion without this elaborate and careful investigation as to the part they have played in plunging the world into war" (Bass 2000: 181). Nevertheless, the trials had gone forward under pressure from the Americans and under Jackson's leadership.[4]

What he brought to this task was not only his intelligence, leadership abilities, and oratorical skills, which were considerable, but also a clear, articulate understanding of the basic principles of legalism. Confronted by the immense lawlessness of the defendants sitting in the Nuremberg dock, Jackson rose to the challenge of showing that even they and their crimes should be punished by legalistic standards based on proofs and evidence rather than summary assumptions of guilt followed by executions. In the process of doing this, he articulated general principles of legalism that apply to other cases of lawlessness, including those described in our study.

How, for example, can we avoid letting emotion subvert the justice process? From his own feelings about a war in which 400,000 Americans had lost their lives, and from his experiences dealing with the British after the Blitz and the Soviets after the horrors of the Eastern Front, Jackson would have understood this problem very well, but he would not have sympathized with vigilante or lawless treatment of criminals in either the twentieth or the twenty-first centuries. As he commented to President Harry Truman in June of 1945, after his consultations with the British and the Soviets, it would have been impossible to free the German war criminals that the Americans had captured. But summary executions of the type demanded by Morgenthau, Churchill, and Stalin (or practiced by Captain Willard or Dirty Harry) were also unacceptable, because "undiscriminating executions or punishments without definite findings of guilt, fairly arrived at ... would not set easily on the American conscience or be remembered by our children with pride." The only other honorable option, he said, was, therefore, "to determine the innocence or guilt of the accused after a hearing as dispassionate as the times and horrors we deal with will permit, and upon a record that will leave our reasons and motives clear" (Jackson 1945b). The last sentence also suggests that Jackson would not be supportive of past or recent efforts to conceal records and motives by using national security as a rationale.

Nor would Jackson have tolerated failure or refusal to follow due process because of inertia or assumptions regarding collective guilt. As the lead prosecutor in a trial that condemned twelve defendants to death, Jackson clearly was willing to punish the guilty to the full extent of the law. But that punishment must occur after a "good faith" trial, because "courts try cases, but cases also try courts. You must put no man on trial ... if you are not prepared to establish his personal guilt. ... on a foundation more certain than suspicion or current rumor," Jackson said in a speech in April 1945, and then added:

> Men of our tradition cannot regard any proceeding as a trial that does not honestly search for the facts, bring forward the best sources of proof obtainable, [and] critically examine testimony. ... . The ultimate principle is that you must put no man on trial under the forms [of] judicial proceedings if you are not willing to see him freed if not proven guilty. ... ; the world yields no respect to courts that are merely organized to convict.
>
> (Jackson 1945a)

Considered from this perspective one of the great successes of the Nuremberg trials was not that they sentenced 12 defendants to the gallows, but that they acquitted three and gave the remainder, such as Albert Speer, prison terms. What this quote also illustrates is a great difference between Jackson's insistence on rationality and due process versus the vigilante mentality and the myth of redemptive violence with their insistence upon rage and punishment.

As the well-known first sentences of Jackson's Opening Statement to the Nuremberg Tribunals show, he could speak with anger that was passionate and powerful, but his greater concern was to subordinate that emotion to reason. "The wrongs which we seek to condemn and punish," Jackson said,

> have been so calculated, so malignant, and so devastating, that civilization cannot tolerate their being ignored, because it cannot survive their being repeated. That four great nations, flushed with victory and stung with injury stay the hand of vengeance and voluntarily submit their captive enemies to the judgment of the law is one of the most significant tributes that Power has ever paid to Reason.
>
> (Jackson 1945c)

When one contrasts the images of Nuremberg in 1945 with images from the war on terror between 2003 and 2008, the contrast is disturbing and enlightening. The infamous images from Abu Ghraib are filled with squalor, degradation, chaos, and brutality; they are symptomatic of a society that had lost control over itself and its dark side. In contrast the images from Nuremberg are exceptionally orderly. Power, the power that Jackson spoke of, is there in the uniformed military policemen who stand behind the defendants' box. In their white helmets and white belts they form a cordon of security that both imprisons and guards the defendants. If the print is clear enough one can see the campaign ribbons and medals on their chests, reminders that they are veterans of a victorious army. They, like the judges and prosecutors, are imposing order on chaos, the moral as well as material chaos created by the defendants. They represent a power that is in control of itself, which has disciplined itself and accepts reason rather than rage as a "moral compass." As for the defendants, they too are orderly. Some of them are, with good reason, deeply depressed, and one of them, Rudolf Hess, is probably insane. But they were not abused or coerced to make confessions; they were allowed to defend themselves, call witnesses to testify on their behalf, and had capable lawyers to defend them. No one tortured them or piled them in pyramids of naked bodies or threatened them with dogs. Instead, they had been treated, as General Washington presumably would have recommended, "with dignity and respect."

What cannot be replicated, however, are some of the historical circumstances that made Nuremberg possible and successful. In 1945 and 1946 the Cold War was just beginning. The trials were one of the last efforts when the United States and the Soviet Union tried to cooperate rather than to compete with one another. American leaders (and their Soviet counterparts) were just beginning to eat the forbidden fruit of the Cold War. The

CIA and a plethora of covert military units were being founded with "missions" that substituted secrecy and James Bond for openness and the concern for rationalism that are characteristic of legalism. In the next decade, the 1950s, that agency would enter into its "glory years" when "few questions were asked of it. Congressional watchdog committees specifically told Allen Dulles they did not want to know about clandestine operations. The President [Eisenhower] and the public took it for granted that the only way to fight the Russians and their KGB (secret police) was to use dirty tricks about which the less that was known, the better. No questions were asked about cost, either." Especially in the Third World, "the application of a little force or a little money could have dramatic results," at least on a short-term basis (Ambrose and Brinkley 1997: 148).

However, overthrowing governments in Iran and Guatemala, consorting with Greek colonels, Argentine generals, Indonesian and Congolese kleptocrats, Central American and Chilean death squads, and the likes of Saddam Hussein, would eventually almost certainly have some negative long-term effects upon America's "moral compass," and contributed to some of our contemporary problems. If nothing else these covert agencies and operations created much of the dark side alternative infrastructure that was so readily available to the Bush administration after 9/11—such as "torture taxis" and secret torture centers in the Middle East and elsewhere.

The cultural climate of the 1970s and 1980s was also changing, as the study indicates. The type of rational characters played by Henry Fonda, Dana Andrews, and Gregory Peck were being displaced by Dirty Harry and his magnificent Magnum, by Popeye Doyle with his .38 "snubby," and by Charles Bronson with his machine gun and bazooka. Vigilante gunmen and rogue cops can be powerful and appealing emblems of valor. In the more or less fantasy world of thriller movies, they can be very persuasive. Questions about guilt and innocence that are so crucial to the legalistic mentality can be finessed in these films. In the *French Connection* the audience is in the chaotic runaway subway train being terrorized by Frog 2. The audience sees him kill a transit policeman and the train conductor, and so it applauds when Doyle leaps out of his battered car, confronts the killer, and kills him. Similarly in *Dirty Harry*, the audience is in the school bus that Scorpio has hijacked. It can hear the screaming children, share their fear, and then can see Harry leaping from an overpass onto the top of the bus, then chasing Scorpio and killing him. As entertainment, it's wonderful, but as a guide to conduct this mentality may be less reliable on the actual streets of Brooklyn and San Francisco.

But don't misjudge us.[5] As long as it is not made the basis for serious foreign policy decisions and wars in places where Americans know little or nothing of the languages or the cultures of the people and the places they are occupying, we acknowledge the appeal of the vigilante mentality. In fact, in its own times and places that mentality could be quite an effective form of justice with warriors seeking revenge for injuries and injustices. Read

Beowulf, for example, set in Denmark in northern Europe over a millennium ago. A king's mead hall is being attacked virtually every night by a grotesque, homicidal monster called Grendel. There is no need to demonize Grendel, because he *is* a demon. Fortunately for the king a hero arrives, Beowulf. When Grendel next attacks, the struggle that follows has no frills or legal niceties, but it succeeds. Beowulf tears off the monster's arm, and the creature runs howling to die in his lair. Soon, Grendel's mother avenges her son's death by killing another Dane who was a favorite of the King. Beowulf tells the king, "Wise Sir, do not grieve. It is always better to avenge dear ones than to indulge in mourning" (Donoghue, Ed. Beowulf 2002: lines 1383–85). Beowulf is right. He follows her to her lair, kills her, and returns victorious. Once again his victory is celebrated with lavish gifts and feasts.

Beowulf is an ideal warrior, but he is also a barbarian. For him and his culture revenge was a matter of physical force, not law, and behavior that would now be considered "barbaric" was highly approved. The decrowning motif that is part of the carnival tradition of justice, for example, is no mere civilized symbolic blow to the head such as the one Vautrin receives in Balzac's novel but an actual decapitation. When Beowulf finds Grendel's corpse in his mother's lair, says the poet, "the warrior determined to take revenge/for every gross act Grendel had committed," he does this by cutting off the monster's head and bringing it back to the mead hall as a trophy. It is "dragged across the floor where the people were drinking /a horror ... to behold" (Beowulf 2002: 1577–78, 1647–49).

Like the end of *Macbeth* when Macduff enters carrying Macbeth's severed head it is barbaric, heroic, carnivalistic, and—from an emotional standpoint—a deeply satisfying image of closure and revenge. But in the twenty-first century, it is also a fantasy: a world without lawyers, Miranda warnings, or due process. It's a world that Charles Bronson, Dirty Harry, or Jimmy Marcus would enjoy. There is no one to question whether Beowulf has killed the right monster, or insisted that even Grendel, like Hermann Goring, deserves his day in court and has an opportunity to defend himself. There would be no Guantanamo or Abu Ghraib scandals, because the detainees, the innocent as well as the guilty, probably would have received summary executions. But what kind of rating would *Dirty Harry* have received if Harry had cut off Scorpio's head and brought it back to the D.A.'s Office in triumph? Or, better yet, if the American Special Forces that captured Saddam Hussein had immediately executed and decapitated him, and General Ricardo Sanchez had brought his head back to Washington, strode into the Oval Office, and presented it to his Commander-in-chief, Congressional leaders, and the assembled cabinet?

The courts may try to fill the revenge function and the emotions it arouses, but they cannot always do this successfully. Yet legalism, based on rationalism and controlled by constitutions is too deeply embedded in our culture to be ignored safely. Eliminate it or subvert it, and it is likely that power will be seized—not by an idealized warrior like Beowulf—but by a Goring or a Pinochet. So we need Justice Jackson for his superb organizational and negotiating skills, his commitment to justice demonstrated at Nuremberg, and Clint Eastwood, not only for his Dirty Harry marksmanship and valor, but for his willingness to moderate the vigilante ethic in *Unforgiven*, to work together, not against one another, and recognize the advantages and the limitations of their respective forms of revenge. But that should not be impossible if they apply Harry's mantra from *Magnum Force*: "a man's got to know his limitations."

Notes

1 Introduction

1 Stalin's idea of a good day was "to plan an artistic revenge on an enemy, carry it out to perfection, and then go home and go peacefully to bed" (Parke 2007).

2 Revenge and the detective tradition: when dogs don't bark and detectives don't tell

1 For the rest of Doyle's list see Doyle 1994: 435–36.
2 Glaspell 1993: 286. In 1900–01 Glaspell was a reporter for the *Des Moines Daily News*, and she wrote extensively about a local murder and trial in which a farm woman, Margaret Hossack, was accused of murdering her husband with two blows with a hatchet or ax while he was asleep. The most damaging evidence against her at her trial was that "she lay asleep by her husband and was not awakened while the murder was taking place." At the first trial Mrs. Hossack was convicted of murder, but the Iowa Supreme Court ordered a retrial that ended in a hung jury, and the prosecution did not seek a third trial. Ben-Zvi 1995: 24–33.
3 Quotations are from Benjamin Flowers, editor of *The Arena*, cited in Shi 1995: 2, 203. Also see Shi 1995: 203–9.

3 Some like it wild: supernatural revenge in Sheridan Le Fanu's "Mr. Justice Harbottle"

1 See our discussion of this topic in Chapter 1.
2 According to Tracy, "Mr. Justice Harbottle" was originally published in *Belgravia* magazine (January 1872) under the title "The Haunted House in Westminister" without any chapter divisions (Le Fanu 1993: 326). Presumably those were added when it was published in *In a Glass Darkly* later in 1872.
3 As Jack Sullivan notes, these "earnest but tortured attempt[s] to reconcile medical science with mystical experience" were a "commonplace exercise in nineteenth- and early twentieth-century weird fiction." Several of the writers, besides Le Fanu, who attempted it were Robert Louis Stevenson, Arthur Machen, Algernon Blackwood, William Hodgson, and H. G. Wells (Sullivan 1978: 27, 138). Some of the other alternatives employed by earlier or less-sophisticated Gothic writers included simply assuming that the supernatural existed (thus risking the sneers of the Enlightened), having the events in the narrative occur and be narrated in an earlier, more credulous age (when everyone believed in ghosts and miracles), or surrendering to rationalism by explaining a novel's or story's supernatural events as being tricks created by trap-doors, mirrors, and other "special effects" (thus anticipating Hollywood).

4 Le Fanu 1993: 117. In "The Familiar," another retribution story in *In a Glass Darkly*, Le Fanu was far more casual about his story's ghost and its ability to intervene in the material world. It sends its victim letters; it travels around Europe to intercept him when he tries to escape from it, and at one point in the narrative it fires a musket at him (Le Fanu 1993: 57).

5 Despite the cleverness of his theories, Hesselius is remarkably incompetent as a psychiatrist in the one story in *In a Glass Darkly*, "Green Tea," in which he tries to cure a patient (Sullivan 1978: 24–25). The haunting in that story may be considered "modern" in the sense that it is so inexplicable that it is absurd. Unlike Harbottle or Captain Barton, the protagonist of "The Familiar," the Reverend Jennings—the protagonist/victim of "Green Tea"—has done nothing that would deserve retribution from the supernatural, except drink too much green tea and read too much Emmanuel Swedenborg. Like the characters in some of Kafka's grim justice narratives, Jennings does not seem to have done anything to deserve his fate, and Hesselius' theories about Jennings and his sufferings are more fatuous than convincing.

4 Law and the romantic ego: conspiracy and justice in Honoré de Balzac's *Le Père Goriot*

1 *Lost Illusions* Balzac 1987: 641, 646, 648. For a survey of Vautrin's assorted conspiracies and villainies in other Balzac novels, see Marceau 1966: 290–93.

2 Balzac, *History of the Thirteen* 1974: 21. This "Preface" was dated 1831, but the novel was written and published two years later. Manfred, Melmoth, and Faust were the Rebel-heroes of works by Byron, Charles Maturin, and Goethe. These were the Romantic or Gothic authors and characters that Balzac himself had imitated in his early 1820s potboilers that were "filled with pirates, freebooters, outlaws of every kind" (Maurois 1965: 258). As Peter Brooks points out, Balzac's novels are also filled with

> organizations such as the Confrérie de la Consolation, Les Grands Fanandels, the Dévorants (otherwise Les Treize); and looser organizations of plotters, the bankers of *César Birotteau*, the Cointet brothers and their associates in the third part of *Illusions perdues*, the various secret police and counter-police in *Splendeurs et misères des courtisanes*, ... and the single figure, benefactor or demon, who manipulates lives— Gosbeck, Doctor Benassis in *Le Médicin de campagne*, Baron de Nucingen, John Melmoth, Vautrin. These organizations, groups, persons are all dedicated to the reorganization and manipulation of life. Their sphere of activity is behind the visible world—the stage of the novel—yet their actions decisively govern the play of the actors in [that] world.
> (Brooks 1976: 119. See also Marceau 1966: 319)

Moreover, as Sarah Maza demonstrates, in the last half of the eighteenth century and just before the revolution, French society had an avid interest in court cases, scandals, and conspiracies, particularly those involving aristocratic or royal personages in shady sexual and/or financial intrigues. See Chapters 4–6 of her study.

3 Recurring characters are, of course, one of the main features of the Comédie humaine. See Maurois 1965: 259–61. In his analysis of Balzac's *A Harlot High and Low*, Prendergast argues that when Vautrin changes from a master criminal to a policeman in the last section of that novel, this "conversion" does not mean there has been any significant change in his values or personality, since "the action of the novel, in continually stressing the moral similarities of the protagonists and antagonists," implies that "Vautrin experiences no difficulties, ... in 'joining' society because the real values of that society are qualitatively no different from his own as a criminal" (Prendergast 1978: 87).

4 Brooks, "Editor's Introduction," Balzac 1998: xii. Also see Proust in Balzac 1998: 239; Saint-Beauve in Balzac 1998: 223–25.
5 Balzac 1998: 125, 103, 62, 164, 15, 152, 123, 153. Baudelaire is in Balzac 1998: 235. See also Albert Béguin in Balzac 1998: 263–72.
6 Conrad, *Heart of Darkness* 1924: 181. See Conrad's *The Secret Agent* where some of the same attitudes are espoused by that novel's nihilists and anarchists as well as by the reactionary Russian diplomat, Vladimir. When paranoid obsessions and/or messianic fantasies are added to this already volatile combination of attitudes, the political consequences can indeed be, as Conrad implicitly warns, very "extreme"—as many nations have discovered during the twentieth and twenty-first centuries. In the words of their respective enemies—the colonial manager in *Heart* and General Corman in *Apocalypse Now*—both Kurtzes use "unsound" methods (Conrad 2002: 169).
7 Balzac 1998: 107. That the specific location of both this and the later meeting between Micheannou and the detective is in the Jardin des Plantes is omitted by Burton Raffel in his translation of the novel. (See Balzac 1998: 1951, 961, 983.)
8 Later Balzac suggests that Gondureau is really the "famous chief of police, Vidocq" (Balzac 1998: 145). An ex-convict who became a policeman, Vidocq (1775–1857) is considered one of Balzac's original sources for Vautrin. See Prendergast, note 3 above.
9 Gautier 1980: 225–28. It is also significant that Gautier identifies this mixing of languages as a sign of Balzac's "modernity." For similar comments on language in Bakhtin, see his *The Dialogic Imagination* 1982: 288–91. Also see Bakhtin (1984: 153) for the "*cris de Paris*" as a carnival motif, one that appears in *Père Goriot* 139–40.
10 Balzac 1998: 42. Vautrin's slapping Goriot's hat is one of several symbolic and literal decrownings that occurs in the novel. The detective Gondereau describes the slang of Paris criminals in which "college professor" ("*Sorbonne*") and "pumpkin" ("*tronche*") are the terms for the human head before and after it is cut off by a guillotine. Balzac 1998: 145, 951, 1004. Because of a special maneuver that Vautrin invents, young Taillefer is killed by a sword thrust to the forehead. Balzac 1998: 134, 148. And Vautrin himself is decrowned when his wig is knocked off by the blow from a policeman. See Balzac 1998: 153. For the significance of "decrowning," see Bakhtin 1984: 124–26.
11 Balzac 1998: 204. In one of his delirious speeches, the dying Goriot rants that his daughters' ingratitude toward him is criminal and that they should be arrested, if necessary, to come to his death-bed: "Call out the police, the Navy, the Marines, everyone! everyone! ... Tell the government, tell the attorney general ... " Balzac 1998: 206.

5 Justice, race, and revenge in Twain's *Pudd'nhead Wilson*

1 See for example Gillman 1989: 55, 70, 83–86, 94–95. For commentaries on the novel's miscegenation theme and its relation to the motif of the "tragic mulatto" see Pettit 1979 in Berger 1980: 347.
2 Quoted Gillman 1989: 12. Despite Twain's (Samuel Clemens') immense popularity as a humorist, the author of an 1898 essay argued:

> there is a serious Mark Twain of whom the world knows little or nothing. Some readers, of course must have recognised that beneath the foaming fun and fancy ... there are deeps of earnest and suggestive thought: and that in his later works, such as 'A Connecticut Yankee at [*sic*] the Court of King Arthur,' and 'Pudd'nhead Wilson,' there are abundant proofs that the writer has quite as firm a grasp of some of the profoundest problems of the day as many of the specialists have. But those who share these views form a very narrow circle of his admirers.
>
> (Carlyle Smythe 1982: 131)

3 Twain, *Life on the Mississippi*, 2007: 236. For an analysis of the cultural attitudes toward dueling in the South, see Hahn 1989: 145–48.
4 Berger 1980: 74. See also Berger 1980: 58. When his supposed nephew, Tom Driscoll, confesses that he has not challenged Count Luigi to a duel after the Market Hall riot, Judge Driscoll responds: "You scum! You vermin! Do you mean to tell me that blood of my race has suffered a blow and crawled to a court of law about it?" Berger 1980: 60. Since York Driscoll himself is a judge, his reaction implies the extent to which the code duello took priority over the rule of law in cases involving gentlemen. Also see Smith in Berger 1980: 249; Turner in Berger 1980: 280.
5 Berger 1980: 39. Earlier in the novel, Twain describes Roxy as being "happy and proud" when she sees "her son, her nigger son, lording it among the whites and securely avenging their crimes against her race" Berger 1980: 22. See also Turner in Berger 1980: 278; Cox 1966: 230.
6 See Cox 1966: 222, 245; Wiggins in Berger 1980: 256, for example.
7 Weisberg 1984: 13. Weisberg's starting point is a number of aphorisms by Nietzsche, mainly on the ressentiment early Christians felt toward Roman and classical values. Some of the major literary examples Weisberg discusses are Flaubert's Frederic Moreau in *A Sentimental Education*, the speaker of Dostoyevsky's *Notes from the Underground*, and Clamence, the protagonist of Camus' *The Fall*.
8 Essex is mentioned very briefly later in the novel (Berger 1980: 22, 43), but he is never characterized or described in any way. Twain mentioning Essex and then excluding him from the narrative can be considered an example of the process described by Forrest Robinson (1993: 113) in which popular culture texts reveal and conceal cultural anxieties. Like Doyle's revelation/concealment of the scandalous secrets of Milverton's victims (see Chapter II), Twain hints at a cultural anxiety, in this case, miscegenation, but he makes that aspect of the slavery system seem less disturbing by almost completely eliminating Tom's white father from the story.
9 In early drafts of the novel, Tom's biological father was Judge York Driscoll, so Twain did consider the possibility of having a "Black" son murder his white father. See Turner in Berger 1980: 276; Pettit in Berger 1980: 350. Also see Cox 1966: 232.
10 Emphasis in original. Twain, "Letter to Fred Hall, 30 July 1893". Also see Gillman 1989: 88–89.

6 The empire strikes back: imperialism and justice in E. M. Forster's *A Passage to India*

1 See, for example, Aziz's political views on Forster 1973: 299. Later in the novel he becomes a convert to the nationalist cause, but his speeches to Fielding—in which he shouts that "India shall be a nation!"—consist of shrill slogans rather than serious political ideas. (See the end of this chapter.)
2 Forster described the massacre in his 1920, "Notes on the English Character," as a "public infamy" (Forster 1920: 13).
3 Mrs. Turton's demand that Indians crawl is a reference to one of the "punishments" inflicted at Amritsar by General Dyer's order: Indian men who entered a lane where the Englishwoman had been assaulted had to crawl down it.

7 Race, sex, fear, revenge in Richard Wright's *Native Son*

1 This is one of the few moments expressing positive carnival humor in the novel; the rest are negative or destructive.
2 Wright 1940: 11. There are two moderately different versions of Wright's novel's manuscript. In one, published in 1940, he deleted or changed passages the Book-of-the-Month Club's editors considered too "offensive" for its readers, plus other changes (such as the

passage just quoted) that he seems to have added for purposes of clarification. Quotes from that version are identified as Wright 1940 in this book. A slightly earlier, "restored" version of the novel, based on Wright's typescript, was published in 1991 by the Library of America and is the one (cited as Wright 1940 in this study) considered definitive.

3 As Max tells the judge, his decision to have Bigger plead guilty is based on the precedent set by Clarence Darrow in the Leopold and Loeb trial (Wright 1991: 798). Darrow assumed that since a jury would surely impose a death sentence, his only hope was to have his clients plead guilty and have the sentence given by a judge who would be more influenced by rational arguments than a jury would be.

4 Despite their celebrity status, these gangsters were still seen as doomed people whose violent deaths proved "crime does not pay."

5 Horton, who was serving a life-sentence for first-degree homicide in Massachusetts and was ineligible for parole, was released for a weekend as part of a furlough program during Michael Dukakis' Governorship. Traveling to Maryland, he held a man captive by beating and stabbing him, then raped the man's fiancée. Despite this event, Dukakis continued to defend the program by claiming it helped to rehabilitate prisoners, and he did not discontinue it until April 1988 (Parmet 1997: 335–36).

8 State terrorism and revenge in André Brink's *A Dry White Season*

1 For discriminatory legislation, see Mandela 1996: 99–103. For the security laws passed between 1950 and 1980, see de Villiers 1983: 395–401.

2 The quote is from Methodist Bishop Peter Storey commenting to the TRC on the Winnie Mandela case (Meredith 1999: 249).

3 Despite the destruction of literally tons of records by the apartheid state's military and security establishment (Meredith 1999: 287–89), substantial amounts of information about these crimes were obtained first by the Richard Goldstone and Jan D'Olivera judicial commission reports and the trials that followed them. Then, on a much larger scale there were the TRC and its hearings. That Commission heard testimony from over 22,000 victims of violence and received more than 7,000 requests for amnesty from perpetrators. Kiss 88. Its testimonies and reports were widely disseminated in the media, including radio and television and a website.

4 Emphasis in original. de Villiers 1983: 401–2. Also see Brink 1984: 62, 71.

5 This statistic is from Attridge and Jolly xiii. According to the TRC, the situation grew worse after Biko's death during the regime of P. W. Botha. Previous apartheid governments had been repressive, but Botha's "adopted a [deliberate] policy of killing its opponents. It was also responsible for the widespread use of torture, abduction, arson, and sabotage" (Meredith 1999: 294).

6 Spegele and Vale 1993: 446. Also see Price 1991: 62–65.

7 Brink 1984: 288. A third carnivalistic figure is Phil Bruwer who is the dualistic opposite of Ben's repressive father-in-law. See above.

8 The issue of lying for *Volk en Vaderland* was raised at one of Eugene de Kock's trials. When asked why he had lied to a commission investigating police criminality, the Colonel replied:

> It was in the interest of the police. It was in the interest of the government. ... .

> [Attorney] ACKERMANN: So you committed perjury for *Volk en Vaderland?*

> DE KOCK: Yes, that is correct. (Cited in Meredith 1999: 48)

9 Brink 1983. The Afrikaner's positive qualities, he said, were his "reverence for life, his romanticism, his sense of the mystical, his deep attachment to the earth, his generosity, his compassion" (Brink 1983: 19).

10 Brink 1984: 160. Also see *Mapmakers* (Brink 1983: 15; LeMay 1995: 23).

11 *Mapmakers* (Brink 1983: 21). For Brink's additional comments on Fischer, see *Mapmakers* (Brink 1983: 55–60). However, despite the *laager* mentality, throughout much of their history both dissident and conformist Afrikaners have demonstrated a formidable capacity for *broedertwis* ("strife between brothers"). Writing about the "ferocity" of Afrikaner politics in 1945, an English South African described the treatment of Afrikaners who dared to support Jan Smuts's United Party rather than the NP:

> Smuts's people in a *dorp* [village] where the majority are Nationalists are liable to be treated ... as outcasts. They live in an atmosphere of ostracism. Boycott, in church and business affairs, never ceases to harass and pursue them. The Boer nature is tough. The followers of Smuts ... have borne this burden of enmity from their own people for years without bating an iota of their political faith. They still bear it. They do far more than bear it; they glory in it. A strange people.
>
> (Le May 1995: 231, 186)

12 *Reinventing* (Brink 1996: 23). Also see *Mapmakers* (Brink 1983: 46–51).

13 The five policemen implicated in the killing of Steve Biko were denied amnesty for a variety of reasons. In its verdict the Commission believed that the

> killing of Biko was not an act associated with a political objective as required by the Amnesty Act. The committee was not satisfied that the applicants had made a full disclosure as further required by the Act. It was not satisfied that the applicants testified truthfully to the events leading to the injury of Biko and further concluded that the applicants' version of how Biko sustained the fatal head injury, to be "so improbable and contradictory that it had to be rejected as false."
>
> (*Infogovza*, "TRC Amnesty Decision" 1999)

14 According to Archbishop Desmond Tutu:

> Ubuntu is a concept that we have in our Bantu languages at home. Ubuntu is the essence of being a person. It means that we are people through other people. We cannot be fully human alone. We are made for interdependence, we are made for family. When you have ubuntu, you embrace others. You are generous, compassionate. If the world had more ubuntu, we would not have war. We would not have this huge gap between the rich and the poor. You are rich so that you can make up what is lacking for others. You are powerful so that you can help the weak, just as a mother or father helps their children.

15 Morgan 2008. In 1995 the Springboks had only one Black player, Chester Williams. By the millennium the team had a world-class Black player, Brian Habbana, and in 2008 they had their first Black coach, Peter DeVillers.

9 Rogue cops and beltway vigilantes

1 In the novel, which is much more pessimistic than the film, both the major and his son commit suicide (Clark 1940: 238).

2 For this approach to Clint Eastwood's films and the relationship of the redemptive violence myth to popular culture texts we are indebted to Ms. Christina Farrell and her paper on "Vigilante Justice in Clint Eastwood's 'Unforgiven' and 'Mystic River.'"

3 For an insightful commentary on this disturbing image, see Errol Morris's "The Most Curious Thing" (2008).

4 Despite his excellent skills as an orator and his organizational abilities Jackson had his limitations, particularly as a trial lawyer. He did very poorly in his cross-examinations at the trial, especially in his confrontation with Goring (Conot 1993: 336–40).

5 For this phrase and the quote at the end of this chapter, see the film *Magnum Force* and the confrontation scenes between Harry and the vigilante cops and Lieutenant Briggs.

Bibliography

Abrams, E. et al. (1997) *Statement of Principals*, Project for the New American Century, June 3. Available at: www.newamericancentury.org/statementofprinciples.htm (accessed August 15, 2009).

Abu Ghraib Timeline (2004) *Associated Press*, May 7. Available at: www.scvhistory.com/scvhistory/signal/iraq/abughraib-timeline.htm (accessed August 1, 2009).

ACLU of Minnesota (2009) *President Obama Orders Gitmo Closed and Ends Torture*, ACLU of Minnesota, January 22. Available at: www.aclu-mn.org/home/news/presidentobamaordersgitmoc.htm (accessed June 14, 2009).

Allende, I. (1988) *Of Love and Shadows*. New York: Bantam.

Ambrose, S. and Brinkley, D. (1997) *Rise to Globalism*, 8th ed. New York: Penguin.

Anonymous (1895) "From The Critic," May 11, Sidney Berger (ed.), *Pudd'nhead Wilson and Those Extraordinary Twins*. New York: Norton Critical Editions, 1980.

Anthropology in the News (2003) "Blood Revenge as a Common Motive in Tribal Warfare," *Anthropology in the News, February 19. Available at: www.unl.edu/rhames/courses/212/anthronews.htm#revenge (accessed February 12, 2008).*

Aristotle (1990) "Nicomachean Ethics," R. Solomon and M. Murphy (eds.), *What is Justice?* New York: Oxford University Press.

Attridge, D. and Jolly, R. (eds.) (1998) *Writing South Africa*. Cambridge: Cambridge University Press.

Bacon, F. (1625) *Essays, Civil and Moral*. The Harvard Classsics, Vol. 3, ed. C. Eliot, p. 15. 1909–1914. New York: P. F. Collier & Sons.

Baker, K. (1999) "Defining the Public Sphere," C. Calhoun (ed.), *Habermas and the Public Sphere*. Cambridge, MA: MIT Press.

Bakhtin, M. (1982) *The Dialogic Imagination*, M. Holquist (ed.) (Translated by Caryl Emerson and Michael Holquist). Austin: University of Texas Press.

——(1984) *Rabelais and His World*. (Translated by Helene Iswolsky.) Bloomington: Indiana University Press.

——(1988) *Problems of Dostoevsky's Poetics*. (Translated by Caryl Emerson.) Minneapolis: University of Minnesota Press.

De Balzac, H. (1951) *Le Père Goriot*. Paris: Editions Gallimard.

Balzac, H. (1974) *The History of the Thirteen*. (Translated by Herbert Hunt.) Hammondsworth: Penguin.

——(1987) *Lost Illusions*. (Translated by Herbert Hunt.) Hammondsworth: Penguin.

——(1998) *Le Père Goriot*. (Translated by Burton Raffel.) New York: Norton Critical Editions.

Bass, G. (2000) *Stay the Hand of Vengeance*. Princeton: Princeton University Press.

BBC News (2004) "Chile Army Admits Rights Abuses," *BBC News*, November 5. Available at: http://newsvote.bbc.co.uk/mpapps/pagetools/print/news.bbc.co.uk/2/hi/ americas/ 3987341.stm (accessed March 13, 2008).

Ben-Zvi, L. (1995) "'Murder She Wrote': The Genesis of Susan Glaspell's Trifles," Linda Ben-Zvi (ed.), *Susan Glaspell: Essays on Her Theater and Fiction*. Ann Arbor: University of Michigan Press.

Berger, S. (ed.) (1980) *Pudd'nhead Wilson and Those Extraordinary Twins*. New York: Norton Critical Editions.

Bond, K. (2007) "Mandela Unites a Nation to RWC Glory," *Rugby News Service*, July 9. Available at: www.rugbyworldcup.com/home/news/newsid=1042046.html (accessed June 6, 2008).

Bonnefoy, P. (2006) "Joy, and Violence, Death of Pinochet," *The New York Times*, December 11. Available at: http://query,nytimes.com/gst/fullpage.html?res=9E07E2DA1431F932A25751C 1A9609C8863&sec=&pagewanted=print (accessed July 1, 2009).

Bontecou Papers (1945) *Agreement for the Establishment of an International Military Tribunal*, World War II File, Harry S. Truman Presidential Museum & Library. Available at: www.trumanlibrary. org/whistlestop/study_collections/nuremberg/documents/index.php?documentdate=1945-00-00 &documentid=18–3&studycollectionid=&pagenumber=1 (accessed August 15, 2009).

Boraine, A. (2000) "Truth and Reconciliation in South Africa: the Third Way," R. I. Rothberg and D. Thompson (eds.), *Truth v. Justice: The Morality of Truth Commissions*. Princeton: Princeton University Press.

Boucher, G. (2008) "Clint Eastwood Targets the Legacy of Dirty Harry," *Los Angeles Times*, June 1. Available at: www.latimes.com/entertainment/news/movies/la-ca-clint1-video-2008jun01,0,4638311.story (accessed August 15, 2009).

Brink, A. (1983) *Mapmakers: Writing in a State of Siege*. London: Faber & Faber.

——(1984) *A Dry White Season*. New York: Penguin.

——(1996) *Reinventing a Continent*. Cambridge, MA: Zoland.

Brooks, P. (1976) *The Melodramatic Imagination*. New Haven: Yale University Press.

Brown, R. (1975) *Strain of Violence*. New York: Oxford University Press.

Brown v. State of Mississippi (1936) *U.S. Supreme Court, 297 U.S. 278*. Available at: http://caselaw. lp.findlaw.com/scripts/getcase.pl?court=us&vol=297&invol=278 (accessed August 15, 2009).

Browne, N. (1951) *Sheridan Le Fanu*. London: Arthur Barker.

Burgis, T. (2004) "Army Honors Prats," *Santiago Times*, October 1. Available at: www. santiagotimes.cl/santiagotimes/index.php/200410015324/news/oldest/army-honors-prats.html (accessed August 1, 2009).

Burns, J. (1997) "Queen Bows Head over Massacre in India," *The New York Times*, October 15, page A1 plus.

Butler, M. (1975) *Jane Austen and the War of Ideas*. Oxford: Clarendon Press.

Butler, R. (1991) *Native Son: The Emergence of a New Black Hero*. Boston: Twayne.

Calvino, I. (1987) *The Literature Machine: Essays Translated by Patrick Creagh*. London: Secker & Warburg Press.

Center for Constitutional Rights (CCR) (2009) *CCR Applauds Spanish Judge's Decision to Open New Criminal Investigation into U.S. Torture Program*. Center for Constitutional Rights. 29 April. Available at: http://ccrjustice.org/newsroom/press-releases/ccr-applauds-spanish-judge's-decision-open-new-criminal-investigation-u.s.-t (accessed July 17, 2009).

Cervantes, M. (1951) *The Portable Cervantes*. (Translated by Samuel Putnam.) New York: Viking.

Chile: Human Rights Development (2001) *Human Rights Watch: World Report*.

CHINAdaily (2006) "Bush: Bring 'em on' was a big mistake," *CHINAdaily*, May 26. Available at: www2.chinadaily.com.cn/world/2006–05/26/content_600998.htm (accessed June 11, 2009).

Christie, A. (1960) *Murder on the Orient Express*. New York: Dodd, Mead & Company.

Churchill, W. (1920) *ASCII Text of Winston Churchill's Amritsar Massacre Speech-July 8th 1920*, UK House of Commons. Available at: http://lachlan.bluehaze.com.au/churchill/am-text.htm (accessed April 24, 2009).

Clark, W. V. T. (1940) *The Ox-Bow Incident*. New York: Modern Library.

Clausen, C. (1984) "Sherlock Holmes, Order, and the Late Victorian Mind," *Georgia Review*, 38 Spring, 104–23.

Clemens, S. L. (1980) *Pudd'nhead Wilson and Those Extraordinary Twins*, Sidney Berger (ed.). New York: Norton Critical Editions.

——(1999) *Adventures of Huckleberry Finn*, Cooley (ed.), 3rd Edition. New York: Norton Critical Edition.

Conot, R. (1993) *Justice at Nuremberg*. New York: Carroll & Graf.

Conrad, J. (1924) *The Secret Agent*. New York: Doubleday.

——(2002) *Heart of Darkness*. Oxford: Oxford University Press.

Cover, R. (1988) "Nomos and Narrative," *Narrative, Violence, and the Law*. Martha Minow et al. (eds.). Ann Arbor: University of Michigan Press.

Cox, J. (1966) *Mark Twain: The Fate of Humor*. Princeton: Princeton University Press.

Crane, C. and Terrill, A. (2003) *Reconstructing Iraq*. Strategic Studies Institute. U. S. Army War College. Carlisle: PA.

Crewdson, J. (2005) "Mysterious Jet Tied to Torture Flights," *Common Dreams News Center*, 8 January. Available at: www.commondreams.org/cgi-bin/print.cgi?file=/headlines05/0108–06.htm (accessed May 6, 2009).

Danner, M. (2009) "Tales from Torture's Dark World," *The New York Times*, March 13.

Darrow, C. (1963) "Realism in Literature," A. Weinberg and L. Weinberg (eds.), *Verdicts Out of Court*. Chicago: Quandrangle.

Death Wish 3 trailer. (1985) *Death Wish 3 Trailer*. Available at: www.youtube.com/watch?v=agyuMM09yAE (accessed July 1, 2009).

Death Wish Script. (1974) *Death Wish Script—Dialogue Transcript*. Available at: www.script-o-rama.com/movie_scripts/d/death-wish-script-transcript-bronson.html (accessed April 6, 2009).

Democracy NOW (2005) "Senate Apologizes for not Enacting Anti-Lynching Legislation, a Look at Journalist and Anti-Lynching Crusader Ida B. Wells," *Democracy NOW, the War and Peace Report*, June 14. Available at: www.democracynow.org/2005/6/14/senate_apologizes_for_not_enacting_anti ≥ (accessed June 2, 2009).

Dickens, C. (1960) *Oliver Twist*. Oxford: Clarendon Press.

Didion, J. (1996) *The Last Thing He Wanted*, New York: Viking, p. 69.

Dirks, T. (2001) *Apocalypse Now (Redux)* (1979) (2001). Available at: www.filmsite.org/apoc2.html≥ (accessed April 22, 2009).

Dirty Harry trailer (1971) *Dirty Harry trailer*. Available at: www.youtube.com/watch?v=YzeV8Sd9pV0 (accessed June 20, 2009).

Dobbs, M. (2003) "For Wolfowitz, a Vision May be Realized," *Washington Post*, April 7. Available at: www.washingtonpost.com/ac2/wp-dyn/A43339–2003Apr6?language=printer (accessed July 17, 2009).

Donoghue, D. (ed.) (2002) *Beowulf*. (Translated by Seamus Heaney.) New York: W. W. Norton & Company.

Donziger, S. (1966) *The Real War on Crime*. New York: Harper.

Dorfman, A. (1999) "Pinochet Menu—Some Post-Decision Comments," Latin American Solidarity Committee, March 24.

——(2002) *Exorcising Terror*. New York: Seven Stories Press.

——(2006) "Spitting on the Dead Dictator," *Los Angeles Times*, December 17. Available at: www.latimes.com/news/printedition/opinion/la-oe-dorfman17dec.htm (accessed March 11, 2009).

Doyle, A. C. (1930) *A Study in Scarlet in the Complete Sherlock Holmes*. New York: Doubleday.

——(1994) "Charles Augustus Milverton," J. A. Hodgson (ed.), *Sherlock Holmes: The Major Stories*. New York: St. Martins.

Economist (2007a) "Slaking a Thirst for Justice," *Economist*, April 12.

——(2007b) "Human Rights in Argentina and Chile," *Economist*, April 12. Available at: www.economist.com/world/americas/displaystory.cfm?story_id=9017531 (accessed July 17, 2009).

Elon, A. (2001) "The Deadlocked City," *New York Review of Books*, 48, October19.

Feitlowitz, M. (2000a) *The Pinochet Precedent: Who Could be Arrested Next?* Crimes of War Project, Expert Analysis. October. Available at: www.crimesofwar.org/expert/pinochet-print. html (accessed July 17, 2009).

——(2000b) *The Pinochet Prosecution: The Genocide Controversy*. Available at: www.crimesofwar. org/expert/pin-marguerite1.html (accessed August 2, 2009).

——(2000c) *The Pinochet Prosecution. Gains, Losses, Lessons*. Available at: www.crimesofwar.org/ expert/pin-marguerite2.html (accessed August 2, 2009).

Forster, E. M. (1920) "Notes on the English Character," *Abinger Harvest*. New York: Meridian Press. 1955: 3–14.

——(1952) *A Passage to India*. New York: Harcourt Brace.

——(1973) *The Manuscripts of A Passage to India*, Oliver Stallybrass (ed.). New York: Holmes and Meier.

Fraenkel, E. (1941) *The Dual State*. (Translated by E. A. Shils.) New York: Oxford University Press.

Frye, N. (1957) *Anatomy of Criticism*. Princeton: Princeton University Press.

Gates, H. L. and Appiah, K. A. (eds.) (1993) *Richard Wright: Critical Perspectives Past and Present*. New York: Amistad.

Gautier, T. (1980) "Balzac's Modernity in Pere Goriot," P. Brooks (ed.), *Père Goriot*. (Translated from French by B. Raffel.) New York: Norton Critical Editions, 1998: 225–28.

Gay, P. (1977) *The Enlightenment*, Volume II. New York: Norton.

Gewirtz, P. (1996a) "Introduction," P. Brooks and P. Gewirtz (eds.), *Law's Stories*. New Haven: Yale University Press.

——(1996b) "Victims and Voyeurs," P. Brooks and P. Gewirtz (eds.), *Law's Stories*. New Haven: Yale University Press, 135–61.

Gibbons, J. (2006) *Conversation with Judge Gibbons*. Personal conversation of Jim Guimond with Judge Gibbons, not published.

Gibbs, P. (1924) *The Romance of Empire*. London: Hutchinson Press.

Gillman, S. (1989) *Dark Twins*. Chicago: University of Chicago Press.

G'laberson, W. (2009) "Pentagon Finds Guantanamo Follows Geneva Conventions," *The New York Times*, February 21.

Glaspell, S. (1993) "A Jury of Her Peers," E. Rabkin (ed.), *Lifted Masks*. Ann Arbor: University of Michigan Press.

Gourevitch, P. (2008) *Errol Morris. Standard Operating Procedure*. New York: Penguin.

Gray, J. (2000) *Two Faces of Liberalism*. New York: New Press.

Green, J. (1985) *Death Wish 3*. Available at: www.fast-rewind.com/deathwishiii.htm (accessed April 14, 2009).

Greenspun, R. (1971) "Review: The French Connection," *The New York Times*, October 8. Available at: www.nytimes.com/packages/html/movies/bestpicture/french-re.html (accessed March 10, 2009).

Guardian.co.uk. (2003) "Full text: George Bush's Speech to the American Enterprise Institute," 27 February. Available at: www.guardian.co.uk/world/2003/Feb/27/usa/iraq2 (accessed December 7, 2008).

Habermas, J. (1996) *Between Facts and Norms*. (Translated by William Rehg.) Cambridge: MIT Press.

Haez, M. (2008) *Suicide Bombers in Iraq*. Washington: US Institute for Peace Press.

Hahn, S. (1989) "Honor and Patriarchy in the Odd South," *American Quarterly*, 36, Spring, pp. 145–53.

Harris, M. (2008) "Mirandize This," *Slate*, June 30. Available at: www.slate.com/toolbar.aspx?action=print&id = 2193951 (accessed June 14, 2009).

Hays, D. (1975) *Albion's Fatal Tree*. New York: Pantheon.

Hochschild, A. (1990) *The Mirror at Midnight*. New York: Viking.

Hodgson, J. (1994) (ed.) *Sherlock Holmes: The Major Stories with Contemporary Critical Essays*. Boston: Bedford/St. Martins.

Holmes Jr., O. W. (1992) *The Common Law* in *The Essential Holmes*, Richard Posner (ed.). Chicago: University of Chicago Press.

Howe, I. (1961) "Eight Men," H. L. Gates (ed.), *Richard Wright: Critical Perspectives*, 1993. New York: Amisted Pub.

Human Rights Watch (2001) "Chile: Keep Pinochet-Era Prosecutions Alive," *Human Rights Watch*, January 12. Available at: www.hrw.org/en/news/2001/01/12/chile-keep-pinochet-era-prosecutions-alive (accessed July 17, 2009).

Hunt, H. (1972) "Introduction," H. de Balzac (ed.), *A Murky Business*. (Translated by Herbert Hunt.) London: Penguin.

Infogovza (1999) "TRC Amnesty Decision on the Death of Steve Biko," *Infogovza*, February 16. Available at: www.info.gov.za/speeches/1999/99218_0bb99999_10160.htm (accessed August 15, 2009).

Jackson, R. H. (1945a) "The Rule of Law Among Nations," *American Bar Association Journal*, 31, April 13. Available at www.robertjackson.org/Man/theman2-7-7-1/ (accessed June 25, 2009).

——(1945b) "International Conference on Military Trials: London 1945," *Report to the President by Mr. Justice Jackson*, June 6. Available at: http://avalon/law.yale.edu/imt/jack08.asp (accessed June 22, 2009).

——(1945c) *Nuremberg Trial Proceedings Volume 2*, Second Day, November 21. Available at: http://avalon.law.yale.edu/imt/11-21–45.asp (accessed June 19, 2009).

Jacoby, R. (1994) *Dogmatic Wisdom*. New York: Anchor.

Jacoby, S. (1983) *Wild Justice: The Evolution of Revenge*. New York: Harper and Row.

Kael, P. (1976) *Reeling*. Boston: Little Brown.

——(1980) *When the Lights Go Down*. New York: Holt Rinheart.

Kiss, E. (2000) "Moral Ambition," R. I. Rothberg and D. Thompson (eds.), *Truth v. Justice*. Princeton: Princeton University Press.

De Klerk, F. W. (1993) *Submission to the Truth and Reconciliation Commission by Mr F W De Klerk, Leader of the National Party*. NP Submission TRC. Available at: www.doj.gov.za/trc/submit/np_truth.htm (accessed December 12, 2006).

Kornbluh, P. (2005) "Letter from Chile," *The Nation*, January 13. Available at: www.thenation. com/doc/20050131/kornbluh (accessed July 17, 2009).

Lal, V. (2008) "Udham Singh: Avenger of Jallianwala Bagh Massacre," MANAS: History and Politics, British India. Available at: www.sscnet.ucla.edu/southasia/British/Avenger.html (accessed August 15, 2009).

Lee, H. (1960) *To Kill a Mockingbird*. Philadelphia: Lippincott.

Le Fanu, S. (1986) *Magical Justice*. (Enchanted World Series.) Alexandria: Time-Life Books.

——(1993) *In a Glass Darkly*. Oxford: Oxford University Press.

Lehane, D. (2000) *Mystic River*. New York: Harper Torch.

LeMay, G. H. (1995) *The Afrikaners*. Oxford: Blackwell.

Lewis, A. (1990) "Revenge or Reconciliation," *The New York Times*, April 10.

Lichtblau, E. and Shane, S. (2008) "Report Details Interrogation Debate," *The New York Times*, May 21. Available at: www.nytimes.com/2008/05/21/washington/20cnd-detain. html?_r=2& ref=world (accessed August 15, 2009).

Longworth, K. (2007) "The Psychology of Torture: Interview with Rory Kennedy," 15 February. Available at: http://newsquake.netscape.com/2007/02/15/the-psychology-of-torture-interview-with-rory-kennedy.html (accessed March 11, 2009).

Los Angeles Times (2008) "Clint Eastwood Targets the Legacy of Dirty Harry," *Los Angeles Times*, June 1. Available at: www.latimes.com/entertainment/news/movies/la-ca-clint1-video-2008jun01,0,2761894,print.story (accessed June 14, 2009).

Magnum Force Script (1973) *Magnum Force Script—Dialogue Transcript*. Available at: www. script-o-rama.com/movie_scripts/m/magnum-force-script-transcript-eastwood.html (accessed April 16, 2009).

Mandela, N. (1994) *Long Walk to Freedom*. Boston: Little Brown.

——(1996) "Preface," A. Brink (ed.), *Reinventing a Continent*. Cambridge: Zoland.

Marceau, F. (1966) *Balzac and His World*. (Translated by Derek Coltman.) New York: Orion.

Maurois, A. (1965) *Prometheus: The Life of Balzac*. (Translated by Norman Denny.) New York: Harper Row.

Maza, S. (1993) *Private Lives and Public Affairs*. Berkeley: University of California Press.

Meredith, M. (1999) *Coming to Terms: South Africa's Search for Truth*. New York: Public Affairs.

Messer, A. E. (2003) "Revenge Motivates Tribal Warfare." Available at: www.eurekalert.org/ pub_releases/2003–02/ps-rmt021203.php (accessed August 15, 2009).

Milbank, D. and Deane, C. (2003) "Bush Proclaims Victory in Iraq," *Washington Post*, May 2.

Mora, A. (2007) *Interview Transcript*. Available at: www.gwu.edu/~nsarchiv/tourturingdemocracy/ interviews/alberto mora.html (accessed March 26, 2009).

Morgan, B. (2008) "Rugby in South Africa," *South Africa Info*, June 3. Available at: www. southafrica.info/about/sport/rugby.htm (accessed June 3, 2008).

Morris, E. (2008) "The Most Curious Thing," *The New York Times*, May 19. Available at: http://morris.blogs.nytimes.com/2008/05/19/the-most-curious-thing/ (accessed June 13, 2009).

Oziebolo, B. (1995) "Suppression and Society in Susan Glaspell's Theatre," L. Ben-Zvi (ed.), *Susan Glaspell: Essays on Her Theater and Fiction*. Ann Arbor: University of Michigan Press.

Paglen, T. and Thompson, A. C. (2006) *Torture Taxi*. Holbroken: Melville House.

Parke, S. (2007) "Simon Parke: Revenge? Or a Kitkat and a whisky?" *Church Times,* Issue 7517, 5 April. Available at: http://www.churchtimes.co.uk/contents.asp?id=37109 (accessed 1 June 2009).

Parmet, H. (1997) *George Bush*. New York: Scribner.

Parrott, T. M. (1904) "The Booklover's Magazine," S. Berger (ed.), *Pudd'nhead Wilson and Those Extraordinary Twins*. New York: Norton Critical Editions, 1980.

Pettit, A. G. (1979) "The Black and White Curse: Pudd'nhead Wilson and Miscegention," S. Berger (ed.), *Pudd'nhead Wilson and Those Extraordinary Twins*. New York: Norton Critical Editions, 1980.

Phil Taylor website (2003) "VP Cheney Elaborates on Pre-emption," September 2003. The Institute of Communications Studies, University of Leeds, UK. Available at: http://ics.leeds.ac.uk/papers/vp01.cfm?outfit=pmt&requesttimeout=500&folder=339&paper=542 (accessed August 15, 2009).

Posner, R. (1988) *Law and Literature: A Misunderstood Relation*. Cambridge: Harvard University Press.

Prendergast, C. (1978) *Balzac: Fiction and Melodrama*. London: Edward Arnold.

Price, R. (1991) *The Apartheid State in Crisis*. New York: Oxford University Press.

Rawls, J. (1971) *A Theory of Justice*. Cambridge: Harvard University Press.

Redmon, A. (2004) "Mechanisms of Violence in Clint Eastwood's Unforgiven and Mystic River," *Journal of American Culture*, September.

Ridley, J. (1998) *Mussolini*. New York: Cooper Square.

Robinson, F. (1993) *Having It Both Ways*. Albuquerque: University of New Mexico Press.

Rohter, L. (2004) "Chile's Army Accepts Blame for Rights Abuses in the Pinochet Era," *The New York Times*, November 6. Available at: www.nytimes.com/2004/11/06/international/americas/06chile.html?_r=1&oref=slogin (accessed March 13, 2008).

Roosevelt, F. D. (1904) *Roosevelt Corollary to the Monroe Doctrine*, US Department of State. Available at: http://www.state.gov/r/pa/ho/time/ip/17660.htm (accessed 1 June 2009).

——(1928) "Our Foreign Policy: A Democratic View," *Foreign Affairs*, Vol. VI, pp. 573–86. Available at: www.websteruniv.edu/~corbetre/haiti/history/occupation/frd.htm (accessed March 27, 2009).

Rosen, N. (2006) "Anatomy of a Civil War," *Boston Review*, November–December.

——(2008) "The Myth of the Surge," *Rolling Stone*, March 6.

Rosenthal, M. (2000) *In the South Bronx of America*. Willimantic: Curbstone Press.

Rozenberg, J. (2004) "Lord Steyn Attacks Fellow Law Lord," *Telegraph UK*, November 27.

Said, E. (1994) *Culture and Imperialism*. New York: Vintage.

Schemo, D. (1993) "A Prison Term of 15 Months for Wachtler," *The New York Times*, September 10.

Scott, W. (1990) "Reviews," V. Sage (ed.), *The Gothick Novel*. London: Macmillan.

Shah, A. (2001) "International Criminal Court: The Pinochet Case," *Global Issues*, September 18. Available at: www.globalissues.org/article/493/icc-the-pinochet-case (accessed July 17, 2009).

Shi, D. (1995) *Facing Facts*. New York: Oxford University Press.

Smith, H. N. (1962) "Pudd'nhead Wilson as Criticism of the Dominate Culture," S. Berger (ed.), *Pudd'nhead Wilson and Those Extraordinary Twins*. New York: Norton Critical Editions, 1980.

Smythe, C. (1982) "The Real Mark Twain," L. Budd (ed.), *Critical Essays on Mark Twain, 1869–1910*. Boston: G. K. Hall.

Spear, P. (1972) *India: A Modern History*. Ann Arbor: University of Michigan Press.

Spegele, R. and Vale, C. (1993) "Theoretical and Practical Implications," D. J. van Vuurven (ed.), *Change in South Africa*. Durban: Butterworths.

Steele, S. (2007) "The Identity Card," *Time*, November 30.

Stone, L. (1987) *The Past and Present Revisited*. London: Routledge & Kegan Paul.

South African Government Information (1999) "TRC Amnesty Decision on the Death of Steve Biko," *South African Government Information*, February 16. Available at: www.info.gov.za/speeches/1999/99218_0bb99999_10160.htm (accessed May 26, 2008).

Sullivan, J. (1978) *Elegant Nightmares*. Athens: Ohio University Press.

Swaminathan, S. A. A. (2002) "General Dyer's Gaurav Yatra," *The Times of India*, September 15. Available at: http://swaminomics.org/articles/20020915_gauravyatra.htm (accessed April 20, 2009).

Taguba Report (2004) *Iraq Prisoner Abuse Investigation of the Hearing 15–16 of the U.S. 800th Military Police Brigade*. Available at: http://news.findlaw.com/wp/docs/iraq/tagubarpt.html (accessed June 30, 2009).

The French Connection trailer (1971) *The French Connection trailer*. Available at: www.youtube.com/watch?v=nP_7ZopT6oM (accessed June 20, 2009).

The New York Times (2007) "Looking for America," *The New York Times*, January 31, A20.

The Ox Bow Incident Script (1943) *The Ox Bow Incident Script—Dialogue Transcript*. Available at: www.script-o-rama.com/movie_scripts/o/ox-bow-incident-script-transcript.html (accessed April 6, 2009).

The White House (2001) *The Vice President Appears on Meet the Press with Tim Russert*, September 16. Available at: www.whitehouse.gov/vicepresident/news-speeches/speeches/vp20010916.html (accessed April 17, 2008).

Tiede, L. (2004) *Committing to Justice: An Analysis of Criminal Law Reforms in Chile*. Center for Iberian and Latin American Studies. San Diego: University of California Press.

Tocqueville (1835) Book 1 Chapter 16, *Causes Which Mitigate the Tyranny of the Majority in the United States*. Available at: http://xroads.virginia.edu/~HYPER/DETOC/1_ch16.htm (accessed March 20, 2009).

To Kill a Mockingbird Script (1962) *To Kill a Mockingbird Script—Dialogue Transcript*. Available at: www.script-o-rama.com/movie_scripts/t/to-kill-a-mockingbird-.html (accessed March 11, 2009).

Touring Democracy (2007) *Touring Democracy*, September 17. Available at: www.gwu.edu/~nsarchiv/torturingdemocracy/interviews/ (accessed August 15, 2009).

Trenton Times (2008) "Judge Orders 5 Gitmo Detainees Freed," *Trenton Times*, November 21, B1.

Truthdig (2008) *Senate Armed Services Committee Inquiry into the Treatment of Detainees in U.S. Custody*, December 12. Available at: www.truthdig.com/report/item/20081212_report_ rumsfeld_responsible_for_detainee_abuse/ (accessed August 15, 2009).

Turner, A. (1968) "Mark Twain and the South: Pudd'nhead Wilson," S. Berger (ed.), *Pudd'nhead Wilson and Those Extraordinary Twins*. New York: Norton Critical Editions, 1980.

Tutu, D. (2004) "Desmond Tutu's Recipe for Peace." Available at: www.beliefnet.com/Inspiration/2004/04/Desmond-Tutus-Recipe-For-Peace.aspx (accessed August 15, 2009).

Twain, M. (1893) "Letter to Fred Hall, 30 July," *Twain quotes.com*. Available at: www.twainquotes.com/Fingerprints.html (accessed August 15, 2009).

——(2007) *Life on the Mississippi*. New York: Modern Library.

USA Today (2003) "Poll: 70% Believe Saddam, 9–11 Link," *USA Today*, September 6. Available at: http://usatoday.com/news/washington/2003-09-06-poll-iraq_x.htm (accessed July 17, 2009).

Verkaik, R. (2003) "Guantanamo Treatment is 'Monstrous', says Law Lord," *The Independent*, November 26. Available at: http://license.icopyright.net/user/viewfreeuse.act?fuid=mjkxmdi4 (accessed March 11, 2009).

de Villiers, D. P. (1983) "Changes in Respect to Security Legislation," D. J. Van Vuuren, et al. (eds.), *Change in South Africa*. Durban: Butterworths.

Virginia Bill of Rights (1776) *Virginia Bill of Rights*, June 12. Available at: www. constitution.org/bor/vir_bor.htm (accessed March 20, 2009).

Waldmeir, P. (1997) *Anatomy of a Miracle*. New York: Norton.

Weber, M. (1954) *Max Weber on Law in Economy and Society*. (Translated by Edward Shils.) Cambridge: Harvard University Press.

Weisberg, R. (1984) *The Failure of the Word*. New Haven: Yale University Press.

Welles, S. (1942) *Sumner Welles, Under Secretary of State Memorial Day Address at the Arlington National Amphitheater*, May 30. Available at: www.ibiblio.org/pha/policy/1942/420530a. html (accessed August 15, 2009).

Wiggins, R. A. (1964) "The Flawed Structure of Pudd'nhead Wilson," S. Berger (ed.), *Pudd'nhead Wilson and Those Extraordinary Twins*. New York: Norton Critical Editions, 1980.

Wink, W. (1999) *The Powers That Be*. New York: Galilee Trade.

Woods, D. (1978) *Biko*. New York: Paddington.

World Affairs. (1904) *Roosevelt Corollary to the Monroe Doctrine*, World Affairs, December 6. Available at: www.u-s-history.com/pages/h1449.html (accessed March 23, 2009).

Worth, R. (2006) "Blast Destroys Shrine in Iraq, Setting Off Sectarian Fury," *The New York Times*, February 22. Available at: www.nytimes.com/2006/02/22/international/middleeast/ 22cnd-iraq.html (accessed February 17, 2008).

Wright, R. (1940) *Native Son*. New York: Harper & Brothers.

——(1991) *Native Son*, Early Works. New York: Library of America.

Index